# Words That Work

# WORDS
## THAT
# WORK

*It's Not What You Say,*
*It's What People Hear*

## DR. FRANK LUNTZ

New York

Excerpts from "Politics and the English Language" from SHOOTING AN ELEPHANT AND OTHER ESSAYS by George Orwell, copyright 1950 by Sonia Brownell Orwell and renewed 1978 by Sonia Pitt-Rivers, reprinted by permission of Harcourt, Inc.

Use of the AT&T Commercial is granted under permission by AT&T Corp.

Use of the Swift Boat Veterans for Truth Advertisement is granted under permission by SBVT.

Library of Congress Cataloging-in-Publication Data

Luntz, Frank I.
   Words that work : it's not what you say, it's what people hear / Frank Luntz.—1st ed.
     p.   cm.
   Includes index.
   ISBN 1-4013-0259-9
   1. English language—United States—Rhetoric.   2. Persuasion (Rhetoric)—Political aspects.   3. Mass media and language.   4. Popular culture—United States.   5. Critical thinking.   6. Communication in politics.   I. Title.

   PE1431.L87  2007
   808'.042—dc22                                                                                     2006043737

Hyperion Books are available for special promotions and premiums. For details contact Michael Rentas, Assistant Director, Inventory Operations, Hyperion, 77 West 66th Street, 12th floor, New York, New York 10023, or call 212-456-0133.

FIRST EDITION

2   4   6   8   10   9   7   5   3   1

This book is dedicated to the 300 million Americans
who make my day-to-day life so
interesting and challenging, often annoying, but always rewarding.
Thanks to you, I am never bored.

# CONTENTS

# ACKNOWLEDGMENTS

This is the part where most authors describe their efforts as a *"labor of love"* and then list all the special people who *"made this book possible."*

I can't. The truth is, this was the single most difficult task I have undertaken—and it ensured that I did not get a decent night's sleep for the past year.

The person most responsible for my lack of fitful rest is my agent, Lorin Rees, from whom I mistakenly took a call on a rare Sunday when I actually wasn't working eight hours. He convinced me to use that afternoon to write up a book proposal that somehow he managed to sell at exactly the minimum amount I was willing to accept. He has never received a pleasant e-mail from me during this entire process. At least he made some money out of it.

Next in line is Jonathan Karl, who has spent the last half decade endlessly nagging me into writing this text. He doesn't know this but on several occasions during the more stressful periods I actually thought about having Dr. Kevorkian pay him a visit. I have to be careful not to say anything bad about him: He's one of the best reporters in Washington, D.C., and he's liable to go out and dig up dirt on me.

The person who has the right to be most angry with me is my editor,

Gretchen Young, who took this assignment after my initial editor departed Hyperion. She must have done something terribly wrong in her previous life to have been given this book. She has suffered the most, and so to her only, I apologize. (If you ever mistakenly consent to write a book, insist that she be your editor. She's a saint.)

I also have to thank the entire Hyperion team, who compassionately laughed at all of my bad jokes and never once made me feel like the linguistic geek that I am.

My staff at Luntz Maslansky Strategic Research also shoulders some of the responsibility. From the interns who sifted through a billion pages of Internet material to help me find the pearls of wisdom to Amy Kramer, who actually read much of this text four times, they got to enjoy my frustration on a daily basis—up close and personal.

Bill Danielson deserves an acknowledgment of his own. Not only did he help with the initial draft of this book but he happens to be one of the best young writers in America today. I also have to personally thank Michael Maslansky, my business partner, for helping me sell my company (and John Wren from Omnicom for buying it) in the midst of this effort. Even if no one anywhere actually buys this book, his success will allow me to enjoy life on eBay forever.

Time is a precious commodity, and so I express particular thanks to Henry Kissinger, Colin Powell, Norman Lear, Bill Maher, Robert Shapiro, Aaron Sorkin, Jack Welch, and Steve Wynn for graciously allowing me to plumb their words of wisdom.

There are certain individuals who had absolutely nothing to do with this book, thank God, but nevertheless had a life-changing impact on my professional life that is deeply intertwined with this text. In chronological order, they are: my parents; Dr. Robert Derosier, the best teacher in America; Senator Jim Buckley, the most principled political figure I ever worked for; Mayor Rudy Giuliani, the most successful leader I ever worked for; Speaker Newt Gingrich, the smartest politician I ever worked for; Tony Blankley and Tony Coehlo, the best personal advisors one could ever hope for; Lawrence Kadish, the definition of a Great American; Frank Fahrenkopf and Steve Wynn, who were responsible for my first Language Dictionary; and Steve Capus, Phil Griffin, and Jonathan Wald, who put my private focus groups on national television. I can never adequately express my appreciation to them for all that they have done for me. This is just my latest failed attempt.

# INTRODUCTION

*"Most people who bother with the matter at all would admit that the English language is in a bad way."*[1]
— GEORGE ORWELL (1946)

September 18, 2004: Writer, socialite, political gadfly Arianna Huffington, a conservative-turned-liberal political-activist-to-the-stars, invites thirty-five of Hollywood's most important power players to her Brentwood home. These are not your run-of-the-mill Democrats. They are members of the Hollywood political elite, deeply concerned about the direction of the U.S. presidential campaign and in outright panic about the state of the nation.

For them, election 2004 is the battle royale for the heart and soul of America. Having watched their "victory" in 2000 "stolen" from them by the Supreme Court, they feel they are witnessing once again the disintegration of a national election before their very eyes. Hollywood Democrats had gladly flocked to John Kerry, but now they think he is blowing it in the wake of the Republican National Convention and the drip-drip-drip of the Swift Boat Vets' attack ads. Bush has surged to a five- to eight-point lead, depending on which poll you believe. Everywhere, Democrats are asking: Why is the President winning when the economy is weak, the war in Iraq isn't going well, and gas prices have climbed above $2 a gallon for the first time ever? Why isn't Kerry connecting with the public? What's wrong with the words he's using? What's the problem with the way he's communicating?

And so the luminaries of the Hollywood Left arrive at Huffington's Brentwood mansion to listen to a guest speaker from Washington, D.C., and talk things through. They drive up in their open-air Mercedes, BMWs, and Jags that cost almost as much as a house in Omaha. Warren Beatty is there, sitting next to Rob Reiner. Larry David walks in a little late and stands off to the side. Norman Lear, creator of *All in the Family, Maude, Good Times,* and a dozen other TV shows, positions himself toward the rear, just behind actress Christine Lahti. Well-known writers, directors, and producers with Oscars and Emmys on the mantels of their pool houses crowd around. People of impeccable Hollywood pedigree, all. And who do they come to learn from?

Remarkably, a "Republican" pollster.

There I am, the man who helped develop the language to sell the Contract with America and deliver a Republican majority in the House of Representatives for the first time in forty years. The man who worked for Rudy Giuliani, two-time Republican mayor of a city where Democratic voters outnumbered Republicans 5-to-1. The man who has been working behind the scenes for the past ten years—in debate prep sessions and television network green rooms, in the halls of Congress and in state capitals across the country—playing my own small part in the Republican ascension and in the Democratic collapse.*

Why have I gone there, into what some of my clients and many of my colleagues would consider enemy territory? More importantly, why do the Hollywood elite welcome me? How do they know I'm not part of some nefarious Karl Rovean disinformation campaign, plotting political pranks and electoral sabotage?

The answer is simple: Although my political clients may come from one side of the aisle, what I do is fundamentally nonpartisan. The ideas and

---

*Twice I was responsible for prepping GOP congressional leaders in their nationwide televised PBS debates, first, in Williamsburg, Virginia, in October 1996, when House Speaker Newt Gingrich and Senate Majority Leader Trent Lott faced off against Democrat House Minority Leader Dick Gephardt and Senate Minority Leader Tom Daschle, and again four years later when GOP House Conference Chairman J. C. Watts and Nebraska Republican Senator Chuck Hagel debated against Senate Democrat Minority Whip Harry Reid and House Democrat Minority Whip David Bonior. At that second debate, held at PBS studios in Arlington, Virginia, I actually had to hide for forty-five minutes in an upstairs bathroom after Reid accused the Republicans on air of being slaves to "Frank Luntz's talking points." I can only imagine what he would have said if he knew I was actually in the building at that very moment.

principles about effective language I was to share with them in Brentwood that afternoon apply equally to Democrats and Republicans. And, frankly, I wanted to see the inside of Arianna's house.

Indeed, the lessons of effective language transcend politics, business, media, and even Hollywood. My polling firm has worked for more than two dozen of the most elite *Fortune* 100 companies. We have written, supervised, and conducted almost fifteen hundred surveys, dial sessions, and focus groups for every product and politician imaginable—representing more than a half million unique individual conversations. What we have learned applies to bankrupt airlines and overbooked hotels, soft drink makers and fast food providers, banks and credit unions. Good language is just as important to twentieth-century trendsetters like IBM and twenty-first-century innovators like Google as it is to blue-blood law firms whose partners' ancestors were on the Mayflower and twenty-one-year-old soon-to-be entrepreneurs who've been in the United States exactly one month.

Language, politics, and commerce have always been intertwined, both for better and for worse. What I presented to that glitterati crowd—and what I proffer to my political and corporate clients every day, seven days a week, 365 days a year (literally)—are the precise tools and insights of political and commercial wordsmithing. These tools apply broadly to almost *any* endeavor that involves presenting a message, whether it's a day-to-day event like talking your way out of a speeding ticket or into a raise, or something more substantial like creating an effective thirty-second commercial, crafting a fifteen-minute speech to your employees, or writing an hour-long State of the Union address.

In the pages that follow, my basic advice to readers will be the following:

**It's not what you say, it's what people hear.**

You can have the best message in the world, but the person on the receiving end will always understand it through the prism of his or her own emotions, preconceptions, prejudices, and preexisting beliefs. It's not enough to be correct or reasonable or even brilliant. The key to successful communication is to take the imaginative leap of stuffing yourself right into your listener's shoes to know what they are thinking and feeling in the deepest recesses of their mind and heart. How that person perceives what you say is even more *real,* at least in a practical sense, than how you perceive yourself.

When someone asks me to illustrate the concept of "words that work," I tell them to read Orwell's *1984*—and then see the movie. In particular, I refer them to the book passage that describes Room 101—or as Orwell basically describes it, the place where everyone's personal, individual nightmares come true. If your greatest fear is snakes, you open the door to a room full of snakes. If your fear is drowning, your Room 101 fills to the brim with water. To me, this is the most frightening, horrific, imaginative concept ever put on paper, simply because it encourages you to imagine your own Room 101. Words that work, whether fiction or reality, not only explain but also motivate. They cause you to think as well as act. They trigger emotion as well as understanding.

But the movie version of *1984* denies the viewer the most powerful aspect that makes Room 101 work: one's own imagination. Once you actually *see* Room 101, it is no longer *your* vision. It becomes someone else's. Lose imagination and you lose an essential component of words that work.

Just as a fictional work's meaning may transcend authorial intention, so every message that you bring into the world is subject to the interpretations and emotions of the people who receive it. Once the words leave your lips, they no longer belong to you. We have a monopoly only on our own thoughts. The act of speaking is not a conquest, but a surrender. When we open our mouths, we are sharing with the world—and the world inevitably interprets, indeed sometimes shifts and distorts, our original meaning.

After all, who hasn't uttered the words "But that's not what I actually meant"?

Just ask former President Jimmy Carter. On July 15, 1979, three years to the day from his triumphant nomination at the Democratic National Convention, he addressed millions of Americans to explain what he called America's *"crisis of confidence."* That phrase means nothing to most Americans—we all know it as his infamous *"malaise"* speech, despite the fact that he never uttered the word malaise even once. What led up to that linguistic misrepresentation of historic proportions will be addressed later in this book.

Or ask former secretary of state Colin Powell, as I did, about the origin of the so-called *"Powell doctrine"* of military success. When it was first articulated in 1991, his exact words referenced the strategy of *"decisive force."* Moreover, "U.S. National Military Strategy," the Pentagon's annual report on military threats to the United States, called Powell's theory *"the theory of decisive force."*

In the hands of the reporters and even the historians, however, it has ended up translated as *"overwhelming force"* and is often now called *"the Powell Doctrine of overwhelming force."* Today, when you search the Lexis-Nexis database for references to *"Colin Powell"* and *"doctrine of decisive force"* in U.S. newspapers and wires from 1990 to 2006, you get a mere seven returns. When you run the same search, but using *"doctrine of overwhelming force"* instead, you get 67 total returns. The same is true for the less limiting phrases of just *"decisive force"* and *"overwhelming force,"* which return 135 and 633 results, respectively. Again, almost five times as many references to *"overwhelming force."*

To the average reader, this may appear to be a difference without a distinction. For Powell, the distinction still matters—a lot. To him, decisive meant *"precise, clean, and surgical,"* whereas overwhelming implies *"excessive and numerical."*[2] The former is smart and sophisticated. The latter: heavy-handed and brutish.

So how did this happen? How does history manage to rewrite itself? The answer is more in the translation than the message itself. Powell did use the phrase *"overwhelming force"* publicly, but just one time, in 1990, and he used it to describe the force necessary to ensure that America *"wins decisively"* every war it engages. In almost every other instance, and even in his 1995 memoir *My American Journey,* Powell reiterates his desire for *"decisive force"* because it "ends wars quickly and in the long run saves lives."

Ultimately, it is the professional—the journalists, historians, and academics who translate words into stories—who hold the key to language dissemination. They have to grab people's attention, and *"overwhelming force"* just sounds more captivating than *"decisive force."* It creates an image in the mind that goes far beyond the dull, policy-based decisive force terminology. *Overwhelming* force is about process. *Decisive* force is about result. Yet no matter how hard Powell has tried to correct and clarify the public record, the world will always think otherwise, and the consequences of that misinterpretation can be seen in Iraq every single day.

Ask former secretary of state Henry Kissinger, as I did, why he chose the word *"détente"* to describe American-Soviet relations in the 1970s. The first diplomatic application has been attributed to an anonymous Russian, spurred by a 1959 meeting between Secretary of State John Foster Dulles and West German Chancellor Konrad Adenauer in which Dulles advocated for open relations with the communist states of Eastern

Europe.[3] So it did have pedigree—but it came with other baggage as well. Said Kissinger:

> *I didn't choose Détente. Someone else gave it to us, and it was a mistake. First, we shouldn't have used a French word, for obvious reasons. And second, it simplified a complex process and helped critics attack the policy. If we had called it an "easing of tensions," which is what it was, no one would have complained.*

The person responsible was probably Raymond Garthoff, a Brookings scholar and former State Department official, who had labeled the concluding of the SALT agreements "the charter of détente."[4] The label not only stuck, but the word proved to be so powerful within its context that it summarized in a neat package nearly an entire decade of international foreign relations, making a complex policy easy to defend . . . and easy to attack. Kissinger, arguably the greatest diplomat of our era, understood—as you soon will—that the simple choice of simple words can and will change the course of history.

This book is about the art and science of words that work. Examining the strategic and tactical use of language in politics, business, and everyday life, it shows how you can achieve better results by narrowing the gap between what you intend to convey and what your audiences actually interpret. The critical task, as I've suggested, is to go beyond your own understanding and to look at the world from your listener's point of view. In essence, it is listener-centered; their perceptions trump whatever "objective" reality a given word or phrase you use might be presumed to have. Again, what matters isn't what you say, it's what people hear.

## IN DEFENSE OF LANGUAGE

For the record, I love the English language. I have built a career attending to matters of rhetoric, to the painstaking and deliberate choice of words. I love the soft twang of Southern belles and the gum-popping slang of Southern California valley girls, the gentle lyricism of the upper Midwest and the in-your-face bluntness of Brooklyn cabbies. I'm enthralled by the bass rumble of James Earl Jones, the velvet smoothness of Steve Wynn, the upper-crust sophistication of Orson Welles and Richard Burton, and the sexy intonations of Lauren Bacall, Sally Kellerman, and Catherine Zeta-Jones. When spoken well, the language of America is a language of hope, of everyday heroes, of faith in the goodness of people.

At its best, American English is also the practical language of commerce. The most effective communication is the unadorned, unpretentious language of farmers, mom-and-pop shopkeepers, and the thousands of businesses located on the hundreds of Main Street USAs, as well as the no-nonsense, matter-of-fact, bottom-line language of men and women who built the greatest companies the world has ever seen.

I am pulled to the language of dreamers and pragmatists both. Of outspoken strivers fighting against the odds, and quiet men and women simply grateful they live in a country that gives them the freedom to spot their neighbors' needs and provide a product or service to meet them. The words of average Americans are at once a language of idealism and a language of common sense. I listen to and love it all.

I am best known for my work in the political sphere, starting with Ross Perot's half campaign, half rant in 1992, followed by Rudy Giuliani's upset victory in New York City in 1993, and capped off with the Contract with America in 1994 that was widely credited with returning control of the House of Representatives to the Republican Party for the first time in forty years. In some fashion, either individually, in small groups, or as an entire caucus, I have advised almost every Republican senator and congressman since then—as well as several prime ministers on several continents—on issues of language. In preparing for this book, I realized with some pride that my firm has polled more than half a million people, and I have personally moderated focus groups in forty-six of the fifty states—and I fully intend to listen to the good people of Idaho, Montana, West Virginia, and Wyoming as soon as they have a reason to hear from me.

I am a committed advocate of political rhetoric that is direct and clear. It should be interactive, not one-sided. It should speak to the common sense of common people—with a moral component, but without being inflammatory, preachy, or divisive. In a perfect world, political language would favor those with enough respect for people to tell them the truth, and enough intelligence not to do so in condescending tones.

In 2005, my 170-page memo on language, *A New American Lexicon,* raised a storm of protest in Washington and the blogosphere because it genuinely sought to establish a common language for a pro-business, pro-freedom agenda. Having served as the pollster of record for the Contract with America a decade earlier, liberal critics took a baseball bat to this work. They came after me with a vengeance for both ideological and political reasons.

Daily Kos, the leading left-wing blog, accused me of "spinning lies into truth." Another blog, thinkprogress.org, asserted that I wanted to "scare" the public about taxes and "exploit" the 9/11 tragedy; they even set up a "Luntz Watch" section of their site just to track and "analyze" my language.[5] And the National Environmental Trust created "Luntz-Speak," a Web site devoted entirely to my messaging of environmental and energy issues, which, in their words, represented "an exciting new way to put a positive spin on an abysmal environmental record." They even created a "Luntzie Award" for the politicians they believed best used my language. As much as I disliked the criticism, I have to admit I did like their cartoon character that was created to look like me: he has better hair, whiter teeth, and a healthy tan.

I wasn't surprised by the reaction. We live in a partisan era, and most Web-generated political language has taken on a vicious partisan tone. I essentially stopped working in domestic political campaigns years ago because they were filled with such a harsh negativity, which seemed to grow more vicious and inhumane with every election cycle. The more ideological Republicans, brilliant minds like William Kristol who understand policy much better than politics, sometimes grumble that my words don't have sufficient bite and that they soften what they think should be the sharp edges of philosophical debate. The more ideological Democrats, particularly the bloggers, object to what they perceive to be my effort to obscure the truth behind gentle-sounding terminology.

To a limited degree, they are both correct. My personal philosophy may be right-of-center, but my political words are always targeted at those essential, nonaligned voters—the not so silent majority of Americans who reject ideological soundness in favor of the sound center. Unlike some of my colleagues, I try very hard not to allow my own beliefs or biases to interfere with my craft. Whether it's a political issue I wish to communicate or a product I wish to sell, I seek to listen, then understand, and ultimately win over the doubter, the fence-sitter, the straddling skeptic. My language eschews overt partisanship and aims to find common ground rather than draw lines or sow separation. The words in this book represent the language of America, not the language of a single political party, philosophy, or product.

Some critics will accuse this book of advocating and even teaching manipulation, but as a retiring magician decides to reveal his tricks and then fade away, I seek only to throw open the doors of the language laboratory and shine a bright light on how words that work are created and used.

I asked the brilliant Hollywood writer Aaron Sorkin, creator of *The West Wing* and *Sports Night*, and someone with a very different political orientation from mine, to explain the difference between language that convinces and language that manipulates. His answer stunned me:

> "There's no difference. It's only when manipulation is obvious, then it's bad manipulation. What I do is every bit as manipulative as some magician doing a magic trick. If I can wave this red silk handkerchief enough in my right hand, I can do whatever I want with my left hand and you're not going to see it. When you're writing fiction, everything is manipulation. I'm setting up the situation specifically so that you'll laugh at this point or cry at this point or be nervous at this point. If you can see how I'm sawing the lady in half, then it's bad manipulation. If you can't see how I did that, then it's good."

Sure, you'll learn what to say to get a table at a crowded restaurant and how to get airport personnel to let you on a flight that has already closed, but is that really language exploitation? You'll learn the language of the twenty-first century, the words and phrases that you'll be hearing more of in the coming years, but is that truly message manipulation? Hardly.

We have certainly seen instances in which language has been used to cloud our judgment and blur the facts, but its beauty—the true power of words—is that it can also be used in defense of clarity and fairness. I do not believe there is something dishonorable about presenting a passionately held proposition in the most favorable light, while avoiding the self-sabotage of clumsy phrasing and dubious delivery. I do not believe it is somehow malevolent to choose the strongest arguments rather than to lazily go with the weakest.

For example, education is not only my own personal hot-button issue—it's the top local issue in America today. The public is demanding further education reform to the "Leave No Child Behind" initiatives that were passed into law—but how those reforms are explained determines their level of support. I have been active in the so-called "school choice" effort, and in my research work I have found that calling the financial component a *"voucher"* rather than the more popular *"scholarship"* trivializes the powerful opportunity and financial award that children from poor families receive when their parents have the right to choose the school they will attend.

In fact, I'd argue that it's more accurate to call it *"parental choice in education"* than *"school choice"* because it really is the parents who are deciding the schooling for their children. Or, considering how such a program equalizes education for rich and poor alike, the most accurate phrase may well be *"equal opportunity in education"*—and it certainly tests best in the polling my firm has done.

Most of the stories you will read in the pages that follow were created for causes and customers that sought to build up rather than tear down, for that is far more memorable than the slash-and-burn of the modern campaign. Even the least political among us has a piece of stirring political rhetoric that touched us when we first heard it and has stayed with us for years, decades and even generations.

"Ask not what your country can do for you . . ."
"The only thing we have to fear is fear itself . . ."
"Some men see things as they are and ask why . . ."
"The shining city atop a hill . . ."
"I have a dream."

In the end, the ongoing battle over political language is more about comprehension than articulation. There are at least two sides to almost every issue, and people on each side believe in the deepest recesses of their souls that they are right. I help communicate the principles of the side I believe in, using the simplest, most straightforward language available. Sure, I seek to persuade. My goal is to fashion political rhetoric that achieves worthy goals—to level the linguistic playing field and to inform Americans of what is truly at stake in our policy debates.

Straightforward communication is equally important in the sphere of private enterprise. American companies have great stories to tell. From the stunning advances in pharmaceutical medications that are prolonging the lives of people with AIDS, to breathtaking innovations in microcomputing and artificial intelligence; from groundbreaking agricultural technologies with the potential to banish hunger around the world, to less disruptive, more environmentally sound techniques for extracting oil and natural gas from the earth—corporate America is imagining and building an exciting new world for the new century. What a tragedy that their language is trapped in a Harvard Business School textbook from the 1950s instead of a plain-speaking John McCain–esque twenty-first-century approach.

True, Enron, WorldCom, Tyco, Adelphia, and even Martha Stewart failed not because they had bad language but because they had bad morals. But for the rest of corporate America (Martha Stewart aside), the convoluted language they continue to use is part of their image problem, not part of the solution. Just pick up almost any 2007 annual report and leaf through to the standard CEO letter. Circle the words, phrases, and concepts you don't understand, you don't like, or you just aren't quite sure about. You'll need a lot of ink.

That's where pollsters and wordsmiths like me come in. This book will offer readers a proverbial look behind the curtain at what has worked for companies in the past, and at the new strategies they are developing for this new millennium. We'll take a historical look at the way political leaders have presented themselves to the American people—and how that process has changed forever. We'll also cover the language being used right now to communicate the hottest issues of the day that are sure to dominate the election cycles ahead. And finally, we will turn our attention to the future, to what companies should be saying now and in the years to come—and to what you can expect the politicians to be talking about in 2008 and beyond.

This is not a book about policy. It doesn't matter, for the purposes of our discussion, whether libertarian comedian Dennis Miller or liberal comedian Al Franken is the better American or whether Bill Clinton or George W. Bush is the better President. This book is addressed equally to Democrats and Republicans, to liberals (or, as they now like to be called, "progressives"—a fascinating change in terminology that we'll get into later) and conservatives alike.

This book will not take sides in the burger wars, the automotive wars, or the cola wars, either. But those who sell products, and the rest of us who buy them, will find just as much value in these pages as those who sell political ideas. For in the end, the best products and the best marketing campaigns involve ideas, not just packaging.

A few—very few—publications have explored the strategic intersection between politics, business, Hollywood, the media, and communication. This book hits at the intersection of all five and introduces a brand-new element: an explanation of how and why the strategic and tactical use of specific words and phrases can change how people think and how they behave. The book recounts personal stories of how commonly identifiable language and product strategies came to be, describing the process that created them as well as the people and businesses who articulated them. And it will provide the reader with the specific Words That Work—and those that don't—in dozens of circumstances. From the political world, we will explore:

- How the *"estate tax"* became the *"death tax,"* turning a relatively arcane issue into a national hot button
- How Rudy Giuliani moved from a *"crime agenda"* to a *"safety and security platform"* in his successful campaign for mayor
- How the Contract with America revolutionized political language in ways its authors never intended
- How *"drilling for oil"* became *"energy exploration,"* frustrating the entire environmental community

From the corporate world, we will explore:

- How effective language can be used to prevent a strike and promote employee satisfaction
- How a large *Fortune* 100 company stalled and then stopped the SEC from implementing popular *"corporate accountability"* measures by reshaping the message and redefining the debate
- How *"gambling"* became *"gaming"* and how Las Vegas impresario Steve Wynn discovered the value of his own name and attached it to the most expensive hotel ever built
- How the CEO of Pfizer, the largest pharmaceutical company in the world, has revolutionized the industry by applying the language of responsibility and accountability and changing the focus from *"disease management"* to *"prevention"*

And from the personal world, your world, you will learn:

- How to talk yourself out of a speeding ticket when you and the officer both know you're guilty
- How to talk yourself into a reservation at a crowded restaurant and onto a plane that has already closed its doors
- How best to apologize when you know you're wrong . . . and make it stick

These are the challenges I face every day, and discovering the answers is the task that I set for myself when I began my professional career nearly twenty years ago. My subjects of study are my fellow citizens—not just in America but worldwide. My laboratory is both the day-to-day life that people lead and organized invitation-only discussions I often host at night.

All of these anecdotes come from my own personal experience, but you'll hear from other, more notable people as well. The lessons I've drawn from a decade and a half of work on behalf of business and political clients are based on empirical studies and quantitative research—not merely opinion. Everything you read here will be based on scientific market research, not idle speculation.

The purpose of this book is to tell you what I tell governors, senators, and members of Congress; what I tell the U.S. Chamber of Commerce and the Business Roundtable; and what I present to CEOs and entrepreneurs every day across this country: ***It's Not What You Say, It's What People Hear.***

This book is part guide, part exposé. It explores how presidents and *Fortune* 500 CEOs craft messages that have the power to revolutionize what we think about politics and products in our day-to-day lives. You will get a peek behind the scenes of the actual process by which some of America's most powerful brands have been created. And you will learn how our country's political and business leaders are developing a brand-new lexicon to address changing public anxiety: the twenty-one words for the twenty-first century.

This book is not merely for politicians or business leaders; it's for everyone who has an interest in or who makes a living using and listening to the language of America. It is for anyone who wants to harness the power of words to improve his or her own lot in life, and to ensure that the true meaning of these words is heard as they intended them to be.

Read the following pages, and you will learn about the language of America. You will also find the words to tell your own story.

# Words That Work

# I

## The Ten Rules of Effective Language

*"Broadly speaking, the short words are the best, and the old words best of all."* —WINSTON CHURCHILL

*"When we disregard the rules altogether we get anarchy or, worse yet, Enron."* —POLITICAL HUMORIST BILL MAHER

Rules govern our daily lives. Some of these rules are explicit, imposed by government: "obey the speed limit," "no parking," "April 15 is tax day." But most are informal, often unspoken cultural norms—rules of politeness, rules of conduct in the business world, rules of interaction between people. Most are commonly understood traditions that have built up over time, habits so ordinary that we usually don't even think about them.

Unfortunately, not all such involuntary habits and subconscious conventions are positive or productive. American business and political communication is rife with bad habits and unhelpful tendencies that can do serious damage to the companies and causes they seek to promote. Just as in every other field, there are rules to good, effective communication. They may not be as inflexible and absolute as the rules against speeding or avoiding your taxes, but they're just as important if you wish to arrive safely at your destination with money in your pocket.

The rules of communication are especially important given the sheer amount of communication the average person has to contend with. We step out of our houses each morning into a nonstop sensory assault: advertising and entertainment, song lyrics and commercial jingles, clipped conversations and abbreviated e-mails. A good deal of noise also comes from inside our homes, from our TVs to our sound systems to our computers and now our iPods. How do you make people hear your words amid all this chatter? "Great language has exactly the same properties as great music," says Aaron Sorkin, the brilliant writer/creator of the hit television drama *The West Wing*. "It has rhythm, it has pitch, it has tone, it has accents."* So in a cacophonous world, how do you ensure that your musical note stands out?

This chapter seeks to examine the principles behind good communication and, in the process, to discourage some of the most common bad habits that plague everyone from senators to CEOs. The ten rules I offer, identified through a career devoted to real-world research, are equally valuable in ad agency conference rooms and political war rooms (and, for that matter, in conversations with an angry spouse or an anxious teenage daughter). When applied, they give rise to language with color and texture. Language that gets heads nodding. Words that pop, the kinds of words and phrases you only have to hear once before they burn themselves into your mind and drive you to action. In short, these ten principles give rise to words that work.

First, allow me a few caveats. This chapter and this book are not concerned with words that are beautiful, words that are timeless, or words that are ideal in some abstract, philosophical sense. Rather, it is concerned, again, with *words that work*—language of everyday utility, language that generates practical results. My concern is with the unadorned, commonsense language of small town, middle America, not the intellectual gamesmanship of the ivory tower. It's with language that has bubbled up from the American people themselves.

There is certainly a time and a place for high-flown, literary language. But to capture a listener's attention the language doesn't need to be urbane or erudite—or use words like, well . . . urbane or erudite. It does not necessarily need the uplifting, ennobling tone of Ted Sorenson (John F. Kennedy's friend and speechwriter) and Peggy Noonan (gifted scribe for Ronald Reagan), the two great speechwriters of our time. The lofty language of Sorensen and Noonan transcends ideologies and generations, moving listeners just as much today as when their words were

---

*Adds Sorkin, "There'll be actual music that I'll hear while I'm driving in my car, and I'll think right there, 'I want to write to a place where that piece of music can come in,' or I want that piece of music under what we're doing."

first spoken by others decades ago. Noonan was once asked to reflect on the craft of wordsmithing and speechwriting, and I think she had it right:

> Most of us are not great leaders speaking at great moments. Most of us are businessmen rolling out our next year's financial goals, or teachers at a state convention making the case for a new curriculum, or nurses at a union meeting explaining the impact of managed care on the hospitals in which we work. And we must have the sound appropriate to us. . . . Your style should never be taller than you are."[1]

In an ideal world, everyone would have all the knowledge they need, a home library, and our political discourse might take place on the elevated level of a Lincoln-Douglas debate or at least *The Newshour with Jim Lehrer*. People would not speak simply, in concise sentences, but obtusely, in dense paragraphs full of tremendous detail, classical allusions, and subtle theoretical insights—more like Bill Buckley than Bill O'Reilly.

That might be a comforting fantasy, but it isn't reality. For most of us, communication has never been and should never be elitist or obscure. It is *functional* rather than an end in itself. For me, the *people* are the true end; language is just a *tool* to reach and teach them, a means to an end. We live in an age when the world is no longer ruled as it once was by the Latin of the elites, but by the common, democratic tongues of the people. And if you want to reach the people, you must first speak their language.

My second caveat concerns the limits of language. Democratic strategist George Lakoff, a Berkeley professor by trade and a linguist by design, has argued that left-wing ideas would have been plenty popular with the public if only they had been "framed" with the right narratives and metaphors. But this ignores the screamingly obvious: *Some policies and ideas really are more popular than others—no matter how they are articulated.* Language is tremendously important—after all, politicians and an increasing number of corporate warriors live and die by it—but it's not everything. Language alone cannot achieve miracles. Actual policy counts at least as much as how something is framed.

When I tell a political client that a given idea is unpopular, it's to his credit if he sticks to his principles and pushes ahead with it anyway, but I'm not serving him well if I explain away the dilemma altogether so that he's never forced to confront that hard choice between conviction and popularity. To me, the truth matters. My job, as I see it, is to remain agnostic on the underlying philosophical issues and keep my personal opinions from infecting my work. It doesn't matter what I think about tax policy or welfare or the minimum wage. Sure, I have opinions, but they remain just that—my opinions. People hire me to tell them, as objectively as possible, what the general public believes on those issues, and why. They want the truth as it is, not as I wish it to be.

You would be amazed and angry if you knew just how little respect the typical pollster, PR guru, or advertising executive has for your opinion. The Republican pollster who gave America Senators Jesse Helms and Al D'Amato once said to me, and I quote, "I don't care what the people think. I only care what I think." A media consultant to three presidents warned me never to "fall in love" with my clients or the people they represent. "They're all flawed."

Perhaps I take a different approach. Before you can create, and certainly before you judge, you have to listen to people and respect them for who they are and what they believe. Just because you may not ultimately accept or endorse someone's subjective perceptions is no excuse for refusing to acknowledge that they exist. I have sought to listen to the American public—not just *hear,* but truly, actively *listen.* It is informed not just by raw data but by intuition and experience. It is empirical more than theoretical, emotional as well as rational. The process is really quite simple. Through national telephone surveys, focus groups, one-on-one interviews, content analysis, and simple day-to-day interaction with people, I learn the language of America. In fact, what you eventually hear either from your elected representatives or in ads for the products and services you use is often spoken first by you and then translated by me.

I'll say it again: What matters is not what you say, but what people hear.

## THE TEN RULES OF SUCCESSFUL COMMUNICATION

### Rule One
### Simplicity: Use Small Words

William Safire, William F. Buckley, and the people who solve the *New York Times* crossword puzzle will resent this first rule: Avoid words that might force someone to reach for the dictionary . . . because most Americans won't. They'll just placidly let your real meaning sail over their heads or, even worse, misunderstand you. You can argue all you want about the dumbing down of America, but unless you speak the language of your intended audience, you won't be heard by the people you want to reach.

Simplicity counts. The average American did not graduate from college and doesn't understand the difference between *effect* and *affect*.* Sophistication is certainly what Americans say they want in their politics, but it is certainly not what they buy. Newt Gingrich is arguably one of the smartest political figures of the past fifty years, yet his overtly intellectual, philosophical approach—which to opponents sounded bombastic and sanctimonious—turned many people away.

Al Gore and John Kerry, legitimately bright individuals with Ivy League backgrounds, suffered the same fate. Where an average critic of the Bush administration could attack its foreign policy for *"going it alone,"* John Kerry felt the need to offer *"a bold, progressive internationalism that stands in stark contrast to the too often belligerent and myopic unilateralism of the Bush Administration."*[2] Huh?

Similarly, Al Gore told audiences that he longed for the days when *"vividness and clarity used to be more common in the way we talk with one another,"* but then went on to attack the *"abhorrent, medieval behavior"* of the Bush administration—in the very same speech.[3] Neither Gore nor Kerry understood that the ideas you might hear in a Harvard seminar will simply not ring true with the stay-at-home mom in Kansas or the department store salesman in Cincinnati.

In fact, using a long word when a short one would suffice tends to raise suspicions: "What is this guy trying to sell me? Does he have an ulterior motive?" The most effective language clarifies rather than obscures. It makes ideas clear rather than clouding them. The more simply and plainly an idea is presented, the more understandable it is—and therefore the more credible it will be.

The same principle holds true in the corporate sphere. From Campbell's Soup's *"M'm! M'm! Good!"* to the *"Snap! Crackle! Pop!"* of Kellogg's

---

*According to the 2005 census, 45% of adult Americans over age 25 have attended some form of college, but only 27% are college graduates. According to a study conducted for the Association of American Universities, as recently as 1970, only 53% of adult Americans had even graduated from high school.

Rice Krispies, product taglines that are so simple and uncomplicated that even kids can remember them are the ones that prove most memorable to their parents as well. It is no accident that the most unforgettable catchphrases of the past fifty years contain only single- or at most two-syllable words. And when they initially haven't been so simple, someone inevitably has stepped in to shorten them. Just ask the makers of the Macintosh (*"Mac"*) computer. And when's the last time you used the words *"International Business Machines"* rather than *"IBM"*? Federal Express is now officially *"FedEx,"* Kentucky Fried Chicken is now *"KFC,"* Oil of Olay is just *"Olay,"* and Dairy Queen now refers to itself as *"DQ."*

This public preference for simple words and acronyms is also reflected in pop culture. For example, take a look at the movie titles at your local multiplex. All the way back in 1991, the movie *Terminator 2* started a trend of truncation when its title was cut down to *T2*—from five syllables down to two. In the years that followed, *Independence Day* was abbreviated to *ID4* and *Mission: Impossible III* became *M:i:III*, just to cite two prominent examples. Many movies have begun dropping the word *the* from their titles, as well. The 1976 movie *The Bad News Bears* was remade in 2005 as simply *Bad News Bears*, and *The Wedding Crashers* became just *Wedding Crashers.*

Even our day-to-day behavior itself has been simplified. We now live in a text messaging world. Teenagers "text" (a newly coined verb for SMS communication) each other all day long, and the twenty-first-century businessman is attached to his BlackBerry like the farmer of the eighteenth century was attached to his plow. Tapping away with one finger on a miniature keyboard to create a message on a tiny screen isn't exactly conducive to multisyllabic SAT words.

Neither is e-mail, for that matter. We process so much more visual and audible information than ever before, that it's no surprise many of us don't have the patience (not to mention the education) to tease out the fine nuances and connotations of a lot of ten-dollar words. At work and at home, in business and in our personal lives, we're actually writing more than ever before—but what we're writing looks less like an old-fashioned letter and more like what you'd see on a vanity license plate.

These changes didn't come about by accident. Good things really do come in small packages—and from small words.

## Rule Two
## Brevity: Use Short Sentences

*"I didn't have time to write a short letter, so I wrote a long one instead."*
—Mark Twain

Be as brief as possible. Never use a sentence when a phrase will do, and never use four words when three can say just as much. When asked how long a man's legs ought to be, Abraham Lincoln said, "Long enough to reach the ground." The best ad-makers and creative artists understand this notion of appropriateness, and they wisely avoid going overboard. Like Goldilocks in the story of the three bears, they look for the phrases that aren't too big or too small, but "just right." This is less about self-restraint than it is a matter of finding exactly the right piece of the language jigsaw puzzle to fit the precise space you're trying to fill.

The most memorable political language is rarely longer than a sentence. *"I like Ike"* was hardly a reason to vote for the man, but the simplicity of the slogan matched the candidate and the campaign. Not many people considered Calvin Coolidge a great president, but to this day we still remember *"Silent Cal"* for his brevity. When Coolidge's dinner guest bet him that she could make him say more than three words, he responded, "You lose"—still considered one of the best political jokes in presidential history. When the prolific British writer G. K. Chesterton was asked for an essay on the topic "What's Wrong with the World?" he wrote: "Dear Sirs: I am. Sincerely yours, G.K. Chesterton."[4] And we've all heard the story about the college philosophy student given the exam question "Why?" who simply responded, "Why not?" Each of these short answers said far more than a thousand-word essay or Castro-like speechathon would have.

Similarly, they say a picture is worth a thousand words . . . or is that ten thousand words? Researchers have traced the origin of that phrase to Fred Barnard, an advertising manager in the 1920s. When selling ad space on the sides of streetcars, he used the words *"One look is worth a thousand words"* to suggest that images are more potent than text in advertisements. At first Barnard claimed the saying came from a Japanese proverb, but shortly thereafter he changed it a bit, to *"One picture is worth ten thousand words,"* and instead credited a Chinese proverb.[5] Some quotation dictionaries now accept Barnard's claim of Chinese origin, and over time this saying has often been credited to Confucius.[6] The origin really doesn't matter, but the rule certainly does. If one visual can say more than a thousand or ten thousand words, use it.

Sometimes two or three words are worth more than a thousand. The most memorable taglines in product advertising are usually not much more than fragments. From the day in 1914 when Thomas Watson joined IBM, then known as the Computer-Tabulating-Recording Company, and coined the phrase *"think"* to communicate the value of the company, some of the most powerful and provocative messages have come in very small packages. *"Easy as Dell"* effectively communicated the ready-to-use functionality of one of the world's most successful personal computer companies. *"The UnCola"* memorably declared to consumers exactly what 7-Up was . . . and was not. If you ask anyone from age five to 65 what cereal is sold based on the slogan *"They're grrreat!"* they'll tell you Frosted Flakes. *"Got Milk?"* has been wickedly parodied by every late-night talk-show host, but it helped make the product cool again. And at three words, three syllables, and eight letters, Nike's *"Just do it"* packed more power, word for word, than any footwear ad ever— and helped cement a global sporting goods empire.

So when it comes to effective communication, small beats large, short beats long, and plain beats complex. And sometimes a visual beats them all.

### Rule Three
### Credibility Is As Important As Philosophy

People have to believe it to buy it. As Lincoln once said, you can't fool all of the people all of the time. If your words lack sincerity, if they contradict accepted facts, circumstances, or perceptions, they will lack impact.

You will read this lesson several times in this book because it really is that important. The words you use become you—and you become the words you use. The political graveyards are full of politicians who learned this lesson the hard way. One recent example was especially memorable. "I actually did vote for the 87 billion dollars [for the Iraq war] before I voted against it" turned out to be the fifteen most damaging words John Kerry spoke during his long and otherwise successful political career. The fact that he himself was appearing to acknowledge a flip-flop on an issue of such importance turned him into a bonafide flip-flopper and undermined everything else he would say and do for the rest of the campaign. Similarly, Al Gore's assertion during the 2000 campaign that he "invented" the Internet and that he and his wife, Tipper, inspired the book *Love Story* had absolutely no credibility and became the source of ongoing late night humor, significantly damaging his electoral hopes.

Companies often commit the same mistake. They launch *"new and improved"* items every day in an effort to get their products noticed and to appeal to a wider consumer base. Yet more often than not, these efforts fail simply because the item in question isn't really new and isn't much improved. Would-be customers don't see enough of a difference and stick with their current brand; current customers are unimpressed and disappointed—and the product loses credibility as a result. Few things are more valuable than reputation—the integrity of a company's brand—and articulating overblown promises as a result of undisciplined language can be an incredibly dangerous game to play.

The most famous "new and improved" flop was New Coke, a sweeter and some say tastier version of traditional Coca-Cola. It was released in 1985 and marketed as a superior version of the popular soft drink with the slogan *"The best just got better."* It was a spectacular failure and a boon for Pepsi. Just three months after New Coke's launch, the company announced it was returning its original formula, "Classic Coke" (they had to rename the traditional brand to give it clarity) as "New Coke" sales dwindled. Sure, consumers in blind taste tests actually preferred the New Coke formula, but New Coke failed anyway because of a deep emotional allegiance to the original brand and a strong sense that *"new and improved"* was a marketing ploy. If they had slowly and secretly changed the formula and left off the *"new and improved"* language, New Coke probably would have succeeded.

In fact, a *"new and improved"* product whose changes are merely cosmetic—the same old same old in different packaging—is a recipe for customer resentment. It's an issue of expectations. If the sales pitch is too over-the-top, even a reasonably good experience with the product is likely to seem underwhelming to the customer. Look at the recent Coors Light can liner campaign. They started marketing a "frost brew liner" that will keep canned beer colder longer. They touted it as a "breakthrough," but the marketplace didn't respond. A customer is going to be a lot more annoyed than she otherwise would have been when she finds out that what's purportedly the greatest thing since sliced bread is actually just "old and unimproved" draped in a lot of new marketing dollars.

Of course, sometimes a product really will live up to the hype that precedes it. When BMW came out with its *"ultimate driving machine"* tagline—a surprisingly cocky assertion—those who test-drove the car agreed with the premise. The boast was perfectly in line with reality. And the rest is history.

The same packaging effort takes place in the political world. Before a debate or primary election, you'll often hear the pundits talk about a campaign "lowering expectations" for its candidate or trying to "raise the bar" for the other guy. The rationale may not be readily apparent, but it's quite smart. If expectations are set low enough, it's often possible for a loser to come out smelling like a winner (think of Bill Clinton's second-place finish in the 1992 New Hampshire primary—thanks to that clever "Comeback Kid" moniker, he was universally declared a winner—all because he trounced the low expectations for his performance).

On the other hand, if you set expectations too high for a candidate or campaign—a statistical win can be seen as a disappointment or, worse yet, a loss. The most famous example was Senator Ed Muskie's first-place finish in New Hampshire in 1972 that still doomed his campaign because he failed to get 50 percent of the vote. He ceased to be a credible candidate simply because he did not win the expected number of votes.

Sometimes just the *expectations* of expectations can destroy a candidacy. In the 1992 New Hampshire Republican presidential primary, early primary day exit polls available to the media had long-shot populist agitator Pat Buchanan within four points of George H. W. Bush—a shocking result for reporters covering the campaign. Even before the real polls closed, the media echo chamber was in full force with the story of the Buchanan surprise and the Bush failure. As the night wore on, Bush's lead began to grow, and yet the media spin did not change. Buchanan's emotional declaration of *"victory,"* delivered live during the 11:00 p.m. newscasts and just as the front pages of the newspapers were being put to bed, ignored the fact that he had dropped to 42 percent in the actual vote count. Now, this was before Al Gore "invented" the Internet, so the news on the front page *was* the news the next morning—even though breakfast television the next day had the accurate returns.

In fact, when all the votes were counted, Bush had achieved a respectable 63% and Buchanan a lackluster 37%—yet to this day there are still people who think Bush lost New Hampshire. But the Bush margin of victory would have been much larger if it wasn't for the damage done by a six-word sentence that brought Republicans to their feet at the 1988 Republican National Convention and had turned them cranky four years later: *"Read my lips: no new taxes."* The combination of broken promises and blown expectations is always a fatal concoction.

Credibility is established very simply. Tell people who you are or what you do. Then be that person and do what you have said you would do. And finally, remind people that you are what in fact you say you are. In a simple sentence: *Say what you mean and mean what you say.*

## Rule Four
## Consistency Matters

Repetition. Repetition. Repetition. Good language is like the Energizer Bunny. It keeps going . . . and going . . . and going.

Too many politicians insist on new talking points on a daily basis, and companies are running too many different ad executions. By the time we begin to recognize and remember a particular message, it has already been changed.

*"It's the real thing,"* the most memorable Coke tagline, was actually created back in 1943, and it is amazing that it got any traction at all, considering that the company launched three other taglines that same year, including the FDR-esque and immediately forgettable: *"The only thing like Coca-Cola is Coca-Cola itself."* Since then, Coke has tried dozens of communication iterations and variations, none of them as simple and effective. While the company refers to itself on its Web site as "the world's most inclusive brand," the constant tinkering with taglines and the inability to stick to a single message have been major factors contributing to its image erosion. On the other hand, the *"We try harder"* Avis campaign was launched in 1962—and Avis has stuck with it for more than four decades, helping to cement the company as the second biggest automobile rental company in the world.

Some slogans that still seem fresh and original today were actually created generations ago, even before the advent of television, and meant as much to your grandparents as they do to you. *"The breakfast of champions"* tagline for Wheaties was first launched back in 1935 and is still going strong today. The *"M'm! M'm! Good!"* campaign for Campbell's Soup was introduced that same year. Hallmark's *"When you care enough to send the very best"* debuted in 1934, and *"Say it with flowers"* for FTD dates all the way back to 1917.

But there are two products that rise above the rest for brand language consistency—and probably 90 percent of you know the taglines to these products even before you read them.

Maxwell House was a well-known hotel in Nashville, Tennessee, that brewed a coffee so rich in flavor that people would stay there just to enjoy the coffee. Around the turn of the century, they began to market their secret brew to nearby establishments, and it became as popular and talked about in the region as Starbucks is today. According to the company, it was President Teddy Roosevelt who coined the phrase *"good to the last drop"* after drinking a cup of Maxwell House coffee in 1907 while visiting the historic estate of Andrew Jackson. That line became the official slogan of the company in 1915 and it still features prominently in the company's advertising and branding efforts almost one hundred years later. And today, Maxwell House is still one of America's best selling in-home coffee brands.

But the all-time most consistent product slogan belongs to a bar of soap that was first launched back in 1879 for ten cents. James Gamble, of Procter & Gamble fame, developed a soap that was so "pure" that it could be used both for the bath and for the laundry. It was to be called P&G White Soap, but Harley Procter (yes, the Procter of Procter & Gamble) insisted on something more creative and memorable. Attending church one Sunday, he heard a reading of Psalm 45:8 that references ivory palaces—and Ivory Soap was born. Three years later, Proctor coined the phrase *"99 and 44/100% pure"* to describe the scientific tests conducted on the soap by college chemistry professors and independent laboratories. The rest, as they say, is history. The slogan, and the additional tag line *"it floats,"* created in 1891, gave Ivory Soap a visual and linguistic hook that has stood the test of time. While P&G goes to great pains to hide the fact that Ivory is no longer a big seller, the product is still among the most beloved in American consumer history. These companies learned an important rule of successful brands: Message consistency builds customer loyalty.

Finding a good message and then sticking with it takes extraordinary discipline, but it pays off tenfold in the end. Remember, you may be making yourself sick by saying the same exact same thing for the umpteenth time, but many in your audience will be hearing it for the first time. The overwhelming majority of your customers or constituents aren't paying as much attention as you are. They didn't read about your tagline in *Adweek* or hear your slogan on C-SPAN's *Road to the White House*. They haven't seen the volumes of internal memos that you've seen or the pages and pages of talking points that have been developed on your behalf. It needs to sound as fresh and vital to your audiences as it did to your own ears the first time you said it.

When it comes to repetition, politicians are seemingly addicted to communication variation. Ronald Reagan was the only politician I ever saw who seemed to enjoy saying the same words over and over again as though it was the first time he had ever spoken them. His message never wavered, and that was a major reason he sustained personal credibility even though a majority of Americans opposed many of his policies during his administration.

The success of President George W. Bush in the 2004 election despite deteriorating conditions in Iraq, high unemployment numbers in key states, and the perception that the economy was sinking was due in part to consistency of his message. He didn't need speech text or a teleprompter in many of his later campaign appearances because the message was always the same and articulated in almost identical language. But what was seen as consistent in 2004 came to be viewed as inflexible and dogmatic during Bush's second term because of an unwillingness to consider alternative ideas, messages, and approaches to governing.

And that leads to rule number five . . .

## Rule Five
### Novelty: Offer Something New

In plain English, words that work often involve a new definition of an old idea.

---

### NOVELTY IN ACTION: CHRISTIAN BRANDO & THE CREATION OF THE *"ACCIDENTAL MANSLAUGHTER"* PLEA

Attorney Robert Shapiro is more than just a lawyer to the rich and famous. He is best known for putting together the defense "dream team" that kept O. J. Simpson on the golf course rather than in jail, and his creative application of English is acknowledged in the legal profession. Shapiro's considerable linguistic skills were put to the test when he was called upon by actor

Marlon Brando in 1990 to defend his son Christian, who had admitted shooting his sister's fiancé at point-blank range—a potential first-degree murder case punishable by death. Shapiro explains:

> After talking with Christian and talking with Marlon and talking to the sister, it became clear to me that it was something more than just a direct and deliberate first-degree murder. When I got into the case it became clear to me that there was a legal theory, but that it would be very, very difficult to explain to laypeople, especially in a twenty-second sound bite on television or newspaper article.
>
> So rather than explain the different degrees of manslaughter that we have in California that would allow for a mitigation of this type of sentence, I wanted to come up with something that would clearly and unequivocally point to what our defense was.
>
> Our defense was twofold:
>
> First, that there was no intent by Christian Brando to commit a crime, so therefore it was accidental.
>
> And second, that the intent that's required is not a specific intent but rather a general intent, and so that would fall under the guise of involuntary manslaughter.
>
> So I coined the phrase "an accidental manslaughter." And each and every time somebody asked me to comment on the case, I said "We will show clearly this was an accidental manslaughter." And that's what the newspapers printed. And to this day, when people talk about it, Christian Brando pled guilty to accidental manslaughter.
>
> The phrase does not exist in law. It came out of my mouth and I repeated it hundreds of times over the course of three months. And it stuck. One-time use. One-time need."

[The phrase *"accidental manslaughter"* was never used before and has not been used since. Christian Brando did plead guilty and spent six years in prison.]

Americans are easily bored. If something doesn't shock or surprise us, we move on to something else. We are always in search of the next big thing, whether it be the next American Idol, a new television "reality" show, a new gee-whiz techno-gizmo, the latest Madonna makeover, or something else that we haven't seen or heard of before. Our tastes change as quickly as the seasons, and we expect the rest of society to keep up.

As individuals, while we appreciate the predictability of friends and family, we also cherish those things that surprise and shock us—provided that the outcome is pleasant rather than painful. It's the reason why many of us, in our free time, prefer to try different vacation destinations, different hotels, different restaurants, and different experiences rather than the tried and true. There is something deep in our character that embraces the pioneering spirit, going where no one has ever gone before, doing what no one has ever done before. If an opportunity is truly new and different, it will attract our attention, our interest, and our participation.

So from a business perspective, you should tell consumers something that gives them a brand-new take on an old idea (and then, in accordance with rule number four, tell them again and again). The combination of surprise and intrigue creates a compelling message. Although often executed with humor, what matters most is that the message brings a sense of discovery, a sort of "Wow, I never thought about it that way" reaction. For example, people knew that Alka-Seltzer was taken for an upset stomach, but market research showed that nobody knew how many they should be taking—so most people were just taking one. But when viewers saw the infamous *"Plop, plop, fizz, fizz, oh what a relief it is"* ads, purchases of Alka-Seltzer nearly doubled almost overnight. The tagline that sold the product became indivisible from the product's *function* because it told consumers something they did not know.

A more humorous example featured the inclusion of religion into advertising to help sell a food product. Not surprisingly, half of the senior executives at Hebrew National, the hot dog company, were Jewish, and their *"We answer to a higher authority"* campaign, suggesting that their hot dogs were made from better ingredients than what the USDA required (personified by a very tall Uncle Sam character), sparked dozens of amusing parodies and millions of sales. The success of the Volkswagen *"Think Small"* campaign in the late 1950s was another example of shifting the thought process in a novel way. At a time when cars and the promotion of them were ever expanding in size, VW took exactly the opposite approach in design and in message. It worked because it made people think about the product in a fresh way.

There's a simple test to determine whether or not your message has met this rule. If it generates an "I didn't know that" response, you have succeeded.

## BAD ENGLISH = A GOOD OUTCOME: THE O. J. SIMPSON TRIAL

A simple but effective mangling of the English language played a major role in the Trial of the Century. Lead defense team lawyer Robert Shapiro desperately needed to find a forensic pathologist to discredit the DNA of Nicole Simpson that was found on the clothing of her estranged husband O. J. Simpson. So he hired Dr. Henry Lee, a chief medical examiner from Connecticut, and a first-generation Asian-American. Shapiro describes the power of words better than I could so I'll let him do the talking:

> It was probably the most dramatic use of language that I've ever seen in a courtroom. When the DNA swabs were being analyzed, the DNA is collected, the blood samples are put in paper and they are folded. The folds should be in a certain way where the blood does not go to the other side, it just stays dry. Otherwise, there is a chance of what they call "cross-contamination."
>
> In this case, somebody made a mistake and had the DNA collected while it was still wet, and folded it. And Dr. Henry Lee, using broken English, which he is more than capable of not using, made a statement that I think will never be forgotten. When the prosecution asked, "What do you conclude from this evidence, Dr. Lee?" he said "Something wrong." I don't know if he thought about it, if he didn't think about it, if it was just spontaneous, but he was asked a question and that was his answer. "How do you account for it?" "Something wrong." Those two words rang loud and true with the jury, and that was the end of that evidence. Two simple words. I wish I was that smart."

### Rule Six
### Sound and Texture Matter

The sounds and texture of language should be just as memorable as the words themselves. A string of words that have the same first letter, the same sound, or the same syllabic cadence is more memorable than a random collection of sounds. The first five rules in this chapter do just that: *simplicity*, *brevity*, *credibility*, *consistency*, and *novelty* stand out because they all end with the same sound.

The phrase *"Snap, Crackle, and Pop"* immediately conjures up images not just of Kellogg's Rice Krispies but of the actual sound of the cereal itself. Some of the most identifiable branding doesn't even involve words. For more than a half century, first on radio and then on television, NBC announced its network programming with three distinctive notes: G-E-C (the initials of parent company General Electric). *"Intel Inside"* is as memorable for its four notes as for the slogan itself.

The sound of music has magical powers that transcend the language it is meant to augment. But while most television writers first craft their words and then add the music, Aaron Sorkin approaches it differently: "There'll be actual music that I'll hear while I'm driving in my car, and I'll think right there, 'I want to write to a place where that piece of music can come in,' or 'that piece of music needs to be under what we're doing.'"

The rhythm of the language is in itself musical—even when there is no tune.*

Besides appealing to people's sense of novelty, Alka-Seltzer's *"Plop, plop, fizz, fizz, oh what a relief it is"* is another good illustration. The rhyme still sticks in people's heads even though the ad has not run for a quarter of a century. Bounty's *"quicker picker upper"* campaign from the 1970s may have mangled the English language, but those three words sounded good together. Likewise, the alliteration at the beginning of the M&M's slogan, *"Melts in your mouth . . ."* helps the tagline stick in the memory.

Another approach is to butcher the English language. The Mac slogan that appeared on billboards and in print ads with pictures of Albert Einstein and other icons, *"Think Different,"* was a grammatical travesty (it should have been *"Think Differently"*), but the company wisely went with the shorter, snappier sounding slogan—and the rules of grammar be damned. Similarly, the latest McDonald's slogan *"i'm lovin' it"* features eye-catching lowercase letters, even when they begin a sentence, and no matter how hard you look, there is no such word as *lovin'* in any English dictionary. But the slogan speaks directly to how customers feel about the experience, and the catchy wordplay has been an important factor in the rise in revenue for the company after a couple years of sales

---

*Says Sorkin: "The greatest speech of all time is 'I Have a Dream.' You read the speech and it's perfect. Listen to the speech, it gets more perfect. The way as the speech moved on, the phrase 'I have a dream' stopped being the beginning of each stanza and began being the end, 'That one day, we will be judged not by the color of our skin, by the content of our character, I have a dream.' That's what jazz musicians do. They take a phrase and they move it. It was phenomenal delivery."

stagnation. Burger King may have it your way, but McDonald's says it their way.


## Rule Seven
## Speak Aspirationally

Messages need to say what people *want* to hear. This is the one area where politicians often have the edge over the corporate community. It's very difficult to craft advertising language that touches people at the most fundamental, primal level, by speaking to their deepest hopes, fears, and dreams. Not many products or services have an impact as serious and significant as abortion, affirmative action, immigration, taxation, and the other topics most often addressed by political figures.

The key to successful aspirational language for products or politics is to personalize and humanize the message to trigger an emotional remembrance. As Warren Beatty, perhaps the best student of the human condition in Hollywood, once told me, people will forget what you say, but they will never forget how you made them feel. If the listener can apply the language to a general situation or human condition, you have achieved *humanization*. But if the listener can relate that language to his or her own life experiences, that's *personalization*. The most memorable example comes from the political world. When Martin Luther King, Jr., uttered the words *"I have a dream,"* the single greatest aspirational speech of the modern era, he was speaking to the individual hopes and dreams of all Americans—the desire to be accepted because of who we are rather than what we look like. Product advertising has a higher hurdle to clear. Consumers have to see themselves in the ad and perceive a genuine benefit and value to themselves from using the product. They have to identify personally with the people in the ads in a profound way, the way you might identify with a special teacher or colleague at work.

Aspirational advertising language doesn't sell the product as a mere tool or as an item that serves a specific, limited purpose. Instead it sells the *you*—the you that you will be when you use the product . . . a smarter, sexier, sunnier you. It's not about creating false expectations, for that would diminish credibility. It's about encouraging the message recipient to want something better—and then delivering it. For example, the current Olay slogan *"Love the skin you're in"* is all about improving self-worth—an aspirational quality for most women. Instead of trying to cover up their natural looks with mounds of cosmetics, this campaign tells women to respect who they already are and embrace what they already look like . . . with the help of Olay. Similarly, L'Oréal's *"because you're worth it"* campaign seeks to empower and embolden women to invest in themselves. By strategically placing beautiful but more natural-looking women in their television commercials and magazine ads, consumers see themselves—not some unattainable model—looking attractive and feeling confident.

A recent De Beers campaign uses the slogan *"A diamond is forever."* But instead of using the traditional message of love and commitment, De Beers has taken it one step farther: eternity. No longer is a diamond a valued and expensive piece of jewelry. Now it offers immortality—both the diamond and the relationship it symbolizes—and that's about as aspirational as you can get.

Experiences can also be aspirational. When JFK challenged America's youth to join the Peace Corps, his message didn't hinge on the actual practicalities of the job—digging wells, distributing medicines, or even teaching living skills. His message was larger than that; it was about what the Peace Corps symbolized . . . and what it meant about *you* as a person when you joined it. In the same way, aspirational advertising language taps into people's idealized self-image, showing them a picture of the other, better life that they wish they had, the life that feels like it's just out of reach right now . . . but that your product may finally help them grasp.

Since women determine the largest percentage of consumer purchases, most successful aspirational language is targeted at them. The *"Look ma, no cavities"* campaign for Crest toothpaste was every mother's dream . . . as was the *"Calgon, take me away"* message, which may seem dated today, but which struck an aspirational nerve when it first aired.

Perhaps the most memorable and effective examples of aspirational language in politics are FDR's assertion that *"The only thing we have to fear is fear itself "* and President Kennedy's *"Ask not what your country can do for you, ask what you can do for your country."* Both make appeals to Americans' most idealistic conceptions of themselves. But even more important is that both statements are essentially *reminders.* Each president was reminding Americans of what Lincoln called "the better angels" of their nature. They were expressing confidence in Americans' bravery (FDR) and their self-sacrifice and patriotism (JFK) and then exhorting them to do even more. Psychologically, these phrases are akin to the parent who tells his child, "You can do it, I have faith in you." FDR and JFK were simultaneously flattering us—by letting us know their confidence in our potential—and challenging us to rise to the occasion and be our better selves. And good advertisements, in a much more minor way, accomplish much the same thing. They make idealists of us all.

## Rule Eight
### Visualize

Paint a vivid picture. From M&M's *"Melts in your mouth not in your hand"* to Morton Salt's *"When it rains, it pours,"* to NBC's *"Must See TV,"* the slogans we remember for a lifetime almost always have a strong visual component, something we can see and almost feel. Allstate's *"You're in good hands,"* first created in 1956, went so far as to include the cupped hands visual in its logo to remind people of its peace-of-mind guarantee.

Recently, more companies are turning to slogans that rely heavily on visuals in order to sell their products. One such product, General Mills' Cinnamon Toast Crunch, has the *"taste you can see."* While the slogan alludes to the very real crystals of sugar and cinnamon visible on the toasted squares, it implies that the taste of the cereal is so incredible that you can actually do the impossible and see it.

Another company that uses visual slogans is Dodge. While we may not all associate grasping onto the head of a ram with driving a truck, the visual that *"Grab life by the horns"* implies says that if you're driving a Dodge Ram, you're doing something active, exciting, and powerful. And that's exactly what truck owners want and expect from their vehicles.*

Ineffective visualization can torpedo even the most potentially popular product. Just ask the makers of Infiniti, arguably the best new car of the past twenty years, who decided, incorrectly, that they should launch their new vehicles invisibly—literally—at exactly the same time that Lexus was using exactly the opposite and much more successful visual approach.

Lexus came out of the gate first with a traditional ad campaign featuring their new car navigating a typical winding road and packaged around the tagline *"The relentless pursuit of perfection."* Solid, but not spectacular. In response, Infiniti refused to use a tagline *or* show their

---

*Most Dodge cars and trucks featured a charging ram on their hoods from 1932 to 1954. They came back to the image of ram tough in the 1980s when sales of their trucks began to lag.

car. Rather, Nissan, the makers of the Infiniti, created a series of nine commercials intended to illustrate the fantasies of potential drivers.

The "fantasy" campaign was a distinct departure from typical car ads because it was based on a Japanese interpretation of luxury that is almost spiritual in its approach rather than the more literal American interpretation, undermining both credibility and relevance. While Lexus packed their ads with facts about their *"European luxury car tradition,"* and beautiful visuals of their car, Infiniti ads were deliberately vague, featuring clear skies, trees, and water shots . . . but never a clear picture of the automobile. None.

So instead of generating winning sales numbers for a great new car, Nissan generated a communication equation for failure: a wholly unrecognizable automotive design + a poorly executed ad design = no visualization. Over the subsequent months, Nissan spent more time defending their ad campaign than pitching their cars, and Infiniti was outsold four-to-one in its first year by Lexus—an automobile that was, from an engineering perspective, an almost identical car.[7] Infiniti simply didn't understand that people will not buy a car if they cannot see themselves in it.

But visualizing has as much to do with words as it does with pictures, and there is one word in the English language that automatically triggers the process of visualization by its mere mention, simply because it has 300 million unique, individual, personal manifestations to match the 300 million Americans. That word: *imagine.* Whether it's the car of your dreams or the candidate of your choice, the word *imagine* is perhaps the single most powerful communication tool because it allows individuals to picture whatever personal vision is in their hearts and minds.

Let me provide one example of the powerful impact of *imagine,* with which I had tangential involvement. Harold Ford, Jr., a centrist member of Congress from Tennessee who was blessed with a velvety smooth style and an intellect beyond that of most politicians, was given the honor of delivering the keynote address at the 2000 Democratic National Convention that nominated Al Gore. At thirty, Ford was one of the youngest keynoters ever, and so the Gore campaign assigned one of its speechwriters, Kenny Baer, to draft the speech to ensure that Ford delivered the "correct" message. The congressman, Kenny, and I all had one thing in common: We all were at the University of Pennsylvania at the same time—the other two as students and me as an adjunct professor. I had known both of them personally for almost a decade, so this should have been a positive experience for all of us.

I had bumped into Ford and one of his aides in a hotel lobby just forty-eight hours before his national debut. They asked me to take a quick look at the speech the Gore campaign had drafted for him because they felt it had not been written in his voice, and the Gore campaign was ignoring their attempts to make fundamental changes to the draft. While Ford went on to shake hands and work the lobby, I went upstairs to his suite to take a look.

What I saw appalled me. It was so partisan, so political, so negative, and so *not* Harold Ford. Class warfare. Rich versus poor. Haves versus have-nots. Greed versus virtue. Good (Democrats) versus evil (Republicans). It painted a picture of a simplistic, black-and-white world. Had Ford delivered that speech as written, he would have come off like every other partisan hack: all politics, no vision.

When Ford returned, I told him I hated the speech because it did not reflect who he was or what he was about. It would sound foreign coming out of his mouth. He needed to talk about something positive and uplifting. And so I recommended that he create a riff on the word *imagine*. Funny that the first time I ever suggested using that word in politics—which I have since advised dozens of politicians to do—it was for a Democrat.

Baer and the Gore people hated Ford's revised speech because it didn't blast a hole in the Republicans. Instead, it was positive and affirming, inclusive and free of partisan sniping. It did not even mention George W. Bush by name. Fortunately, Ford insisted on doing it his way. Now you decide whether the words of Harold Ford are words that work:

> The choice before us is not what kind of America will we have in the next four years, but what kind of America will we have in the next forty?
>
> Imagine if you will for a moment, a debt-free economy strong enough that every American can share in the American dream.
>
> Imagine a health care system where every American receives the medicine he or she needs, and where no senior is forced to stay up late at night deciding whether to buy food or fill a prescription.
>
> Imagine a society that treats seniors with the respect and dignity they deserve.
>
> Imagine a nation of clean coastlines and safe drinking water.
>
> Imagine a world where we give all children a first-class education.
>
> Well, America, it's time to stop imagining. Tonight, I call on all of

my reform-minded Republican and Independent friends to join us in our crusade, to join us in making this bold imagination a reality.[8]

The reviews of Ford's keynote address were solid. Fred Barnes and Mort Kondracke, Fox News commentators, both picked Ford as that convention's "rising star," even suggesting that the thirty-year-old would someday grace a national Democrat ticket.[9] Conservative commentator Sean Hannity applauded the speech, as did Michael Barone, writing for *U.S. News & World Report,* and even GOP leader David Dreier gave it favorable marks.[10] Everyone had high praise—except for the Gore campaign. As Ryan Lizza wrote in *The New Republic:* "As usual, the media wrote laudatory profiles about the 30-year-old, black, Southern New Democrat who represented the future of the party. Behind the scenes, however, Gore's aides were not as praiseworthy."[11] Nope, the people in partisan overdrive were not happy, but everyone else was. By imagining a better America, Harold Ford helped everyone *except* the partisan politicos see a better America.

## Rule Nine
## Ask a Question

*"Is it live, or is it Memorex?" "Where do you want to go today?"* (Microsoft) *"Can you hear me now?"* (Verizon Wireless)

*"Got Milk?"* may be the most memorable print ad campaign of the past decade. The creator realized, whether intentionally or not, that it's sometimes not what you say but what you ask that really matters. A statement, when put in the form of a rhetorical question, can have much greater impact than a plain assertion. If unemployment and inflation are up and confidence in the future is down, telling voters that life has gotten worse, while clearly factual, is less effective than asking voters *"Are you better off today than you were four years ago?"* Ronald Reagan asked Jimmy Carter and the tens of millions of debate listeners this devastating political question in their only face-to-face campaign encounter in 1980. No litany of economic data or political accusation could carry the power of a simple rhetorical question that for most Americans had an equally simple answer. *"Are you better off"* framed not just the debate, held only five days before the election, but the entire campaign, and it propelled Reagan from dead even to a nine-point victory over the incumbent Carter.

An even simpler question was posed hypothetically by former House Speaker Newt Gingrich in the months leading up to the 2006 midterm elections. When asked what he would tell Democrats to say in their campaign against the House Republicans he once led, Newt's response encapsulated several communication "rules." It was just two words, three syllables, and nine letters: *"Had enough?"* It needs no explanation. It needs no clarification. It simply rings true. Apparently, much of America agreed.

The question-rule has day-to-day implications as well. A customer complaining to the store manager that her meat has too much fat in it is less effective than if she asked: *"Does this look lean to you?"* Similarly, asking *"What would you do if you were in my shoes?"* puts direct pressure on the recipient of your complaint to see things your way.

The reason for the effectiveness of questions in communication is quite obvious. When you assert, whether in politics, business, or day-to-day life, the reaction of the listener depends to some degree on his or her opinion of the speaker. But making the same statement in the form of a rhetorical question makes the reaction personal—and personalized communication is the best communication.

This rule comes straight from famed Democratic media consultant Tony Schwartz, and he called it the "responsive chord theory" of communication. Schwartz was best known for creating the advertising campaign for Lyndon Johnson in 1964 that included the "Daisy" ad, the single most devastating political spot of all time, because of its juxtaposition of a little girl counting up the petals on a daisy with a chilling, echoed countdown of a nuclear missile launch. In his work, Schwartz found that people reacted best to language and messages that were participatory—allowing the receiver to interact with the message and the messenger. Rhetorical questions require responses, and responses by definition are interactive.

No profession depends more on the strategic use of the rhetorical question than criminal lawyers (also known as *"attorneys"* by those who actually like what they do and how they do it). The best lawyers use the rhetorical method to remove their clients from the proceedings and in essence put themselves on trial instead. Robert Shapiro explains why:

> My client comes into the courtroom with baggage because we do
> not have the presumption of innocence in America. Truth is, we

have the assumption of guilt, and it starts the minute somebody is arrested. Nobody says "an innocent person was arrested today on suspicion of murder." What happens is the Chief of Police, the District Attorney, and everybody else who is looking to get on television has a press conference and says "We have solved a crime. We have arrested and have in custody the person who did it. He will be prosecuted to the fullest extent of the law." And then a lawyer comes along at some point and either says "no comment" or "my client's not guilty," but nobody believes. So my job as a lawyer is to try to level the playing field.

Shapiro explains and demonstrates the process with a series of questions in his communications tool kit for picking juries. Some of them are designed to raise legitimate doubts, while others are asked merely for emotional impact:

I look right at the jury and I ask each one of them, "Why do you think the person next to me is sitting here? What did he do?" Sometimes I will stand there for 30 seconds in silence—and that's a long time to be silent. I'll wait until they start to get a little bit nervous and a little uneasy. Then I explain to them he's there because a prosecutor has looked at some evidence and decided to issue a charge. Nothing more, nothing less. No trials were heard, no testimony was taken under oath. And then I'll ask, "Do you believe this man did anything?" It's obviously a question that is designed not to have an answer, because they can't answer it. Again silence. And then I say, "Well, this is a demonstration of what the presumption of innocence is. Do you really believe that?" And I stare them straight in the eye.

Shapiro and other successful criminal lawyers use the rhetorical question method to set the context even before the trial begins so that each juror will have an absolute understanding of what the law requires. And the impact on each juror? Says Shapiro: "When I'm done, they believe that the person sitting next to me is no more guilty of any crime than the person sitting next to them in the jury box."

Still, one should think through the consequences of asking a rhetorical question. The *"Does she or doesn't she?"* rhetorical campaign for

Clairol in the 1960s played on the notion that the product was so good that no one could tell the difference between dyed hair and natural color ("Only her hairdresser knows for sure"). The irony was that it also sent a not-so-subtle message that women shouldn't admit that they colored their hair—that this was the kind of thing that ought to be kept hidden in the medicine cabinet. The ad campaign, seemingly simple and straightforward, ended up discouraging satisfied customers from spreading the word about the product.

Nevertheless, the rhetorical question remains one of the most powerful but underutilized communication tools.

## Rule Ten
## Provide Context and Explain Relevance

Context is so important that it serves not only as the last and most important rule of effective communication, but also as its own chapter. You have to give people the "why" of a message before you tell them the "therefore" and the "so that."

Some people call this *framing*. I prefer the word *context*, because it better explains why a particular message matters. Without context, you cannot establish a message's value, its impact, or most importantly, its relevance. *"Have it your way,"* the on-again, off-again Burger King slogan first launched in 1973, spoke to the frustration of fast-food consumers who didn't want their burgers like everyone else's. The line effectively set Burger King apart from the other fast-food chains. Without the underlying context of fast food being a mass-produced, assembly-line proposition, without the idea that all fast food was essentially the same, *"Have it your way"* wouldn't have resonated.

In corporate advertising, as in politics, the order in which you present information determines context, and it can be as important as the substance of the information itself. The "so that" of a message is your solution, but solutions are meaningless unless and until they are attached to an identifiable problem. Finding the right "why" to address is thus just as important as the "how" you offer. Products and services alike must all respond to a felt need on the part of the public.

This is particularly true in politics. From a *"return to normalcy"* in 1920 on behalf of Warren Harding to *"It's morning again in America"* for Ronald Reagan in 1984, campaigns have been using simple phrases to capture the context of the times. Perhaps the best example of a political slogan where the context *is* the message was never really meant to be a political slogan at all. *"It's the economy, stupid"* wasn't created for public consumption. When Democratic strategist James Carville wrote it on a sign that hung on the wall of presidential candidate Bill Clinton's Little Rock campaign office in 1992, he did so to remind the campaign staff what was singularly important. But the phrase caught on—a hallmark of a good slogan—and has been part of our political lexicon ever since. The short and somewhat crude statement (based on the old "Keep it simple, stupid") perfectly encapsulated what the Democrats were trying to get across in 1992.

Context is only half of the framing effort. The other half—relevance— is focused on the individual and personal component of a communication effort. Put most simply, if it doesn't matter to the intended audience, it won't be heard. With so many messages and so many communication vehicles competing for our attention, the target audience must see *individual, personal* meaning and value in your words. The *"Don't leave home without it"* campaign by American Express beginning in the mid-1970s played on people's fears of losing their wallets away from home—a relevant concern for almost every road warrior at that time. Most everyone can relate to that feeling of momentary panic when you realize your wallet isn't in your pocket; we heard the American Express ad and immediately imagined a personal crisis prevented by American Express traveler's checks—and later the American Express card.*

Relevance is one reason market research is so crucial. Until you know what drives and determines a consumer's or a voter's decision-making process, any attempt to influence him or her is really just a shot in the dark. It's relying on luck to hit its target. But once market research has identified the key factors on which a decision turns, then your message can be tailored specifically to those relevant points.

Beyond market research, the most important factor in guaranteeing relevance is imagination. It's important to shed your own perspective and try to put yourself in your audience's position, seeing the world through their eyes. Politicians are notoriously inept at this, constantly mired in Beltway jargon that loses sight of where they came from and what the voters truly care about. A hint: It's not the prerogatives of the

---

*And now it's Visa that is making a case for relevancy, emphasizing all the events and places that do accept Visa cards but don't accept American Express.

Senate or the minutiae of the budget reconciliation process. It's safety, security, and peace of mind.

By the same token, most buyers of Hebrew National don't want to see how those hot dogs are made, and the average buyer of a home computer doesn't give much thought to how a semiconductor works. Don't get so caught up in your own insider's perspective that you lose sight of what the man or woman on the street really cares about. Hassle-free technology is a lot more important to a lot more people than the brand of chip in Dell's laptop computer.

These, then, are the ten rules of effective communication, all summarized in single words: simplicity, brevity, credibility, consistency, novelty, sound, aspiration, visualization, questioning, and context. If your tagline, slogan, or message meets most of these criteria, chances are it will meet with success. If it meets all ten, it has a shot at being a home run. But in the history of political verbiage and product marketing, less than one in one thousand hit it out of the park.

Words aren't everything, of course. If there were a rule eleven, it would address the importance of visual symbols.

It's hard not to acknowledge the staggering impact of visual imagery on modern life. We are all overstimulated—or is it narcotized or lobotomized—by film, television, billboards, and now, the Internet. The amount of information we consume grows ever greater, even as our collective attention span shrinks. To prove this to yourself, simply catch a TV Land rerun of an hour-long popular drama from the 1960s or 1970s. You'll be stunned by the slow, sluggish pacing, by how much it holds the audience's hand, and by dialogue and camera angles that seem to discourage action—and it will hit home how much things have changed. *Hawaii Five-0,* with its striking visuals and more graphic style, was almost revolutionary in its approach to verbal and visual action, and was the top police show in the 1970s, but current fans of Keifer Sutherland's *24* would find it slow and unmemorable today. Even the random flurry of images that appeared so revolutionary when MTV gave birth to the music video in the early 1980s have become antiquated and passé.

Political campaigns are generally very clever at capturing the power of the visual, whether it be standing on the steps of the U.S. Capitol or a multicultural crowd enjoying some random ethnic celebration. In 1984, Lesley Stahl of the *CBS Evening News* put together a lengthy report she thought was highly critical of President Reagan. In Stahl's own words, "I was worried that my sources at the White House would be angry enough to freeze me out." But after the story aired, Deputy White House Chief of Staff Michael Deaver was anything but angry. "Way to go, Kiddo," he said to Stahl. "What a great piece. We loved it." Stahl replied, "Didn't you hear what I said?" Deaver replied, "Nobody heard what you said. . . . You guys in televisionland haven't figured it out yet, have you? When the pictures are powerful and emotional, they override if not completely drown out the sound. I mean it, Lesley. Nobody heard you."[12] The happy pictures of President Reagan—looking strong and amiable and, well, presidential—undermined the *context* for Stahl's harsh critique. Providing proper context is rule number one of communication, but visual impact can obliterate rule number one.

A visual context that supports and reinforces your language will provide a multiplier effect, making your message that much stronger. And, as the Stahl-Reagan anecdote illustrates, a striking visual context can overwhelm the intended verbal message entirely. It's no accident that contemporary politicians have learned to array American flags in the background of their press conferences or speak in front of themed backdrops, pronouncing the subject and message just in case the speech doesn't make it abundantly clear. It's politics for the simpleminded.

No one has done this more often and more effectively than Bush 43 and his White House communication and advance teams. Rarely does the President make official remarks without the topic of those remarks spelled out multiple times on the wall behind him. *"Strengthening Social Security"* or *"Winning the War on Terror"* repeated over and over and over for the television cameras to capture and viewers at home to read . . . and read . . . and read.* Of course this can backfire if the message proves to be false—such as the big *"Mission Accomplished"* sign Bush stood in front of on the U.S.S. *Lincoln* aircraft carrier when he announced the end of "major combat operations" in Iraq on May 1, 2003.

---

*When I got involved in the Social Security messaging effort in the mid 1990s, the official Republican slogan was *"preserve and protect Social Security."* But in my research, I found seniors and pre-retirees much more favorable toward a more proactive and forward-looking approach to the program. While *"preserve and protect"* suggests keeping it just as it is, *"strengthening"* says making it better—and that's what seniors really wanted. Eventually the Republicans adopted the new language. I took a similar approach to Medicare reform. Far more popular than the official House Republican message of "preserving and protecting Medicare" was *"save, strengthen and simplify Medicare."* Dozens of Congressional Republicans agreed.

And of course, no public event in the twenty-first century is complete without the packed stage with the various shades of America huddled on top of each other—all smiling and nodding on cue.*

But deploy the wrong symbol in the wrong way and you're headed for big trouble. While studying at Oxford for my doctorate in the mid-1980s, I made a speech at the hallowed Oxford Union Society arguing that governments take too much money in taxes. I took a British one-pound note (they got rid of them a year later) and began to cut it up with a pair of scissors to illustrate my thesis and visually depict just how much of each pound went to the government in the form of taxes. I thought I was making shrewd use of symbolism, copying the methods used a couple of years earlier by President Reagan.

Now, let's catalogue my mistakes, shall we? There were three of them. (But don't call it a "hat trick"—a hockey symbol for some and a reference to either magic or clothing to others. A majority of women won't know what you're talking about. And if the TV ratings are any indication, many men won't know, either.)

**1.** At the time I had no idea that it was actually illegal to deface the British pound. Strike one. (See how these sports metaphors keep popping up? Suppress the urge. You are not Vin Scully, the "voice" of the Los Angeles Dodgers, and your audience didn't necessarily grow up at Dodger Stadium.)

**2.** I failed to realize that the British do not take kindly to a *foreigner* destroying one of their national symbols. It's not just the substance of the message that's significant, it's also who delivers it. We see this everywhere. David Letterman or Robin Williams can take the most wispy, meaningless nothing of an idea and spin it into comedy gold. Your cousin Lenny tries out the same material, and he comes off about as funny as a stubbed toe.

**3.** Finally, cutting the pound note with scissors was perceived as a violent attack. Before I could finish my speech, I was booed off the dispatch box. I returned to my seat and sunk faster than the exchange rate. The stunt would have worked in the United States, but in England it was too provocative, even sacrilegious. The experience

*The next time you see the President speaking, notice how quickly you stop watching him and scan the faces of the people behind him. They're all nobodies, and yet your eyes will spend as much time focused on their reaction as you do on what the President is saying. We can't help it. It's just the way we process information.

devastated me. I never spoke again at Oxford without a fully prepared text, and even after returning to the States, it took years to shake the embarrassment.

*It's not what you say, it's what people hear . . . and see.*

---

## Words That Worked—Case Study: *"Talk to Me"*

In 1994, I gave 150 Nerf footballs emblazoned with the words *"Talk to Me"* on them to a roomful of anxious Republican members of Congress. The footballs were the antidote for what I thought was wrong with the Republican Party during the previous two-year period when the Democrats were in control of virtually every political level of power nationally.

I knew from my research in 1993 that Americans viewed the GOP as much too uptight and staid, and Republican candidates as too distant and humorless. As the 1994 election approached, Republicans finally began to secure a narrow but noticeable advantage on many of the key political issues facing the country, but Americans still saw them as too stuffy and buttoned-down. The Contract with America was exactly the right approach to demonstrate that this crop of candidates were different not only from the Democrats in charge, but also from the Republicans that had come before. But that wasn't necessarily enough. There had to be a stylistic difference to enhance the substance. They needed a personality transplant.

Enter the footballs—a technique to personalize the otherwise politicized town hall meeting concept. Now, looking at the House Republicans I was advising, I appreciated that they weren't a particularly athletic bunch, and I wasn't sure which they'd have more trouble with, throwing a football or catching one.* So I decided to go Nerf. On the footballs was printed an essential slogan that articulated everything the balls were meant to do: *"Talk to Me."*

The Democrats had controlled Congress for forty years—and over the course of four decades in power they had become distant, closed off, arrogant, and out of touch. *"Talk to Me"* was exactly what voters

---

*Steve Largent and J. C. Watts, elected in the class of 1994, were actual professional football stars in their own right. They were the exception.

wanted to do with their elected officials in 1994, and exactly what too many politicians were not letting them do. I had the balls made blue and white because I wanted them to look patriotic (I was too cheap to add a third color, red). Today, a prototype of those Nerf footballs sits in the Smithsonian Institution.

The words *"Talk to Me"* were important, but so, too, was the symbolism of a congressman playing catch with his or her constituents. The objective: Use the footballs in their town hall sessions to create a *connection* between them and their constituents. More precisely, it was about putting constituents at the center of the communication rather than being the target of it.* The structure of the town halls was supposed to go something like this:

Members would welcome people to their town halls and thank them for coming just as they always had done. But instead of launching into a fifteen- or thirty-minute speech or presentation, members would first ask the audience why they came to the event that day and what they hoped to learn. And the way people would be chosen to speak was by catching the football. The member of Congress would toss the ball to someone in the audience and invite that person to stand and speak. After each person had spoken, he or she would throw the football back to the member, who would then toss it back out to someone else. And this would go on for an hour or ninety minutes.

Everybody wanted to get his or her hands on the football because everyone wanted to be heard. And when somebody caught a pass from the representative, they all felt as if they'd *connected.* Even though the vast majority of attendees never got a chance to speak, everyone left the sessions with a personal sense of involvement. The footballs made what would otherwise have been dull political events into something participatory, interactive, and fun, like catching a foul ball at a baseball game or the bouquet at a wedding reception. By my best estimates, about fifty candidates used the footballs regularly in the 1994 campaign, and you can still see the footballs on display in some of their offices. And in November

---

*My greatest frustration with politicians and corporate leaders is that they talk about being constituent-centered but they don't actually communicate it. For example, instead of reading to children, they should encourage children to read to them. Instead of conducting shareholder meetings that allow limited or no voices from the floor, CEOs should conduct listening sessions where they ask the questions and shareholders do the responding. If a constituent or shareholder is asked a question by a senator or CEO and is given the chance to respond, the entire audience is empowered—and grateful.

1994, *not a single House Republican incumbent was defeated*—despite the anti-incumbent mood of the electorate.

Those three words embroidered on the footballs—*"Talk to Me"*—adhered to almost all of the ten rules of effective language. They were plain, simple, concise, powerful, and effective. Language like that is what this book is all about.

## II

## *Preventing Message Mistakes*

*"Single words really do control the debate. Pro-life, for example, makes the other side automatically pro-death. 'If we're pro-life, I guess the people we're up against are, you know, [laughs] you fill in the blank.'"*
—POLITICAL HUMORIST BILL MAHER

*"It descends from the heavens. Ironically it unleashes hell."*
—AN AD FOR THE BOEING CV-22 OSPREY
THAT SHOWS THE PLANE OBLITERATING A
MOSQUE. BOEING LATER PULLED THE AD.

There's an old joke. A guy is marooned on a desert island, alone, for twenty years, until one day a ship arrives. The ship's captain looks around and notices that there are two synagogues. The castaway says, "I built both of them." The captain replies, "You're here alone?" "Yes." "And you built both?" "Yes," the castaway says. "That one I go to, and that one I'd never set foot in."

That's a classic, traditional Catskills joke. Now, if you're of a certain age, you know what I mean by a "Catskills joke." *Everyone* used to know what that meant, to understand what the Catskills were to American comedy. To young people today, that "Take my wife . . . please" style of humor seems as dated as Sid Caesar.* If you're reading this book as part of a college course, you will probably have to Google "Catskills."

Circumstances change, and so do the meaning of words. You also have to consider the knowledge and frame of reference—the context—of your listener.

---

*When asked why all of Sid Caesar's writers were young and Jewish, Larry Gelbart, a writer for Caesar and genuine comic genius explained, *"It's probably because all of our parents were old and Jewish."*

Few words—indeed, few messages of any kind—whether in politics or in the business world, are ingested in isolation. Their meanings are shaped and shaded by the regional biases, life experiences, education, assumptions, and prejudices of those who receive them. Communicators too often forget this, or absentmindedly acknowledge it but then continue oblivious, making almost calamitous assumptions about where their audience is coming from, figuring that whomever they're pitching their product or policy to is just like they are. They learn too late that most Americans are not denizens of Capitol Hill or the executive suite.

When a CEO asserts publicly that he should receive millions of dollars in options at the same time the company is laying off thousands of workers, no messaging can smooth the hostile reaction from employees and shareholders. When Lee Raymond, former CEO of ExxonMobil, accepted a $400 million dollar exit package in 2006, the very same week that gas prices hit $3.00 for the first time ever, that's a communications disaster for his company and the entire energy industry (notice I didn't call them oil companies). But that's only the public audience—and therefore the public context. Quite another is Wall Street, and they reward a CEO and company for delivering record profits by charging consumers more and cutting costs by laying off employees—as long as it's done in the name of efficiency. That approach is exactly how GE's former CEO Jack Welch got the moniker "Neutron Welch" after he shed some of GE's consumer businesses—the buildings remained, but the people were gone. GE got leaner and, to some observers, meaner, but Wall Street stood up and applauded.

Similarly, when an electricity company's CEO attends a Wall Street analyst meeting, a promise of higher utility rates will encourage investors and shareholders to bid up the stock, even though the same speech will generate outrage among consumers at home. The problem with too many energy CEOs is that they prepare their lexicon for one audience, forgetting that the other audience is listening as well.

When a member of Congress complains about having to support one family and two homes on $160,000 a year, he's announcing to the world that he's out of touch. Likewise, when the first President Bush was caught on camera seeming not to know what a supermarket scanner was, he appeared—unfairly—far removed from the everyday experiences of average Americans. Now, the story itself was misleading: Bush was at a grocery convention, not a supermarket, and he was looking at a new kind of scanner not yet on the market, but the story played into a perception and captured a mood that dogged him until he lost on Election Day because he didn't have the words to dispute it.

Never lose sight of whom you are talking to—and who is listening. Remember that the meaning of your words is constantly in flux, rather than being fixed. How your words are *understood* is strongly influenced by the experiences and biases of the listener—and you take things for granted about those experiences and biases at your own peril.

## DON'T ASSUME KNOWLEDGE OR AWARENESS

The single greatest challenge for those in the world of politics is the inherent assumption that everyone else knows as much as they do. For example, Washington politicians all too frequently toss around inscrutable acronyms that few outside the Beltway can understand or relate to. Here's a test. The following are ten of the most powerful, influential agencies and programs in American government:

1. OMB
2. CBO
3. GAO
4. BLM
5. BLS
6. FERC
7. NRC
8. FICA
9. CRS
10. CMS

How many of these can you name—and explain exactly what each organization does? The answers are in the footnote below—but no peeking!* If you got four or more correct, a failing grade, you did better than

---

*1. OMB=Office of Management and Budget. The White House office responsible for devising and submitting the President's annual budget proposal to Congress.

2. CBO=Congressional Budget Office. The primary congressional agency charged with reviewing congressional budgets and other legislative initiatives with budgetary implications.

3. GAO=General Accounting Office. The investigative arm of Congress, charged with examining matters relating to the receipt and payment of public funds.

4. BLM=Bureau of Land Management. An agency within the U.S. Department of the Interior that sustains the health, diversity, and productivity of the public lands for the use and enjoyment of the people.

95 percent of Americans, but hopefully you learned an important language lesson. So if you really care about the environment, you should call the federal government agency in charge the Environmental Protection Agency—that's a lot more potent and persuasive than its acronym, EPA.

Senators go on television, ostensibly, to communicate with their constituents, but then squander the opportunity by droning on about *"reconciliation"* and *"markup"* and *"cloture."* They have the distinct ability to take a simple issue and mutilate it beyond recognition. In December of 2005, Georgia Senator Johnny Isakson stepped onto the Senate floor to talk about the complicated, unfair system of federal taxation—and instead uttered the sentence that did not end.

> "Simply put [how ironic], we would sunset the current tax code on the Fourth of July, 2008, and command the Congress to take the next three years analyzing consumption taxes, progressive taxes, flat taxes, revenues of all sorts, and the effect each has on the economy and economic policy, and then come back to the American people prior to that date with a new, simplified, fairer, flatter, tax system, or, if failing to do so, the Congress of the United States would then be forced to vote on this floor to extend the existing system we have and all the injustice that goes with it."[1]

Count it: One hundred and three words to say what should have been said in eighteen: "Congress needs to study and simplify the tax code, and they have three years to get it done."

And that's the reason why John F. Kennedy is the only member of Congress in modern times to have gone from Capitol Hill straight to 1600 Pennsylvania Avenue. In fact, you'd have to be more than a hundred years old to have voted for the last legislator to move directly to the

---

**5.** BLS = Bureau of Labor Statistics. The principal fact-finding agency for the federal government in the broad field of labor economics and statistics.

**6.** FERC = Federal Energy Regulatory Commission. Regulates and oversees energy industries in the economic and environmental interest of the American public.

**7.** NRC = Nuclear Regulatory Commission. An independent agency established to regulate civilian use of nuclear materials.

**8.** FICA = Federal Insurance Contributions Act of 1935. Social Security payroll taxes are collected under authority of FICA.

**9.** CRS = Congressional Research Service. A branch of the Library of Congress providing nonpartisan research reports to members of the House and Senate.

**10.** CMS = Center for Medicare. Administers Medicare, Medicaid, and the State Children's Health Insurance Program.

White House prior to Kennedy. (Warren G. Harding, elected in 1920 when the voting age was still twenty-one—meaning you'd have to have been born prior to 1899.) Legislators are handicapped when they run for executive office precisely because they tend to speak a language the American public simply doesn't find compelling.

In 2005, there was an ongoing debate about the use of the filibuster to prevent a floor vote on some of President Bush's judicial nominees. Some Republicans thought the public would be outraged that Democrats were, in their view, abusing the filibuster by exercising it in a historically novel fashion. Some Democrats thought the public would be outraged that the GOP (Grand Old Party—a rare case where the acronym is better known) was, in their view, overturning Senate tradition and steamrolling minority rights by threatening to deny them the filibuster option.

But a better question for both sides to ask might have been: *What percentage of the American public even knows what a filibuster is?* How could anyone expect the public to be outraged about a word and a process that most of them didn't know anything about? For the politician aiming to persuade, and anyone else for that matter, *education must precede motivation* and even *information.* This may be painfully obvious to read, and it is certainly painful to witness when it isn't practiced, but your audience needs to know the basic generalities before you can motivate them to respond to the specifics. You can't short-circuit the communication process. Therefore, teaching always has to be the first step. And to be a good teacher, you have to know from where the pupil is starting.

Again, context.

Fewer than one in five Americans (17 percent) can name three of the nine Supreme Court justices. Now, some might say that that's actually pretty good. By way of comparison, however, consider this: Fully two-thirds (67 percent) of the American people can name all of the Three Stooges (extra credit for Shemp, Joe, and Curly Joe).[2] It's a goofy question, but it makes a serious point: Most people don't live and breathe politics the way its practitioners—and the journalists who cover it—do.

The corporate world is an even more egregious offender when it comes to using unfamiliar words. Microsoft's Bill Gates can be forgiven for talking about the *"binary fashion"* of human perceptions and emotions because that kind of thinking is expected of him.[3] But the leaders of corporate America too often fall prey to the allure of verbosity. If you're eBay CEO Meg Whitman, why must you say that you're *"encouraged by the fundamentals that underlie usage growth on the Net"*[4] when you could say that you're happy that more people are using the Internet. If you're Dell CEO Kevin Rollins, you will tell people that the company needs to "hire in project management capability."[5] Why not simply state that Dell needs to grow its business and expand its workforce?

Too often, corporate chieftains have used language as a weapon to obscure and exclude rather than as a tool to inform and enlighten. When opaque, esoteric, recondite language is used thoughtlessly, either out of laziness, bad habits, or the failure to realize that the listener, no matter how interested or well intentioned, just doesn't come from the speaker's milieu, it is guaranteed to fail.

The words you just read in the previous paragraph are a good example. *"Esoteric," "recondite,"* and *"milieu"* may be great SAT words, and you will certainly be able to impress people at your next cocktail party, but if your primary goal is to communicate, you'd better be cautious about throwing them around. There's a time and a place for showing off the William F. Buckley vocabulary—but it's probably not in a speech to your constituents, a sales pitch to a prospective client, or at a job interview.

One of the best illustrations of the importance of linguistic context is a story told by Aaron Sorkin about cast member D. L. Hughley on his show *Studio 60*. Says Sorkin:

> "He grew up in Inglewood. He was a Blood. I was talking to him about his past, as horrible as can be. He left tenth grade without knowing how to read, and would later teach himself. This is a very brilliant guy. But I asked him back in tenth grade when he left school, or in eighth grade when he saw a friend of his get killed, during these times, was he funny? And the phrase he used to answer me was, 'Oh, I could always talk, and that was my thing. I wasn't athletic. I didn't drive a nice car. The only way I was going to be able to get girls was I could talk.' And I could see how serious a thing it was in his neighborhood. His use of language where he was from was no less important and no less difficult—in fact, probably a lot more important and a lot more difficult—than William Safire's use of language."

There is a time to reach beyond the daily vernacular, and a time to keep it simple. As I often explain to those clients who are in the habit of saying whatever they want whenever they want to—as written in Ecclesiastes, interpreted by Bob Dylan, and sung by the Byrds—to everything there is a season . . . and a time to every purpose.

Yet again, context.

## GETTING THE ORDER RIGHT

The order in which words are presented also affects how we perceive them. To return to the example of the stand-up comic: It's all in the delivery. Miss one beat, or include one beat too many, and it throws off your rhythm. The joke just hovers there, lifeless. Achieving the desired effect requires the presentation of the right information in the right order.

The sequential arrangement of information often *creates* the very meaning of that information, building a whole whose significance is different from and greater than its constituent parts. Film provides perhaps the clearest illustration of this principle. The great Russian director Sergei Eisenstein's theory of montage states that meaning resides in the *juxtaposition* of ideas or images.[6] Two unrelated images are presented, one after the other, and the audience infers a causal or substantive link between them. A shot of a masked killer raising a butcher knife, followed by a shot of a woman opening her mouth, tells us that the woman is scared. But if that same image of the woman opening her mouth is preceded by a shot of a clock showing that it's 3 A.M., the woman may seem not to be screaming, but *yawning*. The mind takes the information it receives and synthesizes it to create a third idea, a new whole.

If you want to truly communicate, to be heard, understood, and have an impact, it's not enough to parrot a few buzzwords and be done with it. This is why my language memos to members of Congress are notoriously long, even though they are filled with concise information. You can't sound-bite complex issues in a sentence, or even a paragraph. Every element of your presentation—the order of your words, the visuals that accompany them, and the way that they relate to what the audience knows of your personality, your history, your character—all of these elements blend to form a single impression. If even one of these elements is off, if they don't work together seamlessly like the pieces of a puzzle . . . you risk losing control of your message or, indeed, sending the wrong message altogether.

The essential importance of the order in which information is presented first hit home for me early in my career when I was working for Ross Perot during the 1992 presidential campaign. I had three videos to test: (a) a Perot biography; (b) testimonials of various people praising Perot; and (c) Perot himself delivering a speech. Without giving it much thought, I'd been showing the videos to focus groups of independent voters in that order—until, at the beginning of one session, I realized to my horror that I'd failed to rewind the first two videotapes. So I was forced to begin the focus group with the tape of Perot himself talking.

The results were stunning.

In every previous focus group, the participants had fallen in love with Perot by the time they'd seen all three tapes in their particular order. No matter what negative information I threw at them, they could not be moved off of their support. But now, when people were seeing the tapes in the opposite order, they were immediately skeptical of Perot's capabilities and claims, and abandoned him at the first negative information they heard. Unless and until you knew something about the man and his background, you would get the impression that his mental tray was not quite in a full, upright, and locked position, as Congressional scholar Norm Ornstein used to say. I repeated this experiment several times, reversing the order, and watched as the same phenomenon took place. Demographically identical focus groups in the same cities had radically different reactions—all based on whether or not they saw Perot's biographical video first and the third-party testimonials second (and were therefore predisposed and conditioned to like him) before or after the candidate spoke for himself.

The language lesson: A + B + C does *not* necessarily equal C + B + A. The order of presentation determines the reaction.

The right order equals the right context.

## THE BATTLE OF THE SEXES

Sex—or *gender,* if you want to be politically correct—can also obstruct understanding. The problem with far too many male politicians and executives is that they tend to make everything into a sports analogy. In my years of interviewing women from all across the country and in all walks of life, I've consistently found that this *drives women insane.* Many women (and, to be fair, also some men) don't know what a "hat trick" is. Men use baseball metaphors, golf metaphors, football metaphors—and often these sports metaphors are graphic and violent.

Indeed, men also tend to compare politics and business to war, which is almost always a mistake. Our day-to-day lives may seem like an endless battle, but there's a big difference between the struggle of a thirty-minute car ride through the streets of New York City and, say, a car bombing in Baghdad. There's altogether too much allusion to *"battles"* and *"charging"* and *"fighting"* in our lexicon—and it's a context most women simply don't appreciate. Sure, we men don't do this deliberately (it's about as natural as loosening the belt around our pants after the Thanksgiving meal), but that doesn't make us any more appealing to women.

But don't ignore tough topics just because your audience is predominantly female. It is totally wrong to assume that women only care about "soft," "touchy-feely" issues such as health care and education, while men only care about "hard" issues like war and economics, even though that's how the political parties often pander. This gross oversimplification ignores the post-9/11 phenomenon of "security moms," women who are every bit as concerned about foreign policy and national defense as their husbands are—and sometimes more so.

When talking to women, you don't have to alter the underlying substance of your message. They don't want to hear only about so-called "women's issues." Ignore the political hacks who demand gender-based politics: There's no need to create a separate "women's agenda." I recently conducted a series of focus groups with California women, and they were adept at differentiating between what is real and what is rhetoric—more so than their male counterparts. The greatest transgression you can commit with women is to be seen as pandering. Women do not want to see a suburban white man with a wedding ring standing before them and pontificating about the challenges facing single African-American or Latina mothers in the inner city. As one woman said: "It's nice to know that you are *aware* of my problems, but don't overemphasize it. I'm a woman. You're not." Authenticity counts.

Still, the language of sports and struggle is just too heated for most contexts. Most Americans' concerns aren't apocalyptic in nature. We're just trying to "muddle through," as the British say, and get through the day. We don't want our leaders badgering us, as if every business decision calls for the Charge of the Light Brigade and every congressional action is a result of this or that crisis. On a more personal level, if you asked Americans which story they would more likely read in their daily newspaper, the carnage in Darfur or how to keep their teeth permanently white, they'll choose teeth whitening almost every time. The more personal the context, the greater the interest. By and large, we're concerned about the realm of our jobs and our families, not the larger unfolding of History with a capital *H*.

In most situations, instead of sounding like football broadcaster John Madden, it's best to adopt a softer, gentler, more down-to-earth Katie Couric–like tone. And the most effective, least divisive language for both men and women is the language of everyday life. For instance, merely conveying to an audience that you identify with parenthood is more effective than all the sports and war metaphors in the world. From getting the kids out of bed, fed, and off to school, to the demands of working outside the home, women are more stressed than ever—and they want to know that the politician understands this or that the product or service they purchase can alleviate it. Even if you are a man, talking about personal experience struggling to meet the demands of work and kids and a spouse can convincingly demonstrate an understanding of the challenges modern women face, and both men and women will spot the parallels to their own lives in your stories. So tell them. That's the context of empathy.

There are definitely differences in outlook and perspective between men and women that require a higher level of communication sophistication. For example, women generally respond better to stories, anecdotes, and metaphors, while men are more fact-oriented and statistical. Men appreciate a colder, more scientific, almost mathematical approach; women's sensibilities tend to be more personal, human, and literary.

The biggest difference between the genders is in response to tone. Women react much more negatively to negative messages than do men. They don't like companies that trash the competition, and they don't like candidates that twist the knife. Cola wars, beer wars, and burger wars are entertainment to men . . . and noise to women. When you articulate what you are *for* or *about,* you reveal something of yourself.

And above all, listen. Listen more than you ask questions, and ask questions more than you "talk." By more than three to one, women say they would choose a candidate who listens really well (73 percent) over a candidate who asks all the right questions (21 percent).[7] It was quite astute of Hillary Rodham Clinton (and quite certainly the result of some market research of her own) to launch her 2000 Senate campaign with a *"listening tour"* of New York. Whenever politicians or companies talk about listening to their constituents or their customers, women reward them with an immediate and positive response.

"Listening"—unlike mere "hearing"—implies consideration because it requires thought. It says that the listener takes the speaker seriously, respects her, and values her opinion. Companies that communicate a listening proposition to their products, services, and how they do business are attuned to what women want.

## IT'S ABOUT THE CHILDREN

One message target stands out above all the rest: the kids. This is the one that comedian Bill Maher has ripped apart so often because to him it sounds so gooey, so saccharine sweet and patently phony. But it's true, and it works. To women, children are the face of the future and the embodiment of tomorrow. From a balanced budget to welfare reform, child-centered arguments consistently score better with women than economic or more factually based messaging. This applies not only to education, health care, and the environment, but also to "hard" issues such as taxes and foreign policy. Products designed for women will also benefit from a child-centered approach. I recently conducted focus groups for the Los Angeles Dodgers with female baseball fans. While they enjoyed attending games with their female friends and particularly liked the tight pants on the field and the male eye candy in the stands, the single greatest motivator to get women to more games was through their children. They can say no to everyone else, but not to their kids.

One of the most powerful examples of the use of children in advertising to appeal to parents can be seen in a 1997 AT&T cell phone service ad. As a mother prepares to go to work, her two daughters complain that they want to go to the beach.

### AT&T

Oldest Daughter: Mom, why do you always have to work?
Mom: It's called food, video, skates . . .
Oldest Daughter: Can we go to the beach?

> Mom: Not today, honey, I've got a meeting with a very important client.
>
> Youngest Daughter: Mom, when can I be a client?
>
> Mom (*after a pause filled with tension and guilt*): You have five minutes to get ready for the beach or I'm going without you.

The mother picks up her AT&T phone, the background music breaks into Cyndi Lauper's "Girls Just Want to Have Fun," and then viewers are transported to the beach to watch Mom and the children frolicking in the sand. As the ad comes to a close, the cell phone rings, Mom answers it, and her daughter screams out, "Hey everybody, it's time for the meeting." Mom gets the job done and makes her family happy thanks to AT&T.*

Parents have an insatiable appetite to please their children, and smart marketers have figured out a way to provide a buffet of value. In one ad, Universal Studios and Toyota team up to appeal to a thirty-something mom by targeting her seven-year-old daughter. The ad begins with the little girl asking a short but incredibly powerful question, *"If kids ruled the world . . ."* which is followed by a series of wishes by various children. Each wish somehow relates to something offered by Universal and is in some way made possible by the Toyota Sienna—and how the combination of both will bring happiness to children—and therefore to their parents. So simple. So effective.

## HOW YOU DEFINE DETERMINES HOW YOU ARE RECEIVED

Of all the components in this book, the following is most likely to generate anger from the language police and negative reviews by the critics because it explains and demonstrates how context is applied in the real world. Positioning an idea linguistically so that it affirms and confirms an audience's context can often mean the difference between that idea's success and failure. The fact is, not all words with similar definitions prompt the same response, and I have built a company and a career by

---

*An equally important lesson of communication is how circumstances and priorities change. Back in 1997, the ability to work almost anywhere, from remote mountain hideaways to secluded beaches, was considered a valuable luxury. Today, it's more often thought of as a nightmare. Back then, technology was seen as an enabler to get people out of the office. Today, it's actually more a connector—so that you can never really escape colleagues, clients, and your boss.

finding the *exact* word for my clients to create the exact context and therefore provoke the *exact* response they want.

In politics, for example, Americans will often come to diametrically opposite conclusions on policy questions, depending on how the questions are phrased—even if the actual result of the policies is exactly the same. In effect, positioning an idea doesn't merely "frame" it so that it carries a certain meaning; it actually defines the terms of the debate itself.

For example, by almost two-to-one, Americans say we are spending too much on *"welfare"* (42 percent) rather than too little (23 percent). Yet an overwhelming 68 percent of Americans think we are spending too little on *"assistance to the poor,"* versus a mere 7 percent who think we're spending too much.[8] Think about it: What is assistance to the poor? Welfare! So while the underlying policy question may be the same, the definition— welfare versus assistance to the poor—and positioning make all the difference in public reaction. If the context is a government program itself, the process and the public hostility is significant. But if the context is the result of that government program, the support is significant.

This apparent hypocrisy is anything but. The word *welfare* didn't used to be a bad word. Prior to the Great Depression there was no national welfare system, though several states ran government programs to help poor families.[9] Welfare, as a national entity, started under President Franklin Roosevelt, but it was the Great Society launched by President Johnson in a commencement address at the University of Michigan in1964 that turned welfare into a household word. In his address, Johnson declared that a great society must mean *"abundance and liberty for all,"* and pledged to use America's vast wealth (at taxpayer expense, some would say) to *"elevate our national life, and to advance the quality of our American civilization."*[10] And for the first few years, welfare itself was widely popular.

During the 1970s, however, welfare took on a wealth of negative connotations. The lexicon of elevation and advancement began to give way to *"welfare queens"* and government *"handouts"* and with that a drop in public support. The term *"welfare queens"* was coined by Lee Atwater, a close advisor to both President Reagan and the first President Bush, and a mentor to Karl Rove. In Atwater's hands, *"welfare queens"* became a means of graphically highlighting people who were taking advantage of the welfare system. By using such a blatantly provocative phrase, Atwater not only shed a negative light on abusers but on the system itself, linguistically paving the way for fundamental welfare reform.

*"Assistance to the poor,"* on the other hand, sounds benign, compassionate, charitable—take your pick. Newt Gingrich added new positioning in the 1990s, promoting welfare reform not because it would punish welfare cheats or save tax dollars but because it would save families and restore the work ethic. Because of this more positive perspective, the American people came to support overwhelmingly the Republican perspective that welfare was a curse rather than the Democrat message that the proposed cuts were "draconian." In fact, in our polling in 1997–98, the American people considered welfare reform to be the most positive accomplishment of Republicans nationwide.

What I am arguing is that *"welfare"* and *"assistance to the poor"* are in fact different topics. To be more specific, while welfare is, by definition, assistance to the poor, not all assistance to the poor comes from welfare. Faith-based organizations like the Salvation Army get little or no federal government assistance, yet they are popular because the public can see the results with their own eyes. Habitat for Humanity and Teach for America work in disadvantaged communities, but they provide a lot more than a weekly check. They teach responsibility, not dependency. Yes, they provide aid of sorts, but it is certainly not *"welfare"* as it is traditionally known.

This is not a question of cravenly molding public policy to fit opinion polls. On the contrary, it's a matter of finding the most appealing and persuasive way to present a preexisting proposition or program in a more accurate light. Several years ago I asked Americans whether they would be willing to pay higher taxes for *"further law enforcement,"* and 51 percent agreed. But when I asked them if they would pay higher taxes *"to halt the rising crime rate,"* 68 percent answered in the affirmative. The difference? Law enforcement is the process, and therefore less popular, while reducing crime is the desirable result. The language lesson: Focus on results, not process.

The assumptions implicit in a polling question about policy also govern the answers it generates. This one is my own personal favorite. Back in the mid-1990s, a majority of Americans (55 percent) said that emergency room care *"should not be given"* to illegal aliens. Yet only 38 percent said it should be *"denied"* to them.[11] The difference in response is attributable to the difference in assumptions. *"Denying"* implies that personal or societal rights are at stake and that someone or something is about to lose that right. It makes us think of a door being slammed in someone's face. But if I refrain from *"giving"* you something, I'm not necessarily impinging on your rights and I'm not necessarily altering the status quo—I'm just opting out. And for many Americans, that's a whole lot easier to live with than *"denial."* Once again, the context determines the public reaction.

The ten rules of effective communication are a necessary first step to words that work, but they are hardly sufficient. Communicators also need to put themselves in the mind-set of their audiences . . . what social status people occupy . . . what they've heard from politicians in the past . . . what their level of education is . . . what gender they are. All these things affect how people will receive a message. The next chapter focuses on this critical element of linguistic context. As we'll see, the meaning of words doesn't stay the same over time. It's constantly changing, in ways that will surprise and amuse you.

# III

## Old Words, New Meaning

*"A man may take to drink because he feels himself to be a failure, and then fail all the more completely because he drinks. It is rather the same thing that is happening to the English language. It becomes ugly and inaccurate because our thoughts are foolish, but the slovenliness of our language makes it easier for us to have foolish thoughts."*
— GEORGE ORWELL
"POLITICS AND THE ENGLISH LANGUAGE"

Most people use the term *Orwellian* to mean someone who engages in *doublespeak*, the official language of the totalitarian government in George Orwell's 1949 novel *1984*. Doublespeak twists and inverts the definitions of words and eliminates terminology the oppressive regime considers politically incorrect in an effort to thereby also eliminate the subversive concepts associated with them.

Because I counsel corporate and political clients on what words work and which expressions to avoid, some have predictably caricatured what I do as Orwellian, painting my message memos as sinister dictionaries of doublespeak. I coach people in euphemism and spin, they charge, clouding the debate rather than clarifying it. But I am not Orwellian in the sense that these critics mean, or in the way Orwellian has been defined by today's popular culture. My explicit aim is to get people to use simple, straightforward language, and if these critics had actually read Orwell's short but powerful essay "Politics and the English Language," they would realize that calling someone Orwellian is not an insult. The term is actually a badge of honor.

And therein lies an essential lesson of linguistic context: Popular perception can overwhelm truth and accuracy in establishing a communication connection. Or, in plain English, it's not what *you say,* it's what *people hear* that matters. Moreover, words that had certain definitions when your grandparents were your age may have an entirely different meaning today.

Two important historic examples immediately come to mind. Niccolò Machiavelli, history's best known student of political conflict, was a brilliant strategic thinker centuries ahead of his time, yet few politicians today would take kindly to being described as *Machiavellian.* It is clear from the breadth of his writings that Machiavelli didn't always endorse the ruthless strategies dissected in his book *The Prince,* and yet the term applied to his teachings has been oversimplified and misunderstood in modern day political culture. So if a contemporary elected official were to praise the contributions Machiavelli brought to the study of leadership, he or she would probably be skewered for committing an unfathomable act.

Similarly, Franz Kafka wasn't in favor of the nightmarish bureaucratic states he described in *The Castle* and *The Trial.* How strange, then, that when somebody calls the maddeningly uncooperative system at the Department of Motor Vehicles (DMV) *Kafkaesque,* he's actually using Kafka's name to describe, and personally affiliating Kafka with, exactly what Kafka satirized and attacked. Rube Goldberg suffered the same fate. He spent a lifetime satirizing machines, technology, and organizational behavior that made simple tasks more difficult. Yet now we use his name to describe exactly what he despised.

That brings me back to George Orwell. The term *Orwellian* has come to be used by most people to mean everything that Orwell most despised—the confusion and misdirection of language. The traditional definition of Orwellian would apply to North Korea, where people are starving to death, eating grass, and boiling corn husks for broth, living like animals. Yet billboards across that country proclaim messages such as *"We Are Happy"* and *"We Have Nothing to Complain About"* and everywhere are pictures of *"Dear Leader Kim Jong Il, who is able to control the weather and make flowers beautiful."*[1] Today's North Korea is probably the closest the world has ever come to the dystopian state of Oceania in Orwell's "1984."

But that is not Orwellian at all. In fact, it is the exact opposite. Two years before he wrote *1984,* Orwell laid out his thoughts on how politically corrupting shoddy language could be in his famous 1946 essay "Politics and the English Language":

> Modern English . . . is full of bad habits which spread by imitation
> and which can be avoided if one is willing to take the necessary

trouble. If one gets rid of these habits one can think more clearly, and to think clearly is a necessary first step toward political regeneration.

*Orwellian* may be a current synonym for linguistic confusion, and yet he himself was the strongest advocate of his time for clear, explicit, uncomplicated political prose. In fact, he argued that streamlining communication and improving its accessibility to the masses would not, as critics today might argue, "dumb down" political discourse but in fact improve the dialogue—and the political system itself. Orwell then complains about how, in political writing:

> The concrete melts into the abstract and no one seems able to think of turns of speech that are not hackneyed: prose consists less and less of words chosen for the sake of their meaning, and more and more of phrases tacked together like the sections of a prefabricated henhouse.[2]

Sound familiar? Orwell puts it far more eloquently than I ever could, but the message is the same. Bad English, whether to sell products or politicians, is abstract and clichéd—designed for the ear but not the intellect. Good English is concrete and alive—and at the same time informative and memorable. Orwell continues:

> The defense of the English language . . . has nothing to do with correct grammar and syntax, which are of no importance so long as one makes one's meaning clear. . . . Though it does imply using the fewest and shortest words that will cover one's meaning. What is above all needed is to let the meaning choose the word, and not the other way around. . . . I have not here been considering the literary use of language, but merely language as an instrument for expressing and not for concealing or preventing thought.[3]

Those last thirteen words are why I have devoted so much space to this essay. The presumed context for "Orwellian thought" is exactly the opposite of what the author actually believed, and history has conspired to propagate this false allusion.

President Bush is a great illustration of this point. His syntax and grammar are often a mess, and he often has trouble completing an off-the-cuff thought, but to Orwell's line of thinking, that is "of no importance" because he "makes his meaning clear." For those who can't fathom why he won the presidency, here's why. He succeeded against opponents who were arguably intellectually his superior in an economic and electoral environment that should have favored the Democratic opponent precisely because voters knew exactly where he stood. You may wince at his butchering of the English language, but he gets his meaning across—which was not always the case with Al Gore or John Kerry. His conviction always came through. Not everyone can speak as glibly and fluently as Bill Clinton. (And not everyone can write as beautifully as George Orwell.) But good communication requires conviction and authenticity; being a walking dictionary is optional.

Orwell also lays out a series of language rules. Every one of them is sound writing advice, whether you're looking for your first job or you've already reached the pinnacle of corporate or political success:

> i. Never use a metaphor, simile, or other figure of speech which you are used to seeing in print.
> ii. Never use a long word where a short one will do.
> iii. If it is possible to cut a word out, always cut it out.
> iv. Never use the passive where you can use the active.
> v. Never use a foreign phrase, a scientific word, or a jargon word if you can think of an everyday English equivalent.
> vi. Break any of these rules sooner than say anything outright barbarous.[4]

I've quoted liberally from Orwell's essay, but you should read the whole thing. Seriously. Put down this book right now, walk—no, run—to your local bookstore and read the full essay, or find it online. I feel like Ferris Bueller at the end of the movie telling the audience to leave the theater and go home. Sure, *Words That Work* should be a page turner—and I shouldn't be encouraging you to set it down even for a moment—but you've already bought the book, unless you happened to flip to this page in the bookstore or library. So go read Orwell's "Politics and the English Language." It will make *Words That Work* a more enjoyable read, and I'll be right here when you get back.

The original title of this book was *Killer Words*. That's not what's on the cover of the book you're holding now, and therein lies a tale of intended versus actual meaning.

I thought the title *Killer Words* was a great way to "grab 'em by the throat." The title was meant to stand out, to be distinctive, just like the attention-grabbing words and phrases that would be found inside the book. *Killer Words* was also meant to convey the mutability of language, the flexible way in which words' meanings are constantly changing as they shed old connotations and take on new nuances. Even the original word itself, *killer,* now means good or "excellent" in some contexts—just as Michael Jackson taught us in the 1980s that *bad* meant "good," just as to today's teenagers and college kids, something *sick* is awesome, something *wicked* is worthy, and something *tight* is what we once thought was cool.

My title was a flop. It was too clever. I tested four different titles in a national survey, and *Killer Words* came in dead last at just 7 percent. *Words That Work:* 31 percent. So I tried a different methodology, focus groups, and the title failed again. Participants scratched their heads and asked: "Is this book about violence and death?" Or worse yet, "What possibly would compel you to study the words of killers?"

Simple and clear is usually best. As my editors pointed out, the average book reader in America is not an under-thirty MySpace-generation skateboarder who peppers his conversations with "killer" and "gnarly." Most of you reading this are, shall we say, more "worldly" (never use the word *"older"*—those who think they are not will be offended, and those who know they are won't appreciate being reminded), and I'll wager that many of you weren't familiar with the ironic, positive use of the word *killer.* You spent your formative years in the company of Johnny Carson and Phil Donahue, not Jon Stewart and Oprah (note how her last name is superfluous).* I was so caught up in what I wanted to say that I didn't give enough consideration to where my primary audience would be coming from. I was fixated on my own subjective interpretation of an idea, not on how the idea might sound to an older American who encountered it cold, on the bookstore shelves, without context or preparation. As Alfred Hitchcock concluded so cynically, the audience is king. And so as I began this book, I found myself relearning the key lesson I had presumed to teach others:

---

*Jon Stewart, host of *The Daily Show,* once referred to me as an "amoral Yoda" because I provided politicians with words that work. Stewart told me that part of his job was to be on the other side of language creation, "debunking" the words and messages that people like me create—using *"death tax"* as a specific example of what he disliked about political discourse. But what he and so many others fail to realize is that as long as the words are accurate, understandable, and credible, they will continue to influence people and move products.

*It's not what you say, it's what people hear.*

In the previous chapter, we looked at how various elements of a person's context can affect the meaning words carry for that specific audience. This chapter is about how the definitions of words change with the generations. Americans are constantly creating new words even as they give old words new meanings. To create words that work, you have to pay close attention to the vitality of the language. You have to understand how people use words today, and what those words have come to mean.

I start with the youth culture because the average reader of this book will have kids using this lexicon and it may help you understand the grunts and groans of your kids if and when you can get them to talk to you. As Figure 1 illustrates below, there really is a whole new lexicon out there.*

## FIGURE 1: CONTEMPORARY YOUTH LANGUAGE AND DEFINITIONS

| WORD | DEFINITION |
| --- | --- |
| Bro | Friend |
| Bling | Bright, flashy jewelry |
| Bootylicious | Very sexually attractive |
| Diss | To disrespect someone |
| Fo' shizzle | An affirmation of a comment or action |
| Ghetto | A description of urban and/or poor culture |
| Got game | Ability that earns the respect of others |
| Hella | Word used to give emphasis to something. Ex: That pizza was hella-good. |
| Holla | A greeting to get one's attention |
| Jonesing | An intense, overwhelming craving |
| Mac Daddy | A man who gets everything he wants |
| Phat | Cool, good-looking |
| Player/Playa | Someone who has many relationships |
| Screen shopping | Window shopping on the Internet |

*A number of websites have sprung up to capture the latest linguistic innovations. The best include Urbandictonary.com and DailyCandy.com.

| Shout out | Hello to |
|-----------|----------|
| Tight | Excellent/outstanding |
| Trippin' | Description of overexuberant behavior |
| Wacked/Whack | Something very abnormal |

What's particularly striking about the new language is that it is coming not from the older elites of society who live in wealthy suburban neighborhoods but from the hip-hop youth culture found in America's urban areas. Even more striking, most of the slang commonly found in pop culture today comes not from the white population but from African Americans and, increasingly, Hispanics. Spread by television, music, and now the Internet, the youth culture in America has created a lexicon all its own. The sixties may be dead and buried, but when it comes to language, the Generation Gap is alive and well.

It's not just individual words that change over time—it's how we as a culture employ language. Twenty years ago, people said the written word was dying. Nobody wrote letters anymore. The flowing letters of our forefathers were replaced by short notes of little meaning, and even they were disappearing, rendered unnecessary by the telephone, the omnipresent answering machine, and the Hallmark card to mark every occasion—with someone else's poetry.

E-mail and the Internet have changed all that. Jack Abramoff, the disgraced Washington lobbyist, is in jail because of his pithy e-mail exchanges with his partners in crime but it's hardly the same significance as the exchange of letters between John Adams and Thomas Jefferson. But when you think about it—flash animation and video files notwithstanding—the Internet is primarily a written medium, though it is becoming more and more visual, adding life to lifeless text. And the written word isn't dead after all; the notes and calling cards of old have just been refashioned for the digital age.

But though the written word is back, the traditional language of written discourse is not. E-mail is informal. It rewards brevity, but brevity and clarity are not always the same thing. E-mail lacks both the inflection and subtlety of speech and (generally) the careful thought and consideration of an old-fashioned letter. E-mail, instant messages, and text messages have a tendency to make inhibitions melt away. They're especially susceptible to misunderstandings. Sarcasm doesn't always come across. Feelings can be hurt. "Flame" wars break out, as people insult each other in far more vigorous terms than they would ever dream of when talking on the phone or face to face.

Don't get me wrong. E-mail is a fantastic thing. I'd have a difficult time choosing between my BlackBerry and, say, oxygen. My point is simply that e-mail has played a role in the coarsening of our language—and that the negativity it sometimes encourages must be actively resisted by those who wish to be great communicators. Hold up on that no-holds-barred, ten-screen-long tirade and pause to consider how the other person is likely to react to your rant. Break your fixation on what you're determined to *say*, and instead think about what she's going to *hear*.

When I talk about the loss of conversational language, at least in the written form, I certainly don't mean to imply that all changes are for the worse. Unlike the Constitution, language is a dynamic, living thing. What were once fresh metaphors become so widespread that they harden into cliché. (When you describe your company's *"track record,"* how often do you think, hey, I'm comparing our business to the 200-meter hurdles? When you refer to *"raising the bar,"* how often do you visualize the high jump?)

Often, words and phrases shift their meanings so much that they bear only the most tenuous relation to what they originally signified. The evolution of words and meanings can be a fascinating, beautiful thing. I have a hard time spelling and even pronouncing the word *etymology,* but a brief examination of how the meaning of commonplace words change will hopefully drive home the point that the English language in general and creating words that work in particular is a living, dynamic, shifting challenge, and that being generationally aware is essential when it comes to effective communication.

Let's look at a few examples.

*Campaign*—Whether you realize it or not, when you talk about an advertising *"campaign"* or a presidential *"campaign,"* you're employing a metaphor; *campaign* originally had an exclusively military meaning: literally, the "open country" suited to battle maneuvers. That's where we get the word *campus,* as well.[5]

*Sad*—The word originally had nothing to do with a person's mood or temperament. It has the same origins as the word *sated,* meaning "full" or "satisfied"—the way you feel after Thanksgiving dinner. Only later did it take on the sense of "heavy" or "weary," and from there it developed into its modern meaning of "unhappy." And it was only about a hundred years ago that *sad* took on yet another meaning: "sorry" or "pathetic."

*Occupy*—We all know what *occupy* means today in the twenty-first century. But did you know that five hundred years ago, it was considered a dirty word? It meant to have sexual intercourse—literally, to "take possession of." Once a taboo word that had all but disappeared from polite language, *occupy* has become completely innocuous today—unless you're a tenant who ignores your landlord's demands to move out.

*OK*—Spelled *okay* in more formal contexts, some scholars believe that it owes its origins to the 1840 presidential campaign, representing the initials of President Van Buren's nickname, Old Kinderhook. Funny how the slang lives on even though the president who inspired it was long ago forgotten. It is also an abbreviation for the German *orl korrect* ("all correct") that entered into the lexicon at the same time.[6]

*Dough* or *bread*—These words have long been slang for "money." *Dough* first appeared as a slang term for "money" in 1851, *bread* not until the 1930s or 1940s. *Breadwinner,* though, dates all the way back to 1818.[7] It takes money to buy bread, so it's easy to see how this usage came about. Think also of the expression/warning *"knowing where your bread is buttered"*—that is, the source of your livelihood.

*Gay*—We're all familiar with this one. If you have elementary school–aged kids and were to sit in on one of their classes, eventually you would probably hear one of the students, reading aloud to the class, come across the word *gay* in a story written fifty or a hundred years ago, or a reference to the so-called Gay Nineties that ended the nineteenth century with a bang. And, equally inevitably, the class would dissolve into giggles. This wouldn't necessarily be because they were thinking specifically of homosexuality, either. For the past few decades, *gay* has been used by young children as a sort of all-purpose put-down, like *dumb* or *lame,* devoid of sexual context.[8] Older kids, of course, know exactly what *gay* implies.

But how did the word *gay* come to represent not just a mood but a lifestyle?

The short answer is that it pretty much always has. For hundreds of years, *gay* has connoted a *"lifestyle."* *Gay* originally meant "happy" or "carefree"—so it's easy to see how its meaning made the transition from "carefree" to "not caring about conventional or respectable sexual morality." As far back as the 1600s, *gay* had a sexual connotation, though not a homosexual one; by the 1800s, it was often used to refer to prostitution. The first use of *gay* to mean "homosexual" was probably by Gertrude Stein in "Miss Furr and Miss Skeene," published in 1922, and in the

1929 Noël Coward musical *Bitter Sweet.* In the 1938 movie *Bringing Up Baby,* Cary Grant also uses the term in a way that implies homosexuality. It wasn't until the 1960s, however, that "gay" started being commonly used by homosexuals to describe themselves.[9]

*Napkin*—In the United States, you wouldn't think twice about asking for a *napkin* in a restaurant. Be careful, though. If it were thirty years ago and you were in Great Britain, asking for a *napkin* might cause the waiter to laugh at you, thinking you wanted a *nappy*—the British word for a baby's diaper. There are countless other linguistic differences between American English and the mother tongue: The Brits say *"flat"* instead of *"apartment"* and *"lift"* instead of *"elevator,"* write *"tyre"* instead of *"tire"* and *"theatre"* instead of *"theater."** One people divided by a small body of water and a common language.

*Humor*—The word *humor* shares the same etymological root as *humid*—both come from *humere,* Latin for moist. So, you ask, how in the world did we get from moisture to laughter and comedy? The answer is that before the birth of modern medicine, *humor* was thought to be a liquid. You may have heard of the four *bodily humors:* blood, phlegm, choler, and melancholy. A person's relative mix of humors was what created and regulated his or her personality. If blood dominated, you were passionate and quick to anger. If it was phlegm, you were *phlegmatic:* calm and unflappable, like Dick Cheney or Clint Eastwood. It was a small step from this understanding of the humors as a sort of lymphatic system that dictated the temperament to the application of *humor* as a temperament itself—to be of "good humor"—and its specifically comedic associations is the word's most recent evolution.

*Bloody*—Speaking of blood, the British epithet or interjection *bloody* used to be considered quite profane, at least in England (those of us who grew up listening to Higgins say it on *Magnum, P.I.* on prime-time TV never knew of its controversial origins). The idea that *bloody* was blasphemous came from the assumption that it was derived from "God's blood" or "Christ's blood" and so the word had a religious context at one time. *Bloody* was also a derogatory reference to the behavior of those with aristocratic or royal *blood*—specifically to the penchant for young lords to get drunk (soused, plastered, hammered, etc.). Later, *bloody*

---

*The pronunciations are different as well. The prime time soap opera *Dynasty* was popular in the early 1990s on both sides of the Atlantic, but the British pronunciation of the series sounded more like dinner than diner.

came to be used as an insult associated with a woman's monthly condition. Eliza Doolittle says it in George Bernard Shaw's play *Pygmalion,* so for a while *bloody* was known as "the Shavian adjective."[10]

*Tawdry*—Some etymologies are so bizarre that no one could ever guess them. The word *tawdry,* meaning "cheap but flamboyant and gaudy," is a contraction of *Saint Audrey.* Audrey was known for wearing eye-catching lace ribbons and necklaces. When she got a fatal tumor in her neck, Audrey viewed it as God's punishment for her vanity. In the town of Ely, at yearly fairs held in her memory, people sold the same kind of lace that she wore, and it came to be known as Saint Audrey's lace. "'t Audrey's lace" or "tawdry lace" was usually inexpensive and of poor quality . . . and the rest is etymological history.

*Geek* and *dork*—These terms currently belong to the same distasteful family as *nerd* and *loser,* but few people consider their genesis when hearing them, and probably no one who uses them to criticize others actually knows their origins. Originally, a *geek* was the objectionable character in a circus sideshow whose talent primarily consisted of biting the heads off chickens or eating bugs down in the "geek pit."[11] And the literal meaning of *dork* is "penis" (first used in 1961 to the best of my knowledge)[12]—not something most tasteful people would discuss in civilized conversation.[13]

*Lame*—Sticking with words that insult, consider the evolution of the word *lame.* Few third graders who call another kid *lame* at recess have any inkling of the word's literal meaning, "disabled" or "limping," but in recent decades it's become a slang term for "stupid" or "pathetic." And speaking of putative insults, we generally use the word *dumb* interchangeably with *stupid,* but its original meaning—"unable to speak" or "mute"—has been widely forgotten.* Similar terms that once had very precise meanings related to levels of awareness and intelligence—*imbecile, cretin, moron*—have also, in popular use, become indistinguishable insults. But the old schoolyard standard, "retard," has become very politically incorrect and is not widely spoken anymore.

Likewise, the word *special* is now used—also out of sensitivity or political correctness—to denote those with problems or disabilities, as in the

---

*Here's a perfect example of the linguistic benefits of rock music. If one had listened closely to the words of The Who's rock opera *Tommy,* one would have heard about the "deaf, dumb and blind boy" and known its real meaning.

term *"special education."* In a laudable effort to avoid stigmatizing those of impeded abilities, we have ventured far from *special's* etymological origins: "appearance, form, beauty," from *specere,* the Latin for "to look."

These changes in the language—this progression of acceptable terminology from *"crippled"* to *"handicapped"* to *"disabled"* to *"special"*—are highly instructive for what they tell us about our culture and its taboos. The word *issue* has taken on a novel definition in the past decade or so. We hear it used every day now, in both business and personal contexts, as a euphemism for *problem,* a term apparently too harsh and stark for our times. Companies face *"issues"* or *"challenges,"* never *"problems."* In fact, the word *problem* has ceased to exist in most corporate lexicons. Now every *"problem"*—or, God forbid, *"threat"*—is spun positively as a *"challenge."* Redefining *"problems"* as *"challenges"* is a profoundly American approach; a *"challenge"* is something to be surmounted—quite literally, in fact, like climbing a mountain. *"Challenge"* implies competition. It means the gauntlet has been thrown down and it's up to us to pick it up. Conversely, *"problem"* is threatening and negative. It suggests failure. A person with personal baggage is said to *"have issues."* Instead of telling a colleague at work, "I disagree," we say, "I have an *issue* with that." Once again, this reveals a great deal about the temper of our times.

My own personal favorite is the evolution of the word *crisis.* Until the 1600s, *crisis* was strictly a medical term that meant the turning point of a disease. Literally, it means "judgment" or "separation," "the decisive moment."[14] It is only in the last two hundred years or so that the word has taken on a more metaphoric definition. But while the word hasn't really changed its meaning in two centuries, it's now applied to almost everything. Just pick up a newspaper: There's a *"health care crisis,"* a *"national security crisis,"* and an *"education crisis"* (which is itself made up of a *"literacy crisis"* and a *"mathematical crisis"*). A run-of-the-mill recession is now an *"economic crisis"* that leads our country to experience a *"crisis of confidence."*

But when *everything* is a crisis, and when all our lives are spent in one crisis or another, what that really means is that *nothing* is. We have put our words on steroids and amped the language up so high that unless we communicate in overdrive and hyperbole, we believe—perhaps correctly—that nobody will hear us. In the process, we've sacrificed nuance and judgment and distinctions, and thereby cheapened the conversation. The thoughtful musings and intellectual discourse of William Safire and George Will were replaced by the verbal slugfests of *Hannity*

& *Colmes* and *The McLaughlin Group*—and while possibly more entertaining, our language has suffered.

The Cuban Missile *Crisis* lived up to its billing: two nations with nuclear capabilities threatening an exchange of military might that could have engulfed the world in a war without end. But do we really believe that the various alleged *"crises"* America faces today constitute as much of a threat to our country's immediate security as nuclear missiles in Cuba did in 1962? Now *that* was a *crisis,* an immediate existential threat to our security and well being. Keep in mind that a *crisis,* by definition, still refers to a decisive moment in time. If something drags on for decades, it may be a chronic problem, it may be of the utmost importance, but it's not a *crisis.*

We are a nation of moderate, cautious people with a reform bent, a conservative temperament, and a can-do spirit. We will rise to every occasion and meet every crisis, but we would rather not. Our leaders need not be unflappable or even-tempered. But neither do we want them to channel Robespierre or George Costanza—and we don't want to be called to some greater purpose any more than we have to.

The broad mass of Americans really does reside in the center and is wary of colorful ideologies of all flavors. They are stubbornly centrist even as politics becomes more polarized than ever before. As liberal Northeastern Republicans and conservative Southern Democrats flirt with extinction, each party grows more ideologically pure, philosophically consistent—and less inclined to compromise. At the same time that this partisan reshuffling takes place, the ranks of the uncommitted independents are growing like never before, more and more registered voters are unaffiliated with either major party, and Americans are practically screaming, in the oft-quoted words of Rodney King: *"Can't we all just get along?"*

Enter a relatively new word that has become the positive antidote to extremism: *bipartisanship.* Bipartisanship is viewed, both by independent voters and by the news media, as synonymous with virtue. Whereas all passionately held, comprehensive belief systems are viewed with suspicion, if not outright hostility, almost anything described as *"bipartisan"* is an automatic winner with the American public. Candidates who can effectively portray themselves as *"bipartisan"* have a marked advantage. Conversely, those credibly accused of *"negativity"* or *"obstructionism"* are in deep trouble. Ironically, one of the most effective negative attacks in politics is to accuse your opponent of being . . . negative.

*Bipartisanship* isn't a philosophy of government. It's more an outlook toward governing. It's a specific word that triggers a specific emotion. To Americans, *"bipartisanship"* or *"nonpartisanship"* means working together to achieve results, as opposed to *"partisanship,"* which has come to be defined as indulging in petty bickering. When people demand *bipartisanship,* they are really demanding *civility* and *practicality* as much as anything else. The hysterics, the over-the-top attacks, the quick resorting to Nazi comparisons one hears from time to time—Americans find it odious, and they've had enough.

Americans weren't always so hostile to ideology and suspicious of passionate commitments to a civic agenda or creed. The word *"liberal"* and the term *"liberalism"* used to be proudly embraced by its adherents. It hadn't yet become a dirty word in 1960 when Democratic presidential nominee John F. Kennedy embraced the *"liberal"* label.

> What do our opponents mean when they apply to us the label "Liberal"? If by "Liberal" they mean, as they want people to believe, someone who is soft in his policies abroad, who is against local government, and who is unconcerned with the taxpayer's dollar, then the record of this party and its members demonstrate that we are not that kind of "Liberal."
>
> But if by a "Liberal" they mean someone who looks ahead and not behind, someone who welcomes new ideas without rigid reactions, someone who cares about the welfare of the people—their health, their housing, their schools, their jobs, their civil rights, and their civil liberties—someone who believes we can break through the stalemate and suspicions that grip us in our policies abroad, if that is what they mean by a "Liberal," then I'm proud to say I'm a "Liberal."

But since then, the term *"liberal"* has taken on a negative connotation in the minds of a majority of Americans. By the 1988 presidential campaign, when Michael Dukakis was pegged as a liberal by then–Vice President Bush, rather than defend his philosophy or the labeling of it, Dukakis tried to deflect the charge by claming *"this election isn't about ideology; it's about competence."*[15] Apparently Dukakis did not realize that presidential *"competence"* was, for most voters, both uninspiring and assumed. *Saturday Night Live* even did a skit called *"The Liberal,"* a spoof of *The Fugitive,* in which guest host Matthew Modine was on the run, the last liberal in America, hunted like Dr. Richard Kimble because being a liberal had become, in 1980s America, synonymous with being marked for personal extinction. Competence was not an effective context for a presidential campaign, and being a liberal was exactly the opposite aspiration of millions of voters.

*Saturday Night Live* had a point. The degree to which politicians on the left have fled from the liberal label is striking. In fact, since the late 1990s, the term *"liberal"* has been widely replaced by *"progressive."* Even the Kennedys have abandoned the labeling that Jack Kennedy so enthusiastically embraced. Like a tired commercial product that needs to be jazzed up and reintroduced to the public, liberals have re-branded themselves. It's now almost universally understood on the American left: Don't call yourself a *"liberal."* Call yourself a *"progressive."* It's a smart move. In polling we did following the 2004 election, a generic Republican beat a generic liberal by 15 points. But a generic progressive beat a generic Republican by two points. Same ideology. Different label. Different result.

Of course, we haven't reached an end point of enlightened terminology—and we never will. What each successive generation deems suitable language will always evolve with the times. But woe to the public figure who violates these unwritten social rules about which terms are acceptable and which have become verboten. For example, the word *niggardly* has gotten people into serious trouble. Washington, D.C., Mayor Anthony Williams fired one of his aides, David Howard, for using the word in a meeting with two city employees.[16] I wonder how many readers know that *niggardly* means "cheap" or "miserly"; it has nothing to do with a racial slur. Howard suffered because of the poor vocabulary of Marshall Brown, the employee who took offense. Mayor Williams quickly rehired Howard, but the damage was done. The next month, a professor at the University of Wisconsin, Madison, Standish Henning, caused controversy by using the same word in a discussion of Chaucer, causing an offended student to call for a new speech code.[17] Making assumptions about the extent of your audience's vocabulary is not only stupid—it can cost you your career.

Some of the most interesting etymology actually does involve race and ethnicity. I am often asked by elected officials to provide the most socially acceptable description for various subgroups in the population because the accepted terminology has changed so radically over the past five decades. As a general principle, people deserve to be described in the language they choose—and that evolves over time. *"Negro"* and *"colored"* are outdated and now considered offensive—but it is worth noting that the highly respected United Negro College Fund and the powerful

National Association for the Advancement of Colored People (NAACP) have not updated their names. Everyone understands their status as organizations of historical importance with a heritage worth preserving—even if they surely would not take the same names today if they were to be created from scratch. Even the dated, old-fashioned term *"colored,"* which fell out of use nearly forty years ago, sheds its offensiveness if it drops the *d* and is preceded by *"people of . . ."*

These days, *"black"* and *"African-American"* are both considered acceptable, although the briefly in vogue *"Afro-American,"* popular in the late sixties and early seventies, has since dropped out of the lexicon. *"African-American"* has emerged as the most commonly acceptable description today, even though not all black people think the term applies to them, either because they are not American or because their ancestors are not from Africa. Not to mention the white Americans who are of African descent (Teresa Heinz Kerry and Charlize Theron come to mind) who could be considered African-Americans too. Interestingly, when Malcolm X introduced the term into his lexicon at a meeting of the Organization of Afro American Unity in the early 1960s, he was violently condemned by many in white America.[18] Seeing that the preferred description of people of color has changed so often in such a short time, it is certainly possible that there will be yet another evolution within the next generation.

*Hispanic versus Latino*—By whatever name, this is the fastest-growing ethnic group in America. Within a few short years, there will be more Latinos than African-Americans. In many American cities, and not just those on the border with Mexico, the ethnic balance has shifted dramatically in recent decades—and in some parts of America you are more likely to hear words spoken in Spanish than in English.

But the descriptive terminology for this segment of the population still remains undefined. At present, there is no commonly and universally accepted term for this ethnic group. The word *Hispanic* comes from *Hispania,* the Latin word for Spain. In the United States, it's actually a government-created designation that refers to those who speak Spanish. In practice, it's used to refer to people from Mexico, Central America, and South America, but it applies just as much to those from Europe. And because it refers to language rather than ethnicity, it's analogous to the term English-speaking, used to describe people as diverse as the British, Americans, Canadians, Australians, and New Zealanders.

This broad-brush approach and lack of precision lead some to find the term offensive. *Chicano,* on the other hand, is a narrow term that comes from *Mejicano,* the Spanish word for "Mexican." However, it is regarded as offensive even by many Mexican-Americans. The term *Latino* (or *Latina,* for women) refers specifically to those from the Americas, in places that speak Spanish or Portuguese (and thus can be more properly applied to Brazilians than *Hispanic* could be), and is increasingly preferred by those of Central and South American descent.

But again, there is no clear consensus. In polling and focus groups, roughly 40 percent prefer to be called *"Hispanic,"* 40 percent prefer *"Latino,"* and 20 percent either don't care or reject both labels. I've seen first-generation Spanish-speaking women vocally and emotionally take both sides, offended that I'd use one term or the other. The easiest solution to the conundrum is to be more specific: *"Mexican," "El Salvadorean," "Argentinean," "Brazilian,"* and so on. As with all discussions of ethnicity and other sensitive topics, the most important thing is to show *respect.*

Not all etymology examines words that are hundreds of years old. Some of it is brand-new.

*Internet*—The root word of *Internet* is actually *network*—and that word dates back to the mid sixteenth century, when it was used to refer to constructs resembling a spider's web. The idea of a network was later used to refer to collections of interrelated things, like a network of islands or a network of telephone lines. The concept of globally connected computers had its origins at MIT in the early 1960s. In its very first origin, J. C. R. Licklider dubbed it the *Galactic Network.* The idea was adopted by the Advanced Research Projects Agency (ARPA), which subsequently added the word *defense* to its name, making it DARPA. Al Gore's claims of Internet patrimony notwithstanding, it was the U.S. military's DARPANET, a network intended to preserve the DOD's command and control functions in the event of a nuclear war with the Soviet Union, that gave birth to the *Internetwork*—which was then shortened to the Internet in 1986.

*Web*—This word came into Old English from the German, and originally meant "woven fabric." Sir Walter Scott wrote of "what a tangled web we weave, when first we practice to deceive" (a line often erroneously attributed to William Shakespeare). Contrary to popular belief, the World Wide Web, "www:", is not synonymous with the Internet. The Web was given its name by Tim Berners-Lee, and was opened to the public on August 6, 1991.[19] The World Wide Web is actually not the interconnected network of computers—that network is the Internet. The World Wide Web is the system for accessing this information. Think of it as a network of addresses for information, or a worldwide, cross-referenced filing cabinet.

Even with the Web's ubiquity, there are other meanings equally as important for certain segments of the population. For example, if you come across a reference to *"a web"* (as opposed to *"the* web") in the entertainment industry trade paper *Daily Variety,* the word is referring not to the Internet, but to one of the television networks. The smaller, now-merged WB and UPN networks were known as *"the weblettes."* The entertainment publication *Variety* has created an entire lexicon all its own that is used and accepted across the industry. They call it *slanguage:*[20]

A Hollywood executive doesn't quit his job, he *ankles.*
There are no writers, only *scribblers* and *scribes.*
It's not Australia, it's *Oz.*
It's not a Western, it's an *oater.*
CBS is *the Eye.*
ABC is *the Alphabet web.*
NBC is *the Peacock web.*
It's not a martial arts film, it's *chop socky.*
It's not an awards show, it's a *kudocast.*
It's not a TV series, it's a *skein* (continuing with that web metaphor).
When a movie (or, rather, a *feature*) plays for a long time, it has *legs.*

Over the past decade alone, the rise of the Web has led to a number of new terms of increasing political and social relevance. Ten years ago, it was unclear exactly how the Internet would change American politics. In 1997, I wrote a piece for *Wired* magazine about *"connected Americans,"* a significant behavioral subgroup of early adopters, somewhat analogous in their characteristics to the active *"investor class"* that we hear so much about today. This youthful, highly educated, forward-looking technology-adopting cohort was indeed the vanguard of political activism in the decade that followed—eventually coalescing around the presidential candidacy and campaign of Howard Dean in 2004.

But the Internet had another impact on politics that none of us anticipated in the mid-1990s—the rise of personal Web diaries, and with it a brand new language: *blog, blogger, blogosphere, netroots, pajamahadeen.*

*Blog* is short for *Weblog,* an online journal that can be updated any-time, day or night. Most blogs are nonpolitical, little more than amateur diaries read by a few friends or family members. But the host sites for these blogs have exploded in use—and financial value. A few years ago, Friendster was the hottest Web site among high school and college kids; today it's MySpace.com—which was recently sold to NewsCorp for an eye-popping $580 million.

In the political realm, blogs have had massive influence on the main-stream media—even though almost none of them are run by professionally trained journalists. And even though more blogs come from a left-of-center perspective, they have had a bipartisan impact. For example, in 2004, they relentlessly drove the Swift Boat Vets attack on John Kerry that the mainstream media initially ignored, and they successfully chal-lenged the authenticity of CBS's fraudulent Bush National Guard memos that led to the resignation of anchor Dan Rather. Neither story would have played out as it did without the political blogs with the strange names. Some of them are:

- *Little Green Footballs*[21] was the first source to show that the Bush National Guard memos publicized by CBS were fake, by re-creating them in Microsoft Word and demonstrating how the line spacing and font matched perfectly those of documents that were supposed to be more than three decades old and created on a typewriter—decades before word processing.[22]
- *PowerLine,* a conservative blog launched in 2002[23] and run by three lawyers, has also broken national stories and influenced the main-stream media, helped along in great measure by contributions and leads from its individual readers. "The secret . . . is 'open-source in-telligence gathering.' . . . We've got a huge pool of highly motivated people who go out there and use the tools to find stuff. We've got an army of citizen journalists out there," says Charles Johnson, one of the founders.[24] In addition to its participation in the Swift Boat in-vestigation, PowerLine also helped lead the charge against Harriet Miers's short-lived nomination to the Supreme Court. PowerLine was named "blog of the year" by *Time* magazine in 2004.
- *Wonkette,* a newly coined female derivative of the term *policy wonk,* is loaded with political gossip that generates incredible attention inside the Beltway even if its reports are occasionally of question-able origin and accuracy.

- *Instapundit,* the granddaddy of all blogs, is run by Glenn Reynolds, a law professor at the University of Tennessee who provides commentary and context twenty-four hours a day, seven days a week. On an average day, he updates his site twenty times.
- *Daily Kos,* named after its founder, Markos Moulitsas Zuniga, is arguably the most influential left-wing blog. It helped launch and sustain Howard Dean's meteoric rise in 2003, and John Kerry, Barbara Boxer, Russ Feingold, and other Democratic politicians have been known to post on the site when they want to communicate to Democrat activists across the country.[25] If you want to find the Democratic base (or what critics dub "the angry left"), this is the place to go.
- *The Drudge Report*, as important to conservatives as Daily Kos is to liberals, but with an emphasis on breaking news rather than traditional ideological commentary.

Of course, this short list is only the tip of the iceberg—and it may have changed by the time you read this. The *blogosphere* is a vast and proliferating thing, constantly changing and reinventing itself, but a few terms are essential to understanding its political typology.

Many left-wing bloggers have taken to calling themselves the "netroots" (a takeoff on *grassroots*), and you can find their posts on sites such as MoveOn.org, Democratic Underground, Atrios, MyDD, Daily Kos, and Arianna Huffington's Huffington Post. Daily Kos's glossary (or *Kossary*) defines *netroots* as: "The Internet-based political grassroots movement; in other words, us."

References to "pajamas" or the "pajamahadeen" signify right-wing bloggers, and a new group of centrist and conservative bloggers led by Roger L. Simon and Charles Johnson named their new blog Pajamas Media. This repeated reference to pajamas is meant as a defiant thumb in the eye to CBS and its former executive, Jonathan Klein (now president of CNN), who defended Dan Rather during the George W. Bush–National Guard memo scandal by deriding his critics as nonprofessionals: "These bloggers have no checks and balances. . . . You couldn't have a starker contrast between the multiple layers of checks and balances and a guy sitting in his living room in his pajamas writing."[26] In response, Jim Geraghty, on his National Review Online blog, The Kerry Spot, accepted the pajamas slur as a badge of honor.[27] Who could have imagined just five years ago that pajamas, George W. Bush, and Dan

Rather would have been mentioned in the same sentence? Our language is still evolving.

One reason why the definitions of words has blurred or changed over time is simply because of their misuse. There are a growing number of examples where the incorrect meaning of relatively commonplace language has become more widespread than the original intention or definition. Just as Orwell, Machiavelli, and Kafka have been misunderstood and misinterpreted, so has the language we use today.

A good example is the word *peruse*. Most people think that to *peruse* something means to "scan or skim it quickly, without paying much attention." In fact, this is the exact *opposite* of what *peruse* really means: "to study or read something carefully, in detail." But the word has been misused so often by so many people, that this second sense of it—the exact opposite of what it actually means—has finally been accepted as a secondary definition . . . and as far as most people know, it's the only definition. Now, imagine that an irate customer sent you a letter about the service he received in one of your stores. If your reply is that you "perused his letter," he's likely to misunderstand, think you're blowing him off, and get even more angry than he was before.

*Factoid* is a good example. Journalists who ought to know better use the term to describe a brief, interesting fact that is definitely true but not necessarily essential to the story. The real meaning of *"factoid,"* however, is the exact opposite. According to Dictionary.com, a factoid is actually *"a piece of unverified or inaccurate information that is presented in the press as factual."* When you see a CNN "factoid" on the air or a *USA Today* "factoid" in a snazzy colorful graphic at the bottom of a page, what they are telling you *is* true and factual information—not the real definition of a factoid at all.

*Fulsome* is another word people misuse all the time. It actually means "complimentary or flattering to an excessive degree."[28] *Fulsome* praise is therefore insincere; in the vulgar vernacular we would call it *brownnosing*. But if you get a letter of recommendation that offers *fulsome praise* of your work, chances are the writer is just using the common, less nuanced version of the term. You'll mistakenly take it as a compliment, as it was meant to be, even though it isn't.

Another word that's been misused so often that its incorrect meaning has become more common than its original sense is *comprise*. Traditionally, *comprise* meant to "consist of" or, literally, "to embrace." It was an active verb that referred to the *whole* rather than the parts that made up that whole: "The Senate *comprises* one hundred senators," not "one hundred senators *comprise* the Senate."[29] *Nauseous* is another good example; its proper meaning is "causing nausea." When you experience nausea yourself, you're *nauseated*, not *nauseous*. So the next time somebody tells you, "I'm nauseous," you'll know to reply: "No, you don't make me want to throw up."[30]

*It's not what you say that matters, it's what they hear. . . .*


It's one thing to insist on proper usage in a piece of formal writing, but if you're speaking or communicating informally—whether to your customers or your constituents—it's really more important to be understood than to be heard. This is not to say that you should knowingly misuse the language; instead, just find a simpler, more readily understandable way to convey what you have to say.

Now that you know the rules of effective communication and the importance of message and messenger, it's time to explore how they are created. While the study of the impact of language may be a science, the actual creation of effective communication is truly an art. It requires technique and creativity, observation and intuition, objectivity and insight. Turn the page to find out how just how difficult it is, and why only a fraction of all the messages created are truly memorable.

## KEEPING UP WITH THE LANGUAGE

| WAS | IS NOW |
|---|---|
| Used car | Pre-owned vehicle |
| Secretary | Administrative assistant |
| Housewife | Stay-at-home mom |
| Stewardess | Flight attendant |
| Waiter/waitress | Server |
| Caretaker | Estate manager |
| Garbage removal | Sanitation services |
| Gay marriage | Same-sex marriage |
| Impotence | E.D./Erectile Dysfunction |

# IV

## How "Words That Work" Are Created

*"If you think about it, talking to a polling company is an odd way to behave. Strangers ask you to give them time and personal information for nothing so that they can profit from it."*
— NICK COHEN, *SUNDAY OBSERVER* (LONDON)

*"If I need five people in a mall to be paid forty dollars to tell me how to do my job, I shouldn't have my job."*
— ROGER AILES, PRESIDENT, FOX NEWS CHANNEL

This story may get me barred from the United States Senate, but it was how I established my credibility with the toughest, most skeptical organization in America. Back in 1998, I was asked to create and then present new language on environmental issues to a meeting of the entire Republican Senate Conference. Helping members of the House is easy: They are open-minded, creative, and focused. The Senate, however, is a different animal entirely. They're generally older, uncompromising, and don't take kindly to others telling them either what to think or what to say. They also demand *proof* that your conclusions and recommendations are based on fact. I knew that to convince these senators that I had created the right language, I had to do something so novel, surprising, and provocative (rule five of successful communication) that even the most determined cynic would accept the results.

And so I arrived there armed with a video presentation that I knew could cost me dearly with four specific senators but would earn me the confidence I needed with everyone else. On that tape were speeches that I had written for these four senators. More accurately, I had written just one speech, and I had four senators read exactly the same text, word for word. I then had the speech "dial-tested" using a Madison Avenue technique described later in this chapter. The presentation video was a compilation of the results—each senator's second-by-second score.

On a big screen in front of the room, the senators watched as computer-generated lines created by a focus group of swing voters rose and fell based on how those thirty individuals felt about each word and phrase. But instead of showing each Senate speech individually, I had the tape edited to show how each paragraph fared, paragraph by paragraph, line by line, senator by senator. Sure enough, it didn't matter whether the speech was well delivered or mangled. It didn't matter whether the senator had a rich southern accent or flat northwestern inflection. The senator's gender didn't even matter. Regardless of the senator or the delivery, the good language scored well and the bad language scored poorly. And so the more than forty senators in the room were mildly amused to see that their four colleagues had unknowingly delivered the exact same speech, but they were impressed and convinced that good language does well no matter how good or bad the speaker. The methodology for creating words that work passed their stringent credibility test, and I have been invited back more than two dozen times.

Here's where I need to address the profession—the methodology—and give you a peek behind the one-way glass and word-laboratory curtain. My editors wanted this section to be very brief: to them, how words that work are created is less important than the words themselves. But I insisted that the process of word creation is and should be just as important as the outcome. So if you are just trying to pick up the language lingo, you may want to skip this section. But if you are in the business of language, or you enjoy the "making of" DVD "extras" as much as the movie itself, read on.

Let's start with the practitioners.

It's hard to tell who is in greater demand today: the Madison Avenue branding experts who are brought in to teach political parties how to define themselves, or the political consultants brought into corporate boardrooms to teach businesses how to communicate more effectively. The tools and techniques invented on Madison Avenue firmly took hold in Washington during the Reagan years—and they continue to drive our politics today. Similarly, more and more companies are turning to political professionals for help achieving the speed, agility, and linguistic accuracy that were once the unique province of electoral campaigns.

Pollsters and the polling they do are unnecessarily shrouded in a cloud of mystery, much of it their own making, in the mistaken assumption that the less people understand about the pollster's craft, the more the pollster can charge. The two best-known pollsters of the modern political era are Pat Caddell, who did the numbers for the Carter White House from 1977 through 1981, and Dick Morris, who became more of a general political advisor to President Clinton for most of his political career. Both men took on almost mythical proportions in the eyes of their clients and the media for their uncanny ability to translate staid numbers into vibrant political and linguistic strategy. And both men broke the first professional rule of thumb (and by the way, the term "rule of thumb" is based on an archaic rule where a husband was not allowed to beat his wife with anything thicker than his thumb) that the pollster is *not* the maker of public opinion but the translator of it.

Nevertheless, they forever changed the world of public opinion gathering. Caddell was the first pollster to test and turn language into a powerful political weapon, applying the art of "wordsmithing" to the science of opinion gathering. Morris, through the actual polling services of Mark Penn and Doug Schoen, was the first outside political advisor to essentially drive White House communication strategy. Between them, they applied the techniques of ongoing public opinion sampling and the application of language as an instrument of policy to create the permanent presidential campaign.

Today, polling is no longer a black art. There is a poll on every possible topic, and some Americans follow polls the way Wall Street follows the market. I am constantly amazed that the Q&A periods following my speeches across the country to various corporate and association audiences are consistently peppered with questions about some specific polling result in the news that day and its veracity—usually asked by someone who holds a contrary point of view.

The truth is, Americans are drowning in polling numbers. National news organizations poll on a monthly or even weekly basis, and the results are given more weight, space in print, and time on air than what the politicians are actually saying. Most recently there have been times when polls about the war in Iraq drowned out the real, actual events of the day. Unfortunately, while the media have all the numbers they can possibly crunch, most surveys and their accompanying analyses are lacking in meaningful insight.

I don't seek to undermine the profession that built my home and pays my mortgage, but telephone surveys have serious limitations that most readers would acknowledge—if they were in fact polled. The first is the increasing difficulty of getting a truly random sample of the population. The increase in cell-phone usage, particularly among those under age thirty, has made it extremely difficult to sample younger Americans (because some cell-phone calling plans charge individuals for incoming calls, it is not acceptable to poll cell phones). Similarly, the rise of "do not call" lists, the increase in unlisted phone numbers, and a general unwillingness of some Americans to answer questions from a stranger are all challenges that pollsters have to overcome every day.

Another problem with telephone polls, and Internet surveys as well, is that Americans don't want to respond yes or no to alternatives that are either unacceptable or require clarification. In the context of today's political environment, there are too many shades of gray, too many "Yes, but what I really think is . . ." attitudes, too many voter priorities that cannot be ranked and explained over the phone. You can test a few words or slogans, but after about fifteen minutes, the respondent will stop responding. Internet surveys have an even shorter patience threshold before respondent fatigue sets in.

Even more problematic is the ordering of questions. Opinion pollsters know full well that *where* they ask a question within the survey exerts tremendous influence on *what* answers they receive. If a pollster has just spent fifteen minutes with you on the phone, grilling you about the frustrations of dealing with your HMO, and then closes the survey by asking you to rate the importance of health care reform against a host of other issues, you're far more likely to pick health care as highly important than you would be if it had been the first question in the survey. Likewise, laying out a new corporate pension policy to your employees will generate a strikingly different reception if you've first explained to them that the current policy is bankrupting the company and will lead to layoffs.

And even if the ordering of questions is correct, too many polls report what voters or consumers *think* without explaining how they *feel*—and why. They measure thoughts and opinions, but they don't provide a deeper understanding of the mind—and the heart. Feelings and emotions are what generate words that work.

That's why I am a committed disciple of focus groups in general and the "Instant Response Dial Session" in particular. A focus group is often nothing more than a formal discussion for ninety minutes or two hours with eight to twelve people who have similar backgrounds, behaviors, opinions, or some other commonality. Madison Avenue has been commissioning focus groups for more than half a century, and virtually every aspect of every major new product launch will involve a dozen or more of these sessions. Political researchers were slower to apply the value of face-to-face discussions to politics, as they are somewhat less profitable and somewhat more labor-intensive than traditional telephone surveys.

Focus groups have been much maligned by the media as a rogue science, designed to learn how to obscure and/or manipulate. True, they do have their limitations, most important among them the scientific inability to project the results of a discussion with two or three dozen people to a population of thousands or millions. They are reflective of the people in the session, not the total population.

But a well-run focus group is the most honest of all research techniques because it involves the most candid commentary and all of the uncensored intensity that real people can muster. As in telephone polling, focus groups begin by gauging respondent awareness and superficial opinions and attitudes. But unlike telephone polling, the superficiality is then stripped away, revealing deeper motivations, associations, and underlying needs. The interaction between a professional moderator and the participants encourages more honesty and less pandering, while measuring the intensity of opinion as well as individual motivation. That's where you'll find the words that work.

A well-run focus group is a laboratory for social interaction and word creation—yet it is one of the most obscure components of audience research. The composition of the focus group must be arrived at scientifically and statistically, and most Americans will never be invited to participate simply because most Americans don't qualify.

A good focus group actually does *not* represent a diverse cross-section of the population. Rather, homogeneity is the key to a successful session. Human behavior studies consistently show that people will reveal their innermost thoughts only to those they believe share a common bond. The people at our sessions are scientifically selected using a screener questionnaire designed to weed out the 80, 90, or, on occasion, even 99 percent of Americans we don't want to talk to. This allows us to find the "target" participants who have very specific demographic, attitudinal, political, or behavioral characteristics.

Participants are told to come a few minutes early to the session are asked to fill out a "pre-screener" when they arrive that provides personal background information and an initial general reaction to the topic that will be addressed that night. One dirty little secret of focus groups is the necessity of recruiting more people than can participate in a session. It's amazing what people will say they are or pretend to be for the opportunity of earning $100 for a two-hour session or $150 for three hours. About 10 percent of would-be focus group participants will lie on the phone, claiming to be something they are not or to believe something they don't, and another 10 percent don't show up despite confirming their participation twice. I have one client, a large national retail chain, where the no-show rate for their employee focus groups consistently reaches 40 percent—and occasionally more.

The pre-screener asks about fifteen questions and is designed to uncover and weed out those who for whatever reason do not belong in the session. But even that process doesn't always work. I once had a woman show up who claimed to watch network news programs on a daily basis, and said so in her screener, but she did not know who Tom Brokaw was and couldn't identify him even when watching a tape of him delivering the news. She was escorted out of the session, but it surely lowered my credibility with my client, the senior NBC executives watching from behind the mirror.

The most common focus group consists of about a dozen people sitting around a long rectangular table in a room about the size of most people's dens.* Nondescript artwork adorns three of the four plain walls if you're lucky, but the fourth wall is a one-way mirror that allows participants to check their hair, repeatedly, while allowing observers in a back room to watch the proceedings undetected—most of the time.

While the participants are doing most of the work in front of the mirror, the real action is happening in the dimly lit back room. The actual focus group participants are treated to a generic deli tray of barely edible sandwiches and stale potato chips—and only if they arrive early enough. But in the back room, the food never stops. Applying the theory that a hungry client is an angry client, back room observers often dine on sushi, fine wine, and gourmet spreads that rival any banquet hall or wedding reception. And thanks to an endless supply of M&M's, miniature

---

*Not all focus groups are conducted in formal settings. I once moderated an impromptu session on board an America West flight. The topic, not coincidentally, was airline satisfaction. The client, however, was Continental—and the America West crew did not take kindly to a discussion of another airline. Despite protests from the passengers, I was ordered to my seat for the remainder of the flight. In Las Vegas in 2002, to test the promos for the NBC fall line-up, I involved an entire section of the Grand Lux Cafe, a restaurant in the Venetian Hotel, in a discussion of Katie Couric. Management again prematurely shut it down.

chocolates, and trail mix that has probably been sitting in the open air since black & white television and has been touched by more hands than Paris Hilton, maintaining a healthy diet is virtually impossible. That's why you will rarely find a successful, skinny focus group moderator.

*[Note to potential focus group participants: Everything you say and do is being watched carefully, and any kind of antisocial behavior such as picking your nose or adjusting your toupee will be noted by the moderator and ridiculed from behind the mirror. A former employee of mine, Gabriel Stricker, was once leading a focus group in Little Rock, Arkansas, for a fledgling online university. At that time, Little Rock was a bastion of poverty; even the pawn shops were going out of business. As moderators do, Gabriel put his wristwatch on the table in front of him to keep track of time. And, in one of the more bizarre cases of focus group antisocial behavior, the people behind the mirror were able to observe as one of the participants in the group attempted to steal his watch when he got up to write something on the whiteboard.]*

In a good focus group, participants are made to feel comfortable talking about what they truly think and feel. The goal, in fact, is to make them feel completely at home and unobserved so that their comments will be as candid and unreserved as possible. I often use self-deprecating humor to encourage participants to open up, and they see this as a license to say things that have been bottled up inside.

Though a focus group is made up of perfect strangers, it is not uncommon for participants to turn on one another at some point. The two coasts are particularly known for their more erratic behavior, and I've moderated sessions where participants have threatened one another and, in one terrible instance, threatened me. I had one situation in Pittsburgh where several heavily tattooed male participants vocally threatened to put me through the one-way mirror, and I could hear in the back through the glass the deliberation among observers as to the proper course of action should I come crashing through; relocating the gourmet dining spread away from the mirror ranked number one on their list. Not particularly helpful.

More problematic is the single dominant voice, more often than not a fifty-something white male originally from one of the five boroughs of New York City or close proximity (no joke). Such a person can cripple open, honest discussion by hijacking the session and intimidating the other participants. As a result, the two-hour conversation can get very heated and occasionally downright ugly.

New York City sessions are notable for their uncontrollable chaos and the frequent use of profanity. New Yorkers like nothing and hate everything—but at least they have opinions and aren't shy about articulating them. When a New Yorker says someone or something is "fair," that's about as good an endorsement of a product, service, or candidate you'll ever get.

By comparison, trying to get people from New England to say anything beyond a simple yes or no is virtually impossible. I once moderated a session in Portland, Maine, for *The MacNeil/Lehrer NewsHour* on PBS. No matter what gimmick I tried, I couldn't get anyone to talk. Only eight minutes of the two hours of discussion actually made it on air because nothing else was salvageable. Of the many words and phrases I've created or popularized during my professional career, not a single one owes its origin to a New England focus group.

While most researchers depend on focus groups to understand the *why* of a topic, I prefer "Instant Response Dial Sessions"—also known as "People Meters"—because they propel the benefits of a traditional focus group a giant leap forward.

The differences between dial sessions and traditional focus groups are significant. Dial sessions have more participants than a focus group, typically about twenty-five to thirty people. They're conducted classroom style, and last longer—usually three hours. Dial sessions are a lot more expensive than focus groups. A typical dial session in 2006 can run from $27,500 up to $40,000 for a difficult recruit, while focus groups can be as cheap as $7,500 and rarely cost more than $12,000. In a well-constructed dial session, it is not uncommon to contact more than fifteen hundred people just to fill the thirty slots. Luckily, e-mail is making it increasingly possible to reach and recruit the right people for an affordable cost.

But what truly differentiates a dial session from a focus group is the dial technology itself. The dials are the research equivalent of an EKG that measures a combination of emotional and intellectual responses and gets inside each participant's psyche, isolating his or her emotional reaction to every word, phrase, and visual. Participants hold small wireless devices in their hands that are about the size of a remote control. Each device has a computerized numerical display that ranges from 0 to 100 and a knob about the size of a quarter on the front that they turn up toward 100 (more positive) or turn down toward 0 (more negative). They do this on a second-by-second basis based on their immediate, visceral, personal reactions to what they are seeing—a videotaped speech, commercials, snippets from a television show or movie, or any sort of communication execution, even a live presentation or conversation. Those reactions are collected in real time on a computer and displayed as a line superimposed on the tested video. Every time the line spikes or plunges, something was said or shown that caused a significant reaction and deserves further group exploration.

The advantages of a dial session over the traditional focus group are significant. True, traditional focus groups and dial sessions both involve listening to *real* people voice *real* reactions. But the sample size in a focus group is too small and the two hours of discussion too brief. The three-hour dial session allows the researcher an unparalleled opportunity to dive deep into an issue or product and test multiple components of a product or politician. And because of its size, you can get a better feel for how people react to competing arguments, advertisements, or executions.

Moreover, unlike those in a traditional focus group, the participants in a dial session are themselves listening and continuously reacting to others—and those reactions are anonymous and therefore free of group dynamics or bias. No one can see when the group dials go up or down, so their reactions are more truthful. The dials measure it all—specifically, scientifically, and immediately. Loud New Yorkers are known to tank focus groups with their dominating personalities, but they can't sabotage a dial session. Quiet New Englanders may not say much, but using their dials, they tell me everything I need to know.

The value of a dial session is often measured in the number of bad words discovered and avoided rather than in the volume of good language created. Even the best speeches have their low points. And even the best advertisements feature words or visuals that undermine or at least detract from its overall effectiveness. Instant Response isolates those low points, helping to fix or improve the words, messages, or themes *before* they reach the general public. For example, if John Kerry had used dial sessions accurately to test his presidential campaign ads, he would have realized that the announcer voice-overs actually undermined the commercial's credibility. When Kerry himself spoke, the dial reaction climbed and climbed—even among Republicans. But when an announcer spoke, the climb abruptly stopped and viewers turned off to the message. Why? Voters wanted to hear directly from the candidate himself, not from some disembodied generic voice. It is such a simple lesson, and frankly so obvious, yet they didn't learn it.

Another essential value of the dials is their ability to capture feelings and emotions and, above all, *intensity*. If you want to understand public opinion and influence private behavior, understanding intensity is the most important component of market research in general and language development in particular. For example, "accountability in government" and "ending wasteful Washington spending" always cause the dials to spike sharply higher because these are basic priorities that everyone agrees with. Similarly, a woman in a two-piece bathing suit lounging in a hammock with the ocean nearby triggers an extremely intense dial reaction. Every woman wants to be in the picture and every man wants to be in that same picture.

In the end, dial sessions are informative, and I use them both to test existing language and to create a new lexicon, but their results cannot automatically be projected onto the entire population. Even a three-hour session with thirty people, conducted by a professional moderator, will have less projectability than a nationwide telephone poll. Nevertheless, dial sessions do provide deep insight into behavioral and emotional patterns that cannot be captured in telephone surveys. And the "words that work" you will read on the pages that follow most likely came from a dial session conducted somewhere near you. Unless, of course, you live in New England.

Arriving at the best language isn't enough in and of itself. The majority of human communication is nonverbal. It involves not only symbolism and imagery but also attitude and atmosphere. As Jules (Samuel L. Jackson) tells Vincent (John Travolta) in *Pulp Fiction,* speaking of Arnold the pig from *Green Acres:* "Personality goes a long way." Those character attributes that together make up personality—that tell us about someone's affiliations and sympathies—are a critical component of communication. When they clash with your listener's expectations, the most precise, tailored, and on-target language in the world won't save you.

Just as it is true that you are what you eat, it is also true that you become what you say. In the elaboration of this theme so far, I have laid out the basic rules for creating words that work and emphasized the importance of paying attention to context. But the most powerful messages will fall on deaf ears if they aren't spoken by credible messengers. Effective language is more than just the words themselves. There is a style that goes hand-in-hand with the substance. Whether running for higher office or running for a closing elevator, how you speak determines how you are perceived and received. But credibility and authenticity don't just happen. They are earned. The next chapter explains how.

## V

### Be the Message

*"I was not very public as a speaker. Nixon didn't want me recorded. He thought my accent wouldn't play in Peoria."*[1]
—HENRY KISSINGER

It's hard to believe today that Henry Kissinger, the most prolific Secretary of State in modern history, would have been muzzled in any way by Richard Nixon, one of the worst presidential communicators of our time. But, as Kissinger acknowledged to me in an interview in 2006, Nixon was concerned that his accent would in some way confuse or undermine the intended communication, and so he was instructed to give background briefings instead of public press conferences. In Nixon's view, the messenger should not be allowed to get in the way of the message.

Character actor James Cromwell, whom readers may remember as Stretch Cunningham in *All in the Family,* the corrupt police chief in *L.A. Confidential,* and the kindly, pig-owning farmer in *Babe,* hosted a party at his home in the summer of 2003 for his preferred presidential candidate, Democrat Congressman Dennis Kucinich. Hector Elizondo and several other actors were in attendance to fete the long-shot candidate. *Los Angeles Times* staff writer Reed Johnson asked Cromwell what distinguished Congressman Kucinich from the rest of the Democratic hopefuls. "Cromwell instantly replied that, first of all, Kucinich was a vegan."

Cromwell elaborated: "'That may sound trivial . . . but it shows that the candidate understands the inter-connectedness between humans and the planet's other occupants.'"[2] Kucinich actually understood what scores of failed candidates never grasp—that connection is a two-way process, and if you do not connect on a personal level, you do not win. Of course, connection alone is not enough; Kucinich was simply much too philosophically extreme, and too out of touch to connect to most Democrats. Still, connecting is a prerequisite. I return to the Warren Beatty mantra once again: "People forget what you say, but they remember how you made them feel." Or, in the words of Roger Ailes, media advisor to Nixon, Reagan, and Bush I; founder of Fox News; and author of *"We report, you decide"* and *"fair and balanced"* (without focus group input), *"The messenger is the message."* Ailes ought to know. He created national celebrities out of Bill O'Reilly and Sean Hannity based as much on their persona as on their philosophy.

The very same principle applies to all political personalities—and I use the word *personalities* advisedly, because that's what separates the political superstars from your typical, run-of-the-mill congressman: A superstar creates a *persona* in the public mind by conveying certain essential characteristics about himself or herself. Successful leaders establish this persona not by *describing* their attributes and values to us, but by simply *living* them.

Evocation of a compelling persona is critical in politics; voters must feel that a candidate speaks to them and is in touch with their personal concerns. It's one reason why the more "likeable" presidential nominee almost always wins the election even when the opponent holds other important attribute advantages.* This is not some breakthrough observation—it has been at the core of successful presidential campaign advertising since all the way back to the time of the first paid political ads, in 1952. That's when the corporate ad makers set their sights on humanizing their flesh-and-blood "product": General Dwight David Eisenhower.

Today, one sure sign of a superstar politician is if he or she is known to the public by his or her first name. It's a short, select list, "Hillary," "Rudy," "Arnold," and "Newt" being the four that spring most immediately to mind. And then there's one that's so powerful that only a middle initial—"W"—tells the world exactly to whom you are referring. The late cabaret singer Hildegarde was credited with starting the single-name

---

*In fact, the only exception since 1952 was Richard Nixon in 1968 versus Hubert Humphrey, although Nixon benefited significantly from what probably could be described as the first candidate makeover in the television era, to humanize his appearance and performance.

vogue among entertainers.[3] Like Hildegarde and those who followed—Elvis, Cher, Madonna, Britney—the "first name politicians" have such vivid, singular personas that we feel as if we really know them. The informality doesn't seem awkward or inappropriate because they are not just public servants, but also celebrities, icons, figures that are larger than life. To borrow a Hollywood metaphor, think of John Wayne or Clint Eastwood. Their movie personas didn't go around *telling* people they were tough; they walked and talked tough. They *personified* toughness.

The same rule applies in politics, only more so. In New Hampshire during his 1992 unsuccessful reelection campaign, the first President Bush famously said: *"Message: I care."* (He wasn't supposed to say anything of the sort. Those words were stage instructions that he blurted out because they were on a note card in front of him.) Bill Clinton, on the other hand, said caring things—and let the voters draw their own inferences about his compassion. The latter approach is far more effective. Tell someone *"two plus two,"* but let him put them together himself and say *"four"*—and he is transformed from a passive observer to an active participant.[4]

Consider the following example from the 2004 presidential campaign. John Kerry referred endlessly to his service in the Vietnam War—as if he were trying to talk voters into viewing him through the prism of his war experience and therefore seeing him as tough and competent enough to serve as commander in chief. His message: as someone who fought valiantly in a bad war, I will keep America out of bad wars. That was sufficient to propel him from an asterisk in the polls a year earlier to the Democratic Party nominee.

On the other hand, George W. Bush, who spent the war stateside in the Texas Air National Guard, spoke about terrorism and Iraq in muscular, unflinching terms. Instead of trying to talk voters into seeing him as a hawk, Bush simply talked in a hawkish manner. Consequently, he came off as much tougher and more determined than the man with the multiple Purple Hearts.

*Show, don't tell.*

Now, it is certainly true that John Kerry was showing rather than telling when he stepped up to the podium at the Democratic National Convention, snapped a salute, and said, "I'm John Kerry and I'm reporting for duty." The gesture was obviously planned and blatantly calculated, and therefore of questionable efficacy.

It broke Aaron Sorkin's most fundamental rule of effective manipulation: Don't let them see it coming. Said Sorkin:

> "I don't remember a single moment of John Kerry's acceptance speech, the most important speech of his life at the Democratic Convention. Not a word or a moment. It was unlikely his—and, believe me, I was rooting for him. I wanted that one to sail out of the park. But his Andrews Sisters salute at the beginning signaled 'I have a dream this ain't going to be.' [Laughing] And it was depressing after that."

In Kerry's mind, and in the minds of his consultants and supporters, the gesture probably made perfect sense. To them, it's what a military man would do. But for the millions of veterans, such a blatant public display smacked of the worst sort of jingoism, like Michael Dukakis and his joy ride in a tank.[5]

The stunt also gave Kerry's opponents considerable ammo with which to attack him. Writing in the *National Review*'s online blog during the convention, Barbara Comstock took the opportunity to ask, "Shouldn't some of that duty involve some accomplishment in his 20 years in the Senate?"[6] and *Unfit for Command* coauthor Jerome Corsi labeled Kerry the "gift that keeps on giving" for his propensity for political stunts.[7] The fact is, candid, genuine expressions of passion and commitment are worth ten times the value of a canned, rehearsed publicity stunt.* But in this case, whether you saw the salute as an inspiring assumption of responsibility by a true hero or merely the goofy gimmick of a poseur had mostly to do with what you were already predisposed to think.

A much more effective example of showing rather than telling was Kerry's practice of traveling accompanied by an entourage of fellow veterans, dubbed his "band of brothers" after the Stephen E. Ambrose book (and subsequent HBO miniseries) about World War II. Merely appearing on stage with them—and particularly his reunion with Jim Rassmann, the man whose life Kerry had saved in Southeast Asia a quarter

---

*Bush reached his all-time height of popularity immediately after his impromptu speech delivered to rescue workers via a megaphone on top of a burned-out fire truck buried in the rubble that used to be the World Trade Center. When one of the workers yelled out, "We can't hear you," Bush responded, "Well, I can hear you. The whole world hears you. And the people who knocked down these buildings will hear all of us soon." Personal, emotional, and spontaneous, he said what every American was thinking . . . and feeling.

century before[8]—bolstered Kerry's credibility considerably. (I was in New Hampshire and watched the two meet for the first time in more than thirty years—not a dry eye in the house. It was authentic, and it was also political theater at its best.)

But the power of Rassmann's personal testimonial was undercut by the arrival of another group of old soldiers, the Swift Boat Veterans for Truth, an issue-oriented political and fundraising organization representing more than 250 Swift boat veterans who served in Vietnam with Kerry. Their denunciations of the Democratic nominee, communicated with a few million dollars in paid advertising and tens of millions more in free media, arguably cost Kerry the presidency. It undercut any benefit his war service provided his campaign but, more importantly, it undercut his perceived integrity. Below is the script of the first ad. See if you can spot the one word that turned this ad from a traditional attack to a genuine killer.

---

### "ANY QUESTIONS?"
### (FIRST AIRED AUGUST 4, 2004)

John Edwards: If you have any question about what John Kerry is made of, just spend three minutes with the men who served with him.

Al French: I served with John Kerry.

Bob Elder: I served with John Kerry.

George Elliott: John Kerry has not been honest about what happened in Vietnam.

Al French: He is lying about his record.

Louis Letson: I know John Kerry is lying about his first Purple Heart because I treated him for that injury.

Van O'Dell: John Kerry lied to get his bronze star. . . . I know, I was there, I saw what happened.

Jack Chenoweth: His account of what happened and what actually happened are the difference between night and day.

Admiral Hoffman: John Kerry has not been honest.

Adrian Lonsdale: And he lacks the capacity to lead.

Larry Thurlow: When the chips were down, you could not count
on John Kerry.

Bob Elder: John Kerry is no war hero.

Grant Hibbard: He betrayed all his shipmates. . . .
He lied before the Senate.

Shelton White: John Kerry betrayed the men and women he served with
in Vietnam.

Joe Ponder: He dishonored his country. . . . He most certainly did.

Bob Hildreth: I served with John Kerry. . . .

Bob Hildreth (off-camera): John Kerry cannot be trusted.

Announcer: Swift Boat Veterans for Truth is responsible for the content
of this advertisement.

From the last night of the Democrat convention right up to election eve, the public was treated to charges and countercharges about Kerry's actual record in Vietnam and his public statements upon returning to the United States. And every day the ads appeared, the Kerry team had to stand by and watch as their candidate's credibility cratered.

So did you find the word that worked? Using the actual people who served with Kerry in Vietnam to make the accusations was powerful. The simplicity, brevity, and credibility of each comment followed the first three rules of communication. But it was the word *"betrayed"* that stuck in the craw of voters—particularly veterans. It's one thing to take a disagreeable position on the Vietnam War—lots of politicians did so and were later elected. But betrayal. Betrayal. That's a crime that can never be forgiven. That's an action that disqualifies someone for life. The focus groups I conducted for MSNBC among swing voters in Ohio instantly seized on that word and would not let go. The ad creators probably never realized that in that one word, *betrayed*, they had found the ingredient to bring down the Kerry campaign.

Yet even though the media tended to focus on the initial Swift boat ad, it was the follow-up thirty-second spot that truly did in Kerry. Again, there is a single comment that stands above the rest—one statement by his accusers that struck a chord, and severed the spinal column of John Kerry's presidential ambitions. See if you can find it.

## "SELLOUT"
## (FIRST AIRED AUGUST 20, 2004)

John Kerry: They had personally raped, cut off ears, cut off heads. . . .

Joe Ponder: The accusations that John Kerry made against the veterans who served in Vietnam was just devastating.

John Kerry: . . . randomly shot at civilians . . .

Joe Ponder: It hurt me more than any physical wounds I had.

John Kerry: . . . cut off limbs, blown up bodies . . .

Ken Cordier: That was part of the torture, was, uh, to sign a statement that you had committed war crimes.

John Kerry: . . . razed villages in a fashion reminiscent of Ghengis Khan . . .

Paul Gallanti: John Kerry gave the enemy for free what I, and many of my, uh, comrades in North Vietnam, in the prison camps, uh, took torture to avoid saying. It demoralized us.

John Kerry: . . . crimes committed on a day-to-day basis . . .

Ken Cordier: He betrayed us in the past, how could we be loyal to him now?

John Kerry: . . . ravaged the countryside of South Vietnam.

Paul Gallanti: He dishonored his country, and, uh, more, more importantly the people he served with. He just sold them out.

Announcer: Swift Boat Veterans for Truth is responsible for the content of this advertisement.

That was John Kerry's actual voice they used. A tape recording of his testimony before Congress still existed, and the ad creators effectively interspersed Kerry's description of what he saw in Vietnam with his critics and accusers. The fact that it was in Kerry's own voice is what made this ad even more devastating than the first one. But there was one line in particular that sent shivers down the spine of voters watching: *"John Kerry gave the enemy for free what I and many of my comrades in North Vietnam, in the prison camps, took torture to avoid saying."* When the MSNBC focus groups saw the ad for the first time, they shuddered and moaned as those words were delivered. Truly words that worked.

But it wasn't over quite yet. On October 22, 2004, just two weeks before Election Day, it all came to a head. John O'Neill, author of the book *Unfit for Command* and one of the most outspoken Swift boat veterans, appeared on MSNBC's *Scarborough Country,* hosted that night by Pat Buchanan. Opposite O'Neill was senior MSNBC political contributor and former Democrat Senate aide Lawrence O'Donnell. Only seconds into the program, chaos erupted. O'Neill began calmly, explaining the political impact of the various Swift boat ads, but O'Donnell quickly interjected and within ten minutes had accused O'Neill no less than twenty-four separate times of lies, lying, and several other derivates of the word.[9] It's impossible to give an exact count; the transcript of the show indicates just how often O'Donnell interrupted and simply talked over O'Neill and even over Buchanan's attempts to regain order. In one particularly contentious ten-second clip, O'Donnell managed to accuse O'Neill six times of lying about whether Kerry personally wrote the after-action report that said the Swift boats Kerry was commanding came under enemy fire:

O'DONNELL: Lies.

BUCHANAN: Oh, let him talk.

O'DONNELL: He just lies. He just spews out lies. Point to his [Kerry's] name on the [after-action] report, you liar. Point to his name, you liar. These are military records. Point to a name.

O'NEILL: I will, if you'll shut up, Larry. You can't just scream everybody down.

O'DONNELL: There's no name. You just spew lies.[10]

I remember the exchange well; I was in the green room of a television studio in New York City preparing to go on the air next and I heard and watched it all unfold. I also remember that video clip reverberating around the Internet for days, earning much broader attention than the actual program itself. Presumably O'Donnell thought he was doing his candidate a service by delivering a relentless attack on the credibility of the attackers. In fact, his efforts undermined the credibility of his own candidate. Voters don't respond well to pundits interrupting and yelling at each other. O'Neill's calm demeanor in the face of O'Donnell's ceaseless tirade convinced some voters in our subsequent focus groups that while both sides may have been playing rather loose with the truth, the benefit of the doubt should go to O'Neill. The Purple Heart persona that

Kerry had labored so long to create was shattered by the Swift Boat Veterans' devastating counternarrative. The message of the Swift boat ads had overwhelmed John Kerry, the messenger.

As a footnote, I am often asked what I would have advised John Kerry if I had been his communications advisor. The answer, and I told this to Kerry early in 2006, may have shocked and offended Bible Belt Republicans, but it would have changed the dynamic of the controversy. I would have asked Kerry to wait until he had a friendly audience in front of him (think visually) and the TV cameras behind him, and then had a reporter call out: "Senator, those people are questioning your patriotism. What do you have to say to them?" I would have had Kerry turn and face the accuser, with the friendly audience now as his backdrop, and I would have told him to deliver the following lines in a stern but controlled voice:

> Let me tell you something, I fought for this country. I was wounded for this country. I'm proud of my service. You tell the people peddling this trash, and the people who support them—including the President and the Vice-President—to go to hell. I went to Vietnam and fought for the American flag. They didn't.*

Unless and until you say something to break the rhythm of a negative story, it will continue. A graphic profanity would have broken the rhythm, changed the focus, and, while a debate about the use of such words in politics would have ensued, that would have been a better debate for John Kerry.

Perhaps he was lucky not to have me as an advisor.

## THE POLITICS OF PERSONALITY

There are three outstanding contemporary case studies of politicians whose personas and language are even more compelling to voters than the philosophy they espouse. The first of these is former New York City mayor

---

*My interview with *The West Wing*'s Aaron Sorkin is what triggered this advice. Says Sorkin: "From time to time I would like to be able to use the language of adulthood. The fact is, when a rescue mission of some DEA agents in Bogota fails, killing the 14 guys, when the President hears this news, I want to be able to write, 'What the f__k happened?' because I know that's what this man would say. I want to be able to say 'Goddamn it' every once in a while." Sorkin calls it "the language of adulthood." I call it reality.

Rudolph Giuliani. In his case, the primacy of personal character traits over issues held true even before September 11 made him so widely known and celebrated around the country and around the world.

In my polling for Rudy's brief senatorial bid in 2000 (which was cut short by health issues), I found that his personal story and record of accomplishment trumped his political philosophy and where he stood on the issues. New Yorkers were more interested in who he was and what he had done than in his beliefs and convictions. Here's a capsule biography of Rudy that poll-tested through the political stratosphere:

> Born to a working class family in Brooklyn, Rudy Giuliani's strong work ethic, values, faith, and sense of responsibility come from his New York upbringing.
>
> Raised and educated entirely in New York, he quickly rose in the legal profession, holding positions as Associate Attorney General and U.S. Attorney for the Southern District of New York, with record-setting prosecutions of organized crime and white collar felonies.
>
> As mayor, Rudy Giuliani presided over the historic New York City comeback . . . lower crime, cleaner streets, hundreds of thousands of new jobs, and record cuts in welfare.
>
> Today, Rudy is motivated by the same things he learned as a child . . . hard work, telling it like it is, a sense of responsibility to community and country, his belief in people, and the power of faith.

New Yorkers responded very positively to language about Rudy's work ethic, his sense of responsibility, and his working class background—in other words, to his *personal values*. They saw in him a fighter—from day one—for them, and that gave voters the confidence to trust that he would do right by them. It also helped Rudy that his public approach to crime, welfare, taxes, and jobs came from emphasizing a values component. He always explained the *why* in his policies as well as the *how*. Perhaps it was the lawyer in him. Perhaps it was an inner need to educate and convince, not just inform. And as long as every "why" was thematically tied to Rudy's pre-established, defined, and winning persona, people were predisposed to give him the benefit of the doubt without belaboring the specifics—which is one reason why he has continued to top virtually every poll for president in 2008 despite the fact that his position on a number of social issues is different from the Republican mainstream.

The second great contemporary case study in political persona is California Governor Arnold Schwarzenegger. In his bodybuilding days and later as a cinematic action hero, Schwarzenegger created a distinct and appealing persona. In fact, notice how wordy—and almost redundant—it seems to give Arnold a title. Three years into his administration, as many people still call him "Arnold" as call him "Governor." Like Rudy and similar political superstars, Arnold's persona *is* his platform. The very fact that he is larger than life—that he is "such a character"—provides him a protected coat of immunity in our celebrity-centered modern American culture. Being a "character" gives a politician such as Arnold a shield of Teflon, as President Reagan was said to have. It also explains how he can go from popular to unpopular and then regain much of his support, credibility, and political aura all in less than eighteen months.

But Arnold is also a perfect case study in the dramatic difference between personal and political communication. Initially, because he was a celebrity turned governor, audiences had a different standard of expectation and judgment. His humor, always sharp and often truly funny, was more important than his substance. But as he shifted from Hollywood character to California governor, so did his fortunes—and misfortunes. The less larger-than-life he became, the less popular he found himself with the people who elected him. The more political his language became, the lower his numbers sunk in the polls. His failure to pass any of his political reforms in the 2005 special election was due in part to his politicizing issues that should have instead been personalized. From attacking "union bosses" instead of standing up for *"hardworking union members who should have the right to control their own union dues"* to condemning the legislature instead of standing up for neighborhoods and communities, his fall from the polling stratosphere took place because he began to walk and talk like a politician. Celebrities are expected to talk like, well, celebrities. Politicians can't.

Still, that first year of the Schwarzenegger administration was unlike any other—anywhere. In addition to the physical strength and relentless energy of his on-screen persona, Arnold brought to Sacramento that infectious and insistent optimism best captured by that favorite word of his: *fantastic*. His unrelenting optimism was one of the most appealing, endearing, and politically helpful characteristics that an American political leader can have. And as a direct result, he scored favorability numbers higher than any other California Republican in decades.

Senator John McCain is the third great contemporary example of a politician whose character *is* his message. McCain's fans revere him because of who he is, because of his compelling and undeniably heroic personal story, because he's the driver of the *Straight Talk Express*—and not, primarily, because of his position on Issue A or Policy B. In fact, many Democrats love the guy even though he has a voting record well to the right of George W. Bush. Why? Because of his independent streak and willingness to criticize other Republicans—and because some of his strange political bedfellows never took the time to learn his record. The mainstream media gives McCain a pass on things they would excoriate another politician for simply because they like him and because he makes such damn good copy. If McCain is elected president in 2008, you can bet that only a handful of his supporters will be with him because of his position on telecommunications regulation, even though he had significant influence there for six years. They'll be with him because of his persona as a man of integrity, a straight shooter, and a courageous war veteran who says what he means and means what he says.

## AUTHENTICITY

Messengers who are their own best message are always true to themselves. *You cannot get away with acting in politics for long.* As soon as an audience catches a politician performing rather than living the role, he is on the road to ruin. President Kennedy "performed" the role of family man, but voters did not know the truth about his private behavior until long after he had died. Ronald Reagan embodied family values, even if it only extended to his wife and not his own children. Yes, Bill Clinton was a performer, but he really was *that good* that even when he got caught, it didn't matter. Hillary Clinton certainly won't be as lucky. Authenticity isn't easy. The best theater and film actors strive their entire careers for honesty and immediacy in their performances, but it's easier for them. They only have to deliver for two hours most nights and matinees on Wednesdays and weekends.[11] Elected officials are on twenty-four hours a day, 365 days a year.

The importance of authenticity cannot be overstated. Whether your arena is business or politics, you simply must be yourself. Few things in this world are more painful—more fingernails-on-the-chalkboard grating—than a politician or a CEO trying to act cool. Except maybe your mom and dad trying act cool around your friends when you were an adolescent. Employees and voters see right through such bad-faith attempts to relate and bond with them. Think of Bill Lumbergh, the egregiously awful boss in the workplace satire *Office Space,* proudly announcing to his staff that Friday will be "Hawaiian Shirt Day"—as if this will deliver them from the drudgery of their cube-farm work lives. Or, for a case study in how *not* to play the "cool boss," consider the character of David Brent, played by Ricky Gervais on the British TV comedy *The Office* (since remade in the United States by NBC), who goes to agonizingly absurd lengths to portray himself as the hip buddy of his employees.

By all means, show don't tell . . . reveal your personality . . . *be* the message rather than *narrating* it, but above all, be *authentic.* When candidate Clinton went on *The Arsenio Hall Show* during the 1992 presidential campaign to wear shades and play the saxophone, he got away with it. It worked because it *fit.* It may surprise readers for me to credit Bill Clinton, of all people, as an example of authenticity. But at least in this particular instance, he was showing people who he really was. Much as conservatives may be loath to admit it, Clinton had a certain genuine cool. He could get away with being a bad boy saxophone player because, audiences could sense, he really did have that naughty side. Even when Clinton discussed his underwear preference on MTV, he was being authentic—equivocating between briefs and boxers—because that was who he really was.

An interesting contrast took place in the 2000 Republican presidential primaries when John McCain and George W. Bush appeared on rival late night talk shows and took decidedly different approaches. McCain, appearing on Leno, was clearly programmed by advisers to be funny and did his best to tell amusing stories and anecdotes to a fairly friendly host and audience. Over on Letterman, Dave took the usual take-no-prisoners approach, leaving Bush nothing much to do except laugh at his own expense.

But here's the surprise. When I showed both clips to focus group dial sessions of Republican and swing voters, Bush outdid McCain. Viewers saw in Bush a man so comfortable in his skin that he could take the ribbing of others and not flinch a bit. Conversely, McCain appeared so insecure that he had to try to dominate the conversation. At the time, most journalists gave the edge to McCain, but they didn't understand (and still don't) that it is often what you don't say that matters to voters.

It was one of the few times during the 2000 campaign when McCain looked and felt rehearsed.

Of course, being yourself doesn't mean you shouldn't put your best foot forward or should be content with being boring or out of touch. It's important to be your *best* self. Back in 1993—in the aftermath of Bill Clinton's defeat of the first President Bush, when the Reagan Revolution was over and the Republicans were going through the soul-searching that every party faces after a major ballot box rejection—I had some blunt words to say about the staid, uptight image of the GOP:

> We don't know as Republicans how to communicate as well as we could because we're still so stuck up. We are still so damn formal. Let me take two senators, Orrin Hatch of Utah and Dick Lugar from Indiana, whom I like very much and I would vote for if I lived in their states. Do they look like the kind of people you could kind of have a beer with and talk to? They look like morticians. They are the people that my mother wishes I dressed like.[12]

That was the first of many instances when my comments got me into real trouble—but no one disagreed with the premise.

We live in an exceptionally informal age. Go back and check out a movie from the 1950s or early '60s. Men and women in the workplace—good *friends* who have known one another for years . . . even people who are *dating*—call one another "Mr. So-and-So" and "Miss Whatever." Every man wears a tie, all the time. Women are in dresses, every day. In today's business world, *everybody* is on a first-name basis, and the days of the starched white shirts and navy blue suits are gone. When you e-mail a business acquaintance you've never met before, chances are you address him by his first name. Politicians and business leaders would be well advised to acknowledge the relaxed, loose, casual world in which the people they are addressing reside. Without trying to be something they're not, without "acting cool," while maintaining their authenticity and avoiding phoniness, they have to *lighten up*.

## THE CORPORATE CEO AS MESSENGER

The business world is particularly plagued by shoddy language. Employees and customers are inundated with jargon and "ad-speak," moribund clichés and windy phrases that signify nothing and are forgotten even before they are remembered. It's stunning how poor the communication skills can be at even the highest levels of corporate America. If you want to be truly depressed about this country's lack of comprehendible economic discourse, peruse (in the true sense of the word) some of the memos and annual messages emanating from the CEOs of some of America's top companies. The CEO is more often than not the de facto messenger for the company he or she leads, and as such is the living, breathing embodiment of whatever product or service it sells—and that's not always a good thing. Right now, there's a *Fortune* 20 CEO out there who is leading a crumbing manufacturing behemoth and doesn't realize that his own unintelligible public statements are contributing to its collapse, and he is certainly not the exception. By the time you read this book, he will probably be gone. By the time the paperback version is published, so may the company.

But there is an equally powerful positive example that other CEOs, business professionals, and Americans at large should emulate: Pfizer's recently retired leader, Hank McKinnell. It may surprise readers that one of the best modern CEO communicators comes from a company and an industry that is seemingly in the bull's-eye of public condemnation.

Pfizer is the perfect example of a corporation where *being* the message through its products is just not enough. It takes a CEO's personal touch. It's incredible that an industry that literally saves thousands of lives every single day would face such hostility. Despite the success in creating breakthrough *medications* (a far more descriptive term than *drugs* or *medicines*) that improve the quality of life of millions of Americans every single year, the progress and innovation that is at the core of the pharmaceutical industry is very quickly forgotten by the people who benefit the most. Americans readily complain about the price they pay for these life-saving pills, as though they were buying another household product. The same people who have no problem forking over $2.65 for a cappuccino at Starbucks will complain bitterly about the cost of a $2.65 pill that keeps them sufficiently healthy and active so that they can consume whatever unhealthy item Starbucks is selling.

Enter McKinnell, with a communication burden no CEO would ever want to carry. He was held to a higher standard because the products he sold were held to higher standards. But the Pfizer products don't speak for the company—McKinnell does, and his language delivers. What makes McKinnell different from other CEOs is that he is consistent (rule four of effective communication), aspirational (rule seven), and always sets the context and relevance for his listeners (rule ten). His presentations are peppered with the *"principles"* of Pfizer, the *"standards"* Pfizer sets for its medications and the employees who make them, and a constant focus on the future—using words like *"progress," "innovation,"* and *"breakthrough"* repeatedly.

---

**FORMER PFIZER CEO HANK MCKINNELL:
WORDS THAT WORK**

At Pfizer, we are developing breakthrough medicines for diseases from Alzheimer's to high blood pressure. We are making significant progress in our efforts to lower cholesterol and reduce heart disease.

But we know our obligations don't end in the lab. With our Pfizer Share Card, we've helped millions of low-income patients gain access to our medicines. Prescription drug access is a major national challenge. At Pfizer we're committed to being a part of the solution. After all, it's not about having the medications, it's about having *access* to the medications.

---

Notice his use of *"obligation"* and *"access."* Here is a CEO of a major company that is putting his name, his face, and his life behind his company. The public commitment is also a personal one—and it effectively aligns him not just to the company he led but to the consumers he served.

It also explains why he appeared personally in Pfizer corporate image advertising. During the period in 2002–03 when corporate America was under sharp attack because of the mounting accounting scandals and ethical lapses, McKinnell was proactively addressing what Pfizer was doing to earn the public trust. And when other CEOs went into hiding rather than face public criticism, McKinnell was willing to take the heat. The language he used was perfect not just for that time but for all time. . . .

---

## MORE MCKINNELL WORDS THAT WORK

As Pfizer's CEO, it is my ultimate responsibility to our customers, employees, and shareholders to ensure that our products are safe and our code of conduct beyond reproach.

Our customers depend on us for honesty. Our health as a business is tied to the health of the people we serve. Science is difficult. Business is complicated. Accountability is not. You've either done the right thing or you've done the wrong thing. It's that simple. There are no shades of gray when it comes to corporate ethics. Ethical failure equals corporate failure.

---

For the pharmaceutical industry itself, words in and of themselves cannot turn back years of bad publicity, complaints about high pricing, and the scourge of medications that have been withdrawn from the market. But they can tip the scales among the still sizeable majority of Americans who don't like the *industry* but who appreciate the product. As McKinnell himself has said, "Now is the time for real answers, not simple ones." If the industry follows McKinnell's advice, the coming years won't be as difficult as the previous ones.

Two other CEOs, one current and the other retired, stand head and shoulders above the rest in how their language embodies the companies they run, the management style they typify, and the leaders they are.

Jack Welch, the venerable former CEO of General Electric, truly practiced what he preached. A tireless worker, Welch led the expansion of General Electric into the powerhouse corporation it is today—and it didn't just happen because of what the company bought and sold. Linguistically, Welch was a dedicated follower and communicator of rules four and ten of effective messaging: repetition and relevance. He certainly lived his life in the public eye, but everything he said and did was designed to promote his company. *"Good business leaders create a vision, articulate the vision, passionately own the vision, and relentlessly drive it to completion."*[13] The incredibly powerful and personal *"GE, we bring good things to life"* ad campaign was launched under his watch, and it perfectly matched his laserlike focus on success.

Steve Jobs, Apple's past and current CEO, is an obvious choice because of his larger than life persona and his candid assessment and lasting impact on the human condition. The parallels between his life and the company he created are remarkable. Though Jobs has been a corporate icon for almost all his business life, and though Apple has consistently introduced cutting-edge technology and products, not everything has gone their way. "I'm the only person I know that's lost a quarter of a billion dollars in one year," Jobs once told an interviewer. "It's very character-building."[14] I guess he never met Enron's Jeff Skilling.

His rags to riches back to rags and once again to riches story is one that should be taught at every business school because it demonstrates the power of personal conviction—and that conviction has defined Apple as well. Responding to a critic who asked why he thought his overly ambitious development plans could be achieved, Jobs declared, *"Because I'm the CEO and I think it can be done."* His unrelenting can-do language and spirit are a perfect reflection of the company he ran. The legendary "1984" Super Bowl commercial set a standard that has still not been surpassed in advertising, and his yearly "rock star" performances for employees and shareholders take on a transformational tone much like a Springsteen concert. While his communication efforts do not meet the rules of simplicity or brevity, Jobs is certainly aspirational, and his language encourages listeners to envision a powerful future.

## BE ALL THAT YOU CAN BE: THE COMPANY PERSONA AND LANGUAGE ALIGNMENT

It's not just CEOs and corporate spokespeople who need effective language to *be* the message. The most successful advertising taglines are not seen as slogans for a product. They *are* the product. From M&M's *"melts in your mouth, not in your hand"* to *"Please don't squeeze the Charmin"* bathroom tissue, from the *"plop, plop, fizz, fizz"* of Alka-Seltzer to *"Fly the friendly skies of United,"* there is no light space between the product and its marketing. Words that work reflect "not only the soul of the brand, but the company itself and its reason for being in business," according to Publicis worldwide executive creative director David Droga.[15]

## COMPANIES WITH ALIGNED PERSONA AND LANGUAGE

| COMPANY/BRAND | PRODUCT | LANGUAGE |
|---|---|---|
| American Express | Financial services | "Don't leave home without it." |
| Anheuser-Busch | Beer | "The king of beers" |
| BMW | Automobiles | "The ultimate driving machine" |
| Cingular Wireless | Cell phones | "Raising the bar" |
| Disney | Theme parks | "I'm going to Disney World." |
| Energizer | Batteries | "It keeps going & going & going." |
| Florida Orange Growers | Orange Juice | "It's not just for breakfast anymore." |
| Fox News Channel | Cable news channel | "We report. You decide." |
| General Electric | Household appliances | "We bring good things to life." |
| Intel | Computer chip | "Intel inside" |
| McDonald's | Quick service food | "i'm lovin' it." |
| Maxwell House | Coffee | "Good to the last drop." |
| Merrill Lynch | Financial services | "Bullish on America" |
| Miller Lite | Beer | "Tastes great. Less filling." |
| Nationwide | Insurance | "Nationwide is on your side." |
| Smuckers | Jams/jellies | "With a name like Smuckers . . . it has to be good." |
| Southwest Airlines | Air travel | "You are now free to move about the country." |
| State Farm | Insurance | "Like a good neighbor, State Farm is there." |
| United Negro College Fund | Education | "A mind is a terrible thing to waste." |
| Verizon Wireless | Cell phones | "Can you hear me now?" |

In the same vein, advertising experts identify a common quality among the most popular and long-lasting corporate icons: Rather than *selling* for their companies, these characters *personify* them. Ronald McDonald, the Marlboro Man, Betty Crocker, the Energizer Bunny—they aren't shills trying to *talk* us into buying a Big Mac, a pack of smokes, a box of cake mix, a package of batteries; they don't even personalize the product. Just like the most celebrated slogans, they *are* the product.[16]

Walk through any bookstore and you'll find dozens of books about the marketing and branding efforts of corporate America. The process of corporate communication has been thinly sliced and diced over and over, but what you won't find is a book about the one truly essential characteristic in our twenty-first-century world: the company *persona* and how words that work are used to create and sustain it.

The company persona is the sum of the corporate leadership, the corporate ethos, the products and services offered, interaction with the customer, and, most importantly, the language that ties it all together. A majority of large companies do not have a company persona, but those that do benefit significantly. Ben & Jerry's attracts customers in part because of the funky names they gave to the conventional (and unconventional) flavors they offer, but the positive relationship between corporate management and their employees also plays a role, even after Ben and Jerry sold the company. McDonald's in the 1970s and Starbucks over the past decade became an integral part of the American culture as much for the lifestyle they reflected as the food and beverages they offered, but the in-store lexicon helped by setting them apart from their competition. (Did any customers ever call the person who served them a cup of coffee a "barista" before Starbucks made the term popular?) Language is never the sole determinant in creating a company persona, but you'll find words that work associated with all companies that have one.

And when the message, messenger, and recipient are all on the same page, I call this rare phenomenon "language alignment," and it happens far less frequently than you might expect. In fact, virtually all of the companies that have hired my firm for communication guidance have found themselves linguistically unaligned.

This manifests itself in two ways. First, in service-oriented businesses, the sales force is too often selling with a different language than the marketing people are using. There's nothing wrong with individualizing the sales approach to each customer, but when you have your sales force promoting a message that has no similarity with the advertising campaign, it undermines both efforts. The language in the ads and promotions must match the language on the street, in the shop, and on the floor. For example, Boost Mobile, which caters to an inner city youth demographic, uses the slogan "Where you at?" Not grammatically (or politically) correct—but it's the language of their consumer.

And second, corporations with multiple products in the same space too often allow the language of those products to blur and bleed into each other. Procter & Gamble may sell a hundred different items, but even though each one fills a different need, a different space, and/or a different category, it is perfectly fine for them to share similar language. You can use some of the same verbiage to sell soap as you would to sell towels, because no consumer will confuse the products and what they do.

Not so for a company that is in a single line of work, say selling cars or selling beer, where companies use the exact same adjectives to describe very different products. In this instance, achieving linguistic alignment requires a much more disciplined linguistic segmentation. It is almost always a more effective sales strategy to divvy up the appropriate adjectives and create a unique lexicon for each individual brand.

An example of a major corporation that has confronted both of these challenges and still managed to achieve linguistic alignment, even as they are laying off thousands of workers, is the Ford Motor Company— which manages a surprisingly diverse group of brands ranging from Mazda to Aston Martin. The Ford corporate leadership recognized that it was impossible to separate the Ford name, corporate history, heritage, and range of vehicles—so why bother. They came as a package. Sure, Ford maintains individual brand identity, through national and local ad campaigns and by creating and maintaining a separate image and language for each brand. For example, *uniquely sensual styling* certainly applies when one is talking about a Jaguar S-Type, but would probably not be pertinent for a Ford F-250 pickup truck. But the fact that the CEO carries the Ford name communicates *continuity* to the company's customers, and Bill Ford sitting in front of an assembly line talking about leadership and innovation in all of Ford's vehicles effectively puts all the individual brands into alignment.

## THE BILL FORD SIXTY-SECOND SPOT

If you look at the Ford Motor Company, innovation has driven everything we've done. We're known for innovation going all the way back to my great grandfather starting with the Model T and the assembly line.

And what we've done is re-committed ourselves to American innovation, dramatically ramping up our commitment to hybrids. We were the first with the hybrid SUV. People like hybrids because they like the technology, and it's one that doesn't require them to do anything differently than they normally would when they drive a vehicle.

Starting next year, we'll have about the same number of vehicles that will be ethanol capable. You can run them either on gasoline, ethanol, or other bio fuels, getting this country less dependent upon foreign oil.

All of Ford Motor Company is dedicated to safety and we're using the best minds from Volvo and elsewhere in the company to dedicate ourselves to safety innovation.

It's a commitment to the technology. It's a commitment to our own engineers that this is the direction that we're taking and that we're not going to back off. Innovation will be the compass that guides this company going forward.

The words he uses—*"innovation," "driven," "re-committed," "dramatically," "dedicated"*—represent the simplicity and brevity of effective communications, and they are wrapped around the CEO who is the fourth-generation Ford to lead the company—hence credibility. The cars are the message, Bill Ford is the messenger, the language is dead-on, and Ford is weathering the American automotive crisis far better than its larger rival General Motors. Again, the language of Ford isn't the only driver of corporate image and sales—but it certainly is a factor.

In fact, the brand-building campaign was so successful that GM jumped on board. But Ford quickly took it a step further. In early 2006, they began to leverage their ownership of Volvo (I wonder how many readers did not know that Ford bought Volvo in 1999 and purchased Jaguar a decade earlier) to communicate a corporate-wide commitment to automotive safety, across all of its individual brands and vehicles. Volvo is one of the most respected cars on the road today, and aligning all of Ford behind an industry leader is a very smart strategy indeed.

So what about the competition?

General Motors, once the automotive powerhouse of the world, has an equally diverse product line and arguably a richer history of technology and innovation, but their public message of cutbacks, buy-backs, and lay-offs was designed to appeal to Wall Street, not Main Street, and it crushed new car sales. At the time of this writing, GM is suffering through record losses, record job layoffs, and a record number of bad stories about its failing marketing efforts.

It didn't have to be this way.

The actual attributes of many of the GM product lines are more appealing than the competition, but the product image itself is not. To own a GM car is to tell the world that you're so 1970s, and since what you drive is considered an extension and expression of yourself to others, people end up buying cars they actually like less because they feel the cars will say something more about them.

Think about it. Here's a company that was the first to develop a catalytic converter, the first to develop an advanced anti-tipping stabilization technology, the first to develop engines that could use all sorts of blended gasolines, and most importantly in today's market, the creator of OnStar—an incredible new-age computerized safety and tracking device. Yet most American consumers have no idea that any of these valuable innovations came from General Motors, simply because GM decided not to tell them. So instead of using its latest and greatest emerging technology to align itself with its customers, GM finds itself in a deteriorating dialogue with shareholders. No alignment = no sales.

Another problem with GM: No one knew that the various brands under the GM moniker were in fact . . . GM. Even such well-known brands as Corvette and Cadillac had become disconnected from the parent company. Worse yet, all the various brands (with the exception of Hummer, which couldn't get lost in a crowd even if the brand manager wanted it to) were using similar language, similar visuals, and a similar message—blurring the distinction between brands and turning GM vehicles into nothing more than generic American cars. Repeated marketing failures were just part of GM's recurring problems, but as that issue was completely within their control, it should have been the easiest to address.

When products, services, and language are aligned, they gain another essential attribute: authenticity. In my own market research for dozens of *Fortune* 500 companies, I have found that the best way to communicate authenticity is to trigger *personalization:* Do audience members see themselves in the slogan . . . and therefore in the product? Unfortunately, achieving personalization is by no means easy.

To illustrate how companies and brands in a competitive space create compelling personas for themselves while addressing the needs of different consumer groups, let's take a look at cereals. Anyone can go out and buy a box of cereal. But different cereals offer different experiences. Watch and listen carefully to their marketing approach and the words they use.

Most cereals geared toward children sell energy, excitement, adventure, and the potential for fun—even more than the actual taste of the sugar-coated rice or wheat puffs in the cardboard box. On the other hand, cereal aimed at grown-ups is sold based on its utility to the maintenance and enhancement of health—with taste once again secondary.

Children's cereals are pitched by nonthreatening cartoon characters—tigers, parrots, chocolate-loving vampires, Cap'ns, and a tiny trio in stocking caps—never an adult or authority figure. Adult cereals come at you head-on with a not-so-subtle Food Police message, wrapped in saccharine-sweet smiles, exclaiming that this cereal is a favorite of healthy and cholesterol-conscious adults who don't want to get colon cancer! Ugghhh. Kids buy Frosted Flakes because *"They're grrrreat!"* Adults buy Special K because we want to be as attractive and vigorous as the actors who promote it. When it comes to cereal, about the only thing parents and kids have in common is that the taste matters only slightly more than the image, experience, and product association—and if the communication appears authentic, they'll buy.

And cereal certainly sells. From Cheerios to Cinnamon Toast Crunch, more than $6 billion worth of cold cereal was sold in the United States alone in 2005. If you were to look at the five top-selling brands, you would see a diverse list targeted to a diverse set of customers. The language used for each of these five brands is noticeably different, but in all cases totally essential.

In looking at the first and third best-selling brands of cereal, one might initially think that only a slight variation in ingredients mark their distinctions. Cheerios and Honey Nut Cheerios are both based around the same whole-grain O-shaped cereal, but are in fact two very different products, beyond the addition of honey and a nut-like crunch.

The language behind Cheerios is remarkably simple and all-encompassing—*"The one and only Cheerios."* Could be for kids . . . could be for young adults . . . could be for parents. Actually, Cheerios wants to sell to all of them. As its Web site states, Cheerios is the right cereal for "toddlers to adults and everyone in between." The subtle heart-shaped bowl on each box suggests to the older consumer that the *"whole-grain"* cereal is a healthy start to a healthy day. But the Web site also has a section devoted entirely to younger adults, complete with testimonials and "tips from new parents" talking about how Cheerios has helped them to raise happy, healthy children. The language behind Cheerios works because it transcends the traditional societal boundaries of age and adds a sense of authenticity to the product.

While you could probably live a happy and healthy existence with Cheerios as your sole cereal choice, there is a substantial segment of the cereal market that demands more. For the cereal-consuming public roughly between the ages of four and fourteen, a different taste and linguistic approach is required. Buzz the Bee, the kid-friendly mascot of Honey Nut Cheerios, pitches the *"irresistible taste of golden honey,"* selling the sweetness of the product to a demographic that craves sweet foods. While the parent knows that his or her child wants the cereal because of its sweet taste (as conveyed through the packaging), Honey Nut Cheerios must still pass the parent test. By putting such statements as *"whole-grain"* and *"13 essential vitamins and minerals"* on the box, the product gains authenticity, credibility, and the approval of the parent.

Two different messages on one common box effectively markets the same product to both children and parents alike, helping to make Honey Nut Cheerios the number three top-selling cereal in 2004. So with the addition of honey and nuts, General Mills, the producer of the Cheerios line, has filled the gap between toddlers and young adults, and completed the Cheerios cradle-to-grave lifetime hold on the consumer.*

To take another example, if you want people to think you're hip and healthy, you make sure they see you drinking bottled water—and the fancier the better. No one walking around with a diet Dr Pepper in hand is looking to impress anybody. These days, there's almost a feeling that soft drinks are exclusively for kids and the uneducated masses. There's a cache to the consumption of water, and expensive and exclusive brands

---

*Kix cereal did it even more overtly with its "Kid tested, Mother approved" slogan. That proved to be a lot more successful than its "Atomic Bomb Ring" promotion effort years earlier.

are all the rage. Now, there may be a few people who have such extremely refined, educated taste buds that they can taste the difference between Dasani and Aquafina (I certainly can't), but the connoisseurs of modish waters are more likely than not posers (or, to continue the snobbery theme, *poseurs*). You won't see many people walking around Cincinnati or Syracuse clutching fancy bottled water. Hollywood, South Beach, and the Upper East Side of New York City are, as usual, another story.

There's one final aspect of *being* the message that impacts what we hear and how we hear it. How our language is delivered can be as important as the words themselves, and no one understands this principle better than Hollywood.

At a small table tucked away in the corner of a boutique Italian restaurant on the outskirts of Beverly Hills, I had the opportunity to dine with legendary actors Charles Durning, Jack Klugman, and Dom DeLuise. The entire dinner was a litany of stories of actors, writers, and the most memorable movie lines ever delivered. (Says Klugman, an Emmy Award winner, "A great line isn't spoken, it is delivered.") Best known for his roles in *The Odd Couple* and *Quincy,* Klugman told a story about how Spencer Tracy was practicing his lines for a movie late in his career in the presence of the film's screenwriter. Apparently not pleased with the reading, the writer said to Tracy, "Would you please pay more attention to how you are reading that line? It took me six months to write it," to which Tracy shot back, "It took me thirty years to learn how to say correctly the line that took you only six months to write."

Spencer Tracy knew how to be the message—and his shelf of Academy Awards proved it.


*It's not what you say, it's what people hear—and see.* This chapter has examined the importance of developing a concrete persona in the political and business spheres. As we have seen, it is not enough to blindly apply the ten rules of effective communication, nor is it enough to consider the audience's context as well. You have to go further and *be* the message. That, at least, is the theory. In the next part of this book, we'll explore how the approach I've outlined has played out in real-life situations. As we shall see, getting the words right can lead to some pretty dramatic results. In some cases, in fact, it makes all the difference between success and failure.

# VI

# *Words We Remember*

> *"You talking to me?"*  — TAXI DRIVER
>
> *"I'm going to make him an offer he can't refuse."*
> — THE GODFATHER
>
> *"Here's looking at you, kid."*  — CASABLANCA
>
> *"Rosebud."*  — CITIZEN KANE *

In a career spanning five decades, Larry King has interviewed quite literally thousands of celebrities, politicians, world leaders, and other famous and infamous individuals of note. But when I ask him to pick out the one interview out of those thousands he won't hesitate a second:

> I was with Martin Luther King, Jr., in 1961 when he was trying to integrate a hotel in Tallahassee, Florida. The hotel won't give him a room even though he has a reservation, and the police squad cars are coming because he's blocking the entrance. He knows he's going to be arrested. I'm there right next to him because I was invited there by his lawyer. So King sits down on this porch in front of this small twenty-room hotel. The owner of the hotel comes out, very straightforward but not belligerently, walks up to King and asks, *"What do you want?"* King says nothing, so the owner asks again in the same direct tone,

---

*"Let's get outta here" was the most common scripted line in all Hollywood productions. According to Filmsite.org, it was used at least once 84 percent of the time from the late 1930s through the mid 1970s. That said, it is the writers of these memorable lines, not the actors who spoke them, who deserve the credit.

*"What do you want?"* And Martin Luther King just looked up at him and said, *"My dignity."* And that word has stuck with me to this day.

That defines this chapter: words we remember. These are not the common words of common people. These are the political, corporate, and cultural words that have been burned into our brains. Some are serious, others frivolous. We may forget our passport or our license plate number, but this chapter is about the words that will always be with us. Forever.

*"Great movie quotes become part of our cultural vocabulary."* So said Jean Pickler Firstenberg, director and CEO of the American Film Institute, when in 2005 AFI released its list of the top 100 memorable movie lines. The jury assembled (made up of directors, actors, screenwriters, critics, historians, and others in the creative community) to select the top quotations was instructed to make their picks based on a quotation's "cultural impact" and legacy. It says something about American culture and priorities that a lot more of us can recite lines voiced in movies released fifty years ago than can tell you what our United States senator said this week, last week . . . ever.

When it comes to movie language, fiction is often more powerful than reality. Think about it. A lot more people know that Arnold Schwarzenegger delivered a defiant *"I'll be back"* (AFI rank #37) guarantee in the blockbuster film *The Terminator* than know that General Douglas MacArthur declared *"I shall return"* as he fled the Philippines from the advancing Japanese in that blockbuster military conflict World War II. Other than the infamous *"If it doesn't fit, you must acquit,"** no real courtroom language is more immediately recognizable than the make-believe *"You can't handle the truth"* (#29) outburst by Jack Nicholson in the Aaron Sorkin–penned *A Few Good Men.* How many people know that *"Keep your friends close but your enemies closer"* from *The Godfather* (#58) is almost identical to what philosopher John Stuart Mill wrote 150 years ago and what Machiavelli advised almost 500 years ago? Surely not many.

My own favorite movie quote, *"What we've got here is failure to com-*

---

*If Robert Shapiro had his way, *"If it doesn't fit, you must acquit"* would never have entered the public lexicon. The most memorable phrase from the O. J. Simpson trial was delivered by Johnnie Cochran, but it wasn't spontaneous. In fact, they weren't even his words. They were written for him by another lawyer on the Simpson defense team, Gerald Uelmen, and Shapiro hated the phrase. "When I first heard it, I thought, 'Oh, God, I don't like that.' It's not something I would have been comfortable saying. But it worked for Cochran."

*municate,"* from *Cool Hand Luke,* came in at #11—but for many businesses, it should be Number One. That clip, which ends in the unfortunate death of the Paul Newman character, is quoted and occasionally played at corporate retreats because it accurately sums up the reoccurring problem: listening to customers and understanding employees. Labor negotiations in particular have collapsed because of the failure to communicate. Wal-Mart even went so far as to shut down a store in Canada in early 2005 simply because company executives and local union leaders failed to properly communicate one another's positions. And the disastrous four-month strike of supermarkets in Southern California in 2004 is seen primarily as a result of labor leaders communicating faulty information and corporate management communicating almost no information at all.

Then there's the Howard Beale character in the film classic *Network,* a movie that lays bare the never-ending pursuit of ratings and revenues. In the midst of an on-air nervous breakdown, he pleads with his viewers to "go to the window, open it, stick your head out and yell: 'I'm mad as hell, and I'm not going to take this anymore.'" That line ranks #19 on the AFI list, and it's on the lips of every disgruntled employee even today. Yet while it comes from a make-believe movie, the words have been co-opted by very real political groups angry with the status quo. From Ross Perot's quixotic campaign in 1992 to the Freedom Alliance founded by Col. Oliver North, who actually named an April 2006 policy memo on immigration *"I'm Mad As Hell and I'm Not Going to Take It Anymore,"* that mad-as-hell language says exactly what you mean and means exactly what you say.

But those lines pale in impact to the top movie line of all time: *"Frankly, my dear, I don't give a damn,"* from *Gone with the Wind.* Short words, assertive tone, delivered spectacularly by Clark Gable and repeated countless times ever since. But in addition to being a classic movie quotation, *"Frankly, my dear . . ."* is also a perfect example of *words that work.* Though it seems tame by today's standards, "I don't give a damn" was considered extreme profanity in the cultural context of 1939. It was debated, condemned, ridiculed . . . and it helped to expand the American lexicon in new directions.

Profanity continues to make a point even in today's coarsened lexicon. On the same day in 2004 that the Senate approved the Defense of Decency Act by a rather sizeable 99 to 1 vote, Vice President Dick Cheney told Vermont senator Patrick Leahy to *"go fuck yourself"* on the Senate floor. Guess which got more publicity. Two years later, at the 2006 G-8 Summit, George W. Bush whispered to British prime minister Tony Blair near an open microphone that *"what they need to do is get Syria to get Hezbollah to stop doing this shit and it's over"* in reference to the escalating military conflict between Israel and Hezbollah. The media pounced on that one word, all but ignoring the much more significant political statement. In a rare moment of exactness and candor, the *New York Times*, the *Washington Post*, and most major national newspapers gave readers the unedited version. This case was *"an exception,"* according to *Pittsburgh Post* executive editor David Shribman. *"The president was quoted in our paper and in others because the actual quote—the actual word—was incontrovertibly part of the story. Indeed, it was the story,"* said Mr. Shribman.[1] But as comedian George Carlin would sadly note, both words are still among the seven that still cannot be said on broadcast television. All four networks bleeped it out.*

Other entries in AFI's top 100 movie lines transcended their original celluloid delivery into fields of impact well beyond their initial intentions. *"Go ahead, make my day,"* #6 on the list, was delivered with clenched jaw by Clint Eastwood as Detective Harry Callahan in 1983's *Sudden Impact*. That same expression of bravado and supreme confidence gave way to George H. W. Bush's memorable *"Read my lips, no new taxes"* line at the 1988 Republican Convention and a surge in public support that propelled him from a seventeen-point deficit into an eight-point victory on election day. Bush the elder could have easily said that there won't be any additional taxes while he's in office.

Similarly, Bush the younger could have said that the terrorists who attacked the U.S. on 9/11 should either be captured or killed, but he didn't. Instead, he drew his inspiration from popular culture; his *"Dead or Alive"* comment about Osama bin Laden could have come right from a John Ford western. Even more memorable, *"Bring it on"* conveyed a swagger that would have made John Wayne proud. But those three simple words, *"bring it on,"* will also prove to be the worst three words of his entire presidency. Even former secretary of state Colin Powell ad-

---

*At the risk of losing a slot in the Conservative Book of the Month Club, the word *shit* also appeared in the *New York Times* on July 10, 1973, in the published transcript of the Watergate tape in which Nixon said, *"I don't give a shit what happens. I want you to stonewall it, let them plead the Fifth Amendment, cover-up or anything else."* But that word did not appear in the accompanying news stories about the tapes.

mitted to me that those words made him cringe. It was unfortunate timing for Powell because he had worked feverishly and successfully to launch a $15 billion international HIV/AIDS relief program, one of the largest humanitarian relief efforts in American history. But at the White House press conference to announce the naming of a global AIDS coordinator and lay out the details of the program, a much different story emerged:

---

### WORDS THAT *DON'T* WORK

Q: A posse of small nations, like Ukraine and Poland, are materializing to help keep the peace in Iraq, but with the attacks on U.S. forces and casualty rates rising, what does the administration do to get larger powers like France and Germany and Russia to join in?

BUSH: Well, first of all, you know, we'll put together a force structure that meets the threats on the ground. And we got a lot of forces there ourselves. And as I said yesterday, anybody who wants to harm American troops will be found and brought to justice.

There are some who feel like that if they attack us that we may decide to leave prematurely. They don't understand what they're talking about, if that's the case.

[*attempted interruption*]

Let me finish.

There are some who feel like that, you know, the conditions are such that they can attack us there. My answer is **BRING IT ON**. We got the force necessary to deal with the security situation.

---

For the first time in the *"War on Terror,"* Bush had the wrong words. Said Powell:

"Looking at Bush as he was speaking, it's the kind of phrase that I immediately knew wouldn't translate or play well in Europe. It came across as sharp, arrogant, and frankly, it had that cowboy aspect to it that I knew wouldn't sound good to European ears."

It didn't sound good to American ears either. In my focus groups for MSNBC, even Republican women recoiled at the phrase. In a session I conducted for MSNBC in Ohio, one Republican mom said in a quivering but firm voice, *"I don't want them to bring it on. I don't want them to target our boys. That could have been my son over there."*

Those same words that proved so disastrous for President Bush offered an unparalleled opportunity for his opponent. In an incredible act of political jujitsu, Andrei Cherny, John Kerry's twenty-eight-year-old chief campaign speechwriter, captured that line and crafted an alternative refrain that challenged Bush to debate and defend his national security record, which took Kerry from boring presidential wannabe to dynamic frontrunner. But even though the partisan Democrat crowds loved it, Kerry eventually dropped it from his stump speech (and Cherny from the campaign) based on the faulty advice of campaign message-meister Bob Shrum who, according to *Newsweek,* thought that attack was too *"undignified"* and Cherny's suggested rhetoric too *"punchy."*

And now, a word from our sponsor . . .

> *"Two all-beef patties–special sauce–lettuce–cheese–pickles–onions–on a sesame seed bun."*
> *"Fly the friendly skies."*
> *"They're magically delicious."*
> *"Have it your way."*

Almost no adult in America would have the slightest trouble identifying these advertising slogans, yet they were created decades ago. If you're a typical American today, you know these slogans—and the thousands like them—the way you know your own name. They are second nature, embedded deep within every one of us—part of the ambient noise of our lives, surrounding us like wallpaper, inescapable. Some are funny. Some are matter-of-fact. Some are genuinely annoying. The best are truly unforgettable.

See how long it takes you to name the last six presidents—if you can. Now see how many of the following six top advertising slogans of the past forty years you can identify:[2]

1. *"Just do it"*
2. *"Tastes great, less filling"*
3. *"Where's the beef?"*

**4.** *"Let your fingers do the walking"*
**5.** *"Melts in your mouth, not in your hand"*
**6.** *"We bring good things to life"*\*

These short, innocuous bursts of words are actually more memorable than the people who have occupied the most powerful position in the world, and they have convinced most of us, at one time or another in our lives, to buy one of the products they trumpet. Good advertising slogans and catchphrases are closely associated with their companies or products. But it is that rare combination of words, thoughts, and emotion that becomes an intrinsic part of the American idiom. And each of them abides by multiple rules of effective language. Think about it. . . .

*"Just do it"* has the values of simplicity, brevity, and is clearly aspirational.

*"Tastes great, less filling"* has all three of those characteristics as well as a fourth: novelty. "Wow," thought consumers. "Finally, a light beer with fewer calories and more drinkable."

*"Where's the beef?"* finally asked out loud in a humorous way the simple rhetorical question that consumers had been thinking about for years.

*"Let your fingers do the walking"* is about as visual and relevant as you can get. To this day, older Americans still remember this ad even though it hasn't run on television in decades.

*"Melts in your mouth, not in your hand"* is also about context and relevance. Finally, a chocolate candy that doesn't make a mess—and it earns its credibility every time you have one.

*"We bring good things to life"* is a simple definition of aspiration—a company that makes the good life possible for people like me. And the more one learned about GE products, the more credible the slogan became.

In fact, many of the most endearing homespun sayings began their lives as pitch lines for well-known products. For example, most people today don't realize that *"When it rains, it pours"* was popularized by Morton Salt in 1912 and was not something your great uncle with the bum knee came up with.[3] Some may remember that the phrase *"Loose lips sink*

---

\***1.** Nike
  **2.** Miller Lite
  **3.** Wendy's
  **4.** Yellow Pages
  **5.** M&M's
  **6.** General Electric

*ships"* comes from a World War II public service campaign.[4] But do you know the origins of the expression, *"Always a bridesmaid, never a bride"?* Would you believe it comes from a 1923 advertisement for Listerine?[5]

Tonight, when you're sitting at the dinner table, and someone states that they "can't believe they ate the whole thing," they'll be paraphrasing an Alka-Seltzer advertisement from the 1970s.[6] Or tomorrow morning, when you pick up the newspaper to see an analysis of what makes Americans tick, know that Chevy's *"heartbeat of America"* campaign has led to the resurgence of the phrase.[7]

Ad copy is conquering more and more of our brains' territory. A decade ago, popular Yale history professor Jaroslav Pelikan would regale his students with the tale of how, at the age of twelve, he had memorized Homer's *Odyssey*—in *Greek.*[8] Unfortunately, when they were twelve, most of his students were busy memorizing: *"Two-all-beef-patties-special-sauce-lettuce-cheese-pickles-onions-on-a-sesame-seed-bun."* Not exactly the language of *"wine-dark sea"* or *"rosy-fingered Dawn."*

Much of this advertising language saturation—and our subsequent ability to recall it—is involuntary. That's one of the definitions of words that work: We remember even when we're not trying. Not that we seek to ignore them. Effective commercial jingles are lodged in our memories every bit as indelibly as the Pledge of Allegiance or the childhood alphabet song—and often, not surprisingly, carry the same nostalgic power. Like the lyrics of the Bugs Bunny version of *The Barber of Seville* (my own personal favorite) or ABC's *Schoolhouse Rock* ("Conjunction Junction, what's your function?"—I bet you're singing it now), they hibernate for decades in some seldom-visited alcove of our minds—but it doesn't take much for them to awaken and burst back into our consciousness. Not that long ago I attended a performance of *The Barber of Seville* in Moscow. During the overture, I began to sing the Bugs Bunny lyrics quietly. Several Americans within earshot turned, smiled, and nodded knowingly. Like magic, these words are truly *part of us,* never to be forgotten.

There is no doubt that in the creation and dissemination of language, nothing in day-to-day life plays a more significant role than television. But the real question for those who seek to understand and then apply the power of words is whether television mirrors society or leads it. From television pioneer Norman Lear's perspective, his groundbreaking programming merely shined a bright light on words and situations that were all too familiar in real life, even if they had never been discussed on television.

"There wasn't anything on *All in the Family* that I didn't think one could hear in a schoolyard anywhere in the country. The accents would change, the inclination to certain phrases might change, but the basic sentiment was 'people speak,' 'ordinary folk talking.' You heard it either from the armchair from your favorite uncle or father or you heard it on the playground."*

Lear may claim that his characters reflected the words of the people, but his shows clearly pushed the language limit to the breaking point—and beyond. He enjoys telling the story about the first time *"son-of-a-bitch"* appeared on television:

> We did an episode of *Maude* where Walter comes close to committing some form of infidelity. The audience knows, and when Maude learns this at that at the very end, she embraces him and says "you son-of-a-bitch." That was the tagline.
>
> So I hear from the guy that runs Program Practices, and he says, "You're kidding Norman, you're not going to do that." We got into a long conversation about it, maybe a couple of conversations, and his argument to me was she could say something else just as successfully fitting and every bit as good. And I said, "Tell you what I'll do, Bill. You find it, you call me and tell me 'Norman, this is every bit as good,' and if you can look me in the eye on the telephone, metaphorically, and say 'I think it's as good,' I'll do it."
>
> So he called me in a day or so and said "Goddamn, I can't. I haven't found it." So he let me do it, and we did it, and nothing happened. The American public did not give a damn.

George Will may bemoan the dumbing down of America, but our frame of reference and common bond as Americans has become pop culture, not the classics.† We are much more likely to bond over an episode of *The Sopranos* than we are over a public reading of the *Federalist Papers*. Sadly, even the core democratic institutions and the people who gave birth to this country are less familiar to the next generation of American adults than the latest *American Idol/Survivor* phenomenon. In

*From *All in the Family* to *Maude, Good Times,* and *The Jeffersons,* the shows Lear created in the 1970s had an incredible impact on the American psyche. His insistence that he only *mirrored* American culture is more a reflection of personal modesty than accuracy.

†I once invited Will to attend one of my focus groups to learn what's on the minds of the American voter. His response: "Heavens no. What makes you think I want to know what 'real people' are thinking?"

a poll of teenagers I conducted for the Constitution Center in Philadelphia a few years ago:

- Fewer than 2 percent of American teenagers knew that the man considered the father of the Constitution was James Madison, yet 90 percent knew that the male star of *Titanic* was Leonardo DiCaprio.
- Fewer than 2 percent of American teenagers could name then–Chief Justice William Rehnquist—yet 95 percent could tell you that the Fresh Prince of Bel Air was Will Smith.
- Fewer than 9 percent of American teenagers knew the name of the town where Abraham Lincoln lived for most of his adult life and which he represented in Congress (Springfield)—yet 75 percent knew the name of the town where Bart Simpson "lives" (Springfield).[9]

We know so much about things that don't really matter because we see them on television—and therefore it matters to us—yet we are so remarkably ignorant about what should matter—our own national heritage, culture, and traditions—because no one ever explained why we should care. *Relevance* sells—and seeing it on television makes even the most obscure and trivial seem relevant.

Popular entertainment in general, and the thirty-second spot in particular, need not be corrosive of the lexicon or the culture. Truth is, not all ads are bad. From the ads promoting Radio Free Europe that dramatically captured life behind the Iron Curtain in the 1960s to the infamous frying egg *"This is your brain; this is your brain on drugs"* in the 1980s and the fantastically successful *"Know when to say when"* campaign by Anheuser-Busch over the past decade, some promotional efforts have been enlightening, informative, and occasionally even influential.

And not all ads have to air hundreds of times for us to remember them. Two ads stand above all the rest for their impact, even though they were officially broadcast just once: the aforementioned "Daisy" spot that helped sink Barry Goldwater in 1964, and the infamous "1984" commercial for Apple that aired during that year's Super Bowl—forever connecting Hollywood production with Madison Avenue creativity. That spot, designed to introduce the much-anticipated Macintosh computer, was put together by the dream of award-winning director Ridley Scott and advertising powerhouse Chiat/Day—and *Advertising Age* named it the top spot of the decade.

Advertising certainly didn't start out to be corruptive or manipulative. The modern advertising age is said to have begun with the "creative revolution" touted by William Bernbach of the Doyle Dane Bernbach agency (DDB), who wrote, ambitiously, that: "good taste, good art, good writing can be good selling."[10]

DDB's 1959 campaign for Volkswagen, titled *"Think Small,"* was named by *Advertising Age* as the top ad campaign ever.[11] Just two words, brief and simple, but the contextual surprise signaled a new sophistication in American advertising, marking a subtle but influential shift in the way products would be sold from then on. The most memorable ads of the past fifty years as chosen by the industry itself do indeed rely on Bernbach's "good writing" equals "good selling" formulation.[12] And here's the pleasant surprise for family-oriented consumers: Almost all of the best of the best involve mainstream themes, everyday people, a positive outcome, and simple language. Among *Advertising Age's* top 100 ad campaigns of all time:

- Only eight involve sex.
- Only seven feature celebrities.
- Only four play on consumer fear and insecurities.[13]

The *idea* has primacy. Accessible language rules.

The best advertising taglines abide by the Ten Rules of Effective Communication and are therefore easily remembered. In a recent national survey, the most recognized product and corporate taglines slogans included:

- *"You're in good hands,"* overtly visual, aspirational, and therefore not surprisingly recognized as Allstate's slogan by 87 percent of the American public.
- *"Like a Good Neighbor,"* again aspirational, and with a jingle written by Barry Manilow that enhances the memorability, recognized as State Farm's tagline by 70 percent.
- *"Always Low Prices. Always."* Overtly repetitive and unquestionably credible, Wal-Mart's tagline is identified by 67 percent.
- *"Obey Your Thirst,"* a relatively new tagline for Sprite, recognized by 35 percent of the population because of its novelty, twist of language, and visualization.
- *"Think Outside the Bun,"* Taco Bell's tagline, recognized by 34 percent, for reasons similar to Sprite's.

- *"i'm lovin' it,"* the latest and greatest for McDonald's, already at 33 percent despite being less than a year old, because it hits more than half of the rules: simplicity, brevity, credibility, aspiration, and relevance.
- *"What's in your wallet?"* the rhetorical question from Capital One that earns a 27 percent recognition level.[14]

---

**MEMORABLE COMMERICALS, JINGLES, AND WORDS THAT WORK WRITTEN, PERFORMED, OR PRODUCED BY BARRY MANILOW**

| LANGUAGE | PRODUCT |
|---|---|
| "You deserve a break today" | McDonald's |
| "Like a good neighbor, State Farm is there" | State Farm Insurance |
| "I am stuck on Band-Aids . . ." | Band-Aids |
| "Grab a bucket of chicken" | KFC |
| "The most original soft drink ever" | Dr. Pepper |
| "Give your face somethin' to smile about" | Stridex Medicated Pads |
| "Feelin' free" | Pepsi |

---

These are all obviously attention-grabbing. The vast majority of advertising taglines—perhaps as high as 99 percent—never achieve widespread recognition or become part of the American lexicon because they lack creativity, simplicity, or relevance. For every jingle you can remember from childhood, or last year, you have probably forgotten a hundred of them. They simply didn't contain the words that work or the catchy tunes that last.

Curiously, it's not uncommon for companies to abandon incredibly successful slogans for new ones that flop. Someone needs to ask senior corporate management at General Electric and the marketing whizzes at the various ad agencies why they found it beneficial to abandon *"We bring good things to life"* (recognized by 39 percent of Americans) in 2002 in favor of *"Imagination at work,"* which is recognized by a scant 5 percent?[15] Yes, imagination is important, vital, in the twenty-first century, but applying that imagination to everyday life is an even higher priority. Think about it: Do you have more respect for a company that is imagining the future, or making the future better for you personally?

Why did the U.S. Army jettison *"Be all that you can be,"* surely one of the most widely known taglines in the world, for the rather odd and uninspiring *"An army of one"?* Especially when an "army," by definition, is more than one person. While it is understandable for an organization like the military to want to individualize and personalize what it does, that's just not a believable or credible selling point.

Why did Burger King replace its successful *"Have it your way"* slogan, devised in 1974, with immediately forgettable taglines such as *"Best darn burger"* (1978), *"Burger King Town"* (1986), and the *"The Whopper says"* (2001), before finally returning to *"Have it your way"* in 2004?[16] When it comes to fast food, or "QSR" (Quick Service Restaurants) as those in the industry like to call themselves, individualizing and personalizing the product really does matter.

The success of language in business is measured at the cash register and in the stock price. In politics, success is measured on Election Day. In business, words that work are words that sell. In politics, words that work are words that *win*. But what they both have in common is the timeless nature of truly memorable language.

On rare occasion, great words even live beyond the lives of the people who spoke them.

Great words have helped to end segregation *("I have a dream")* . . .

Restore hope *("The only thing we have to fear is fear itself")* . . .

Inspire a generation *("Ask not what your country can do for you; ask what you can do for your country")* . . .

Urge personal responsibility *("Be the change you wish to see in the world")* . . .

End tyranny *("Mr. Gorbachev, tear down this wall")* . . .

Dream dreams *("Some men see things as they are and ask why; I dream of things that never were and ask, why not").*

If a face can launch a thousand ships, a few good words can change history. And what all those great phrases of the ages have in common is in their inspirational and aspirational tone: each is positive, uplifting, and delivers a call to action. They were written and spoken to raise souls and touch something deep within us.

But not all that is memorable is also politically successful. While most of this chapter is devoted to the Language Hall of Fame, one should not ignore the Language Hall of Shame. In fact, some of the most memorable political language of the past fifty years has proven to be quite destructive to the individual speaking it.

Two examples immediately come to mind.

It's been almost thirty-five years since Richard Nixon uttered the words *"I am not a crook,"* thus confirming the perception in the public mind that he was, in fact, a crook. He broke a cardinal rule of political communication: never repeat a criticism as part of your rebuttal. Even today, most college students who would flunk the most basic civics test can identify the author of that line.

Even more enlightening is the story of a single word associated with a single speech that would dog and eventually destroy the president who came to office as a response to the corruption of Watergate. I am of course referring to Jimmy Carter and his infamous "Crisis of Confidence" speech in the summer of 1979 that most of you will know as "The Malaise Speech." Delivered almost thirty years ago, no political speech in my lifetime offers more language lessons for what *not* to do.

Carter's popularity and America's patience had collapsed thanks to the economic tailspin, rising inflation, and lengthening gas lines. Pessimism, cynicism, and overt anger had swept the country, and Carter's advisors, led by pollster Patrick Caddell, correctly concluded that he needed a nationally televised address to tackle the public's frustration head-on. Said Caddell:

> What was really disturbing to me was for the first time, we actually got [polling] numbers where people no longer believed that the future of America was going to be as good as it is now. And that really shook me, because it was so at odds with the American character.[17]

It was Caddell, not Carter, who used the word *"malaise"* to describe the mood of the country, and so, based on the polling and recommendations of his pollster, Carter withdrew to Camp David to engage in what may have been the first political "listening session" in which Americans from all walks of life made the sixty-five-mile trek to the president's mountaintop retreat for what was essentially a ten-day-long focus group. The problem for Carter was that he listened *too well*, internalizing all the negativity and filtering out all the hope, and so the speech he eventually gave left everyone even more depressed.

He began by reminding Americans that he had promised to be a president *"who feels your pain,"* a line that will now forever be credited to Bill Clinton. But then the speech disintegrated. He spoke of *"the crisis of the spirit in our country,"* setting a political precedent that every downturn in anything important to the public would be labeled a crisis, and how we were no longer the nation of *"the ballot, not the bullet,"* that our armies were no longer *"invincible,"* that the economy was no longer *"sound as a dollar."* Never in American history had a president attacked every essential American institution all in one speech. But it was his direct assault on American values that shook listeners to their very core.

> In a nation that was proud of hard work, strong families, close-knit communities, and our faith in God, too many of us now tend to worship self-indulgence and consumption. Human identity is no longer defined by what one does, but by what one owns.

Having reread the speech for the first time since hearing it as a child, even I got depressed. It was a litany of despair and defeat that Americans had never heard from their president until that night. And, while he took some responsibility, the message heard by the American people was that it was America's fault. (Remember, it's not what you say but what people hear that matters.) The speech was a reminder not of what Americans *could* be if they dared to dream, but rather a declaration of what they had in fact become in that particularly dark period of our history. Instead of appealing to American aspirations, the malaise speech harped on their anxieties and insecurities. It was gloomy rather than optimistic, telling us to get our heads out of the clouds, put our feet back on the ground, and see just how badly we had lost our way.

But Americans didn't appreciate the lecture. Over the subsequent weeks, the country collectively decided that there was nothing wrong with the American people—the problem was, in fact, the occupant in the White House. Carter's popularity and his presidency were essentially destroyed. He apparently didn't understand rule seven of effective communication: speak aspirationally. He never realized that it is better to smile through the downpour secure in the knowledge that a rainbow is on the way than to frown and complain about the weather. And the public realized, malaise or no malaise, that he was not the man who was capable of leading them out of the storm. Playing to weakness rather than strength, Carter revealed his own crippling weakness. And the American electorate rewarded the optimism of Ronald Reagan as a result.

Nixon, Carter, and an endless stream of political wannabes learned the hard way: Everything stupid you say or do can and will be used against you. In the end, politicians are often their own worst enemy, but they have plenty of help. Journalists are about as popular within the political community as Dr. Kevorkian at an AARP convention. When it comes to memorable language that destroys careers, the words come from the politician, but the media provides the weapon. As political humorist Bill Maher so appropriately observed:

> "I was watching Andrea Mitchell . . . talking about debates, and she said, 'A sighing Gore, a sweating Nixon, a seemingly bored Bush, those unfortunate, unscripted moments that voters sometimes remember most.' And I thought, yeah, they remember most because you show it on a loop on your media twenty-four hours a friggin' day! That's why they remember it most! It's not the voters who [choose]. It's what the media pick. The media picks out a few moments and they show it over and over again. And then people go, 'Well, Gore sighed; he's toast.'"[18]

The Dean Scream of 2004 is the perfect illustration. It was played so many times that it became the defining moment of his candidacy. In the end, it was the repetition, not the event, that did him in.

Politics generally does not lend itself to lasting language because Americans don't really like politics. We remember a few of the great political speeches because they inspired us, or because they were repeated over and over again on television, but campaign language and State of the Union addresses, when speechwriters trot out their best stuff, are almost always forgotten simply because we'd rather remember something else.

Again in the Hall of Shame category, the most explosively controversial presidential slogan of all time was surely the *"extremism in the defense of liberty"* label embraced by Arizona Senator and Republican presidential nominee Barry Goldwater in 1964 in his unsuccessful effort to defeat incumbent Lyndon Johnson. The full quote, delivered from the podium of the Republican National Convention in San Francisco as Senator Goldwater accepted the nomination, reads a little like something you might find in a Shakespearean play:

> I would remind you that extremism in the defense of liberty is no vice. And let me remind you also that moderation in the pursuit of justice is no virtue.

Here is a prime example of how it's what people hear that matters, not what the speaker intends. Goldwater's statement was completely defensible on a theoretical, intellectual level. But that didn't matter because what Goldwater actually said was not at all what people heard. The point Goldwater thought he was making, a strong unwavering declaration for freedom, was far too rarified for the *context* of a presidential campaign. By appearing to describe *himself* as an extremist—actually using that highly charged word—Goldwater's own language reinforced the image his opponents had created for him as a finger-on-the-nuclear-button extremist.

But the story doesn't end there. Goldwater's linguistic carelessness was amplified by President Johnson's incredibly aggressive media team, led by creative genius Tony Schwartz. While it doesn't qualify as the memorable "language," Johnson's team did create one of the most memorable television ads of all time. A blond-haired little girl sits in an open field pulling petals from a daisy, counting them slowly as they fall to the ground. As she counts and glances upward quizzically, the camera suddenly freezes and slowly zooms in on her face, her voice replaced by an emotionless male voice counting down. When the count reaches zero, a mushroom cloud fills the screen and President Johnson breaks in with a chilling voice-over:

> These are the stakes. To make a world in which all of God's children can live, or to go into the dark. We must either love each other, or we must die.

An announcer concludes, "Vote for President Johnson on November 3. The stakes are too high for you to stay home."[19]

The ad never mentions the word *"extremism,"* nor does it mention Goldwater. It simply encourages the audience to make the disturbing connection between what Goldwater said and the ad's suggested consequences. The "Daisy" ad aired officially only once (even though it was played on various national news programs repeatedly)—it created such an immediate uproar that the campaign quickly pulled it—but the damage had been done. The official Goldwater campaign slogan, *"In your heart you know he's right,"* was mocked by buttons that read *"In your gut you know he's nuts,"* and Johnson never gave his opponent a chance to explain himself via a national debate. The result was a landslide defeat for Goldwater.

That one single word—*"extremism"*—spoke stronger and louder than everything else said or done during the 1964 campaign. There was no explaining it away, no chance for qualifying statements or clarifications after-the-fact to be heard. Goldwater had become an icon of extremism every bit as firmly as the Energizer Bunny is today an icon of indefatigable motion. And extremism doesn't sell. Ever. Every elected official knows this in his or her bones—the mainstream is the place to be.

Yet incredibly, the Republicans made the same mistake in the aftermath of their smashing success in 1994 by calling their takeover of Capitol Hill a *"revolution"* and by talking in grandiose terms about *"remaking Western civilization"* itself. In fact, anytime a candidate or political party invokes the word *civilization,* know that they are at a minimum breaking communication rules one (simplicity) and three (credibility). This sort of overcooked rhetoric has always led to political trouble—and it eventually led to the downfall of Newt Gingrich—arguably the best and worst wordsmith of our generation. Republicans have long borne the brunt of the extremism charge, as in the 2000 presidential campaign when Al Gore rarely missed an opportunity to label George W. Bush *"extreme"* or refer repeatedly to his *"risky schemes."*

Of course, the appearance of immoderation can wound Democrats, as well. Even though this is essentially a book about words, sometimes it is how those words are delivered that determines the outcome. Howard Dean is a case in point. The famous "Dean scream" on the evening of the Iowa caucuses in 2004 fixed Dean's image in the public mind in a way that has been impossible to undo. A transcript of the event would record a rather thorough and reasonable listing of states Dean planned to campaign in, but along with it came a sound that had not come from a presidential candidate before—or at least not caught live on every network. It was that sound, a Western yee-haw delivered with a New England twang and a guttural New York intensity, along with relentless re-airing of the video, that did him in. He had certainly delivered communication rule eight (visualize)—only in exactly the opposite way that he intended. Viewers got a chance to imagine and visualize Governor Dean as President Dean—and it frightened them.

Incredibly, the perception of extremism had little to do with Dean's actual position on the issues or record in office. As many in the media eagerly and repeatedly pointed out, Dean wasn't a particularly left-wing governor, at least by Vermont standards. By most objective measures of their professional careers, John Kerry was in fact more liberal than Dean.* But Dean's persona, his rhetoric, his attitude, were much less restrained and much more volatile than Kerry's stoic personality. Perception is everything—and the scream made Dean appear extreme and therefore unpresidential. It will also be one of the video snippets from 2004 that will be replayed every election cycle.

In examining each of these famous linguistic suicide missions, it's easy to believe that most politicians are fated to flub—destined to utter some line in the most public of settings that causes even his or her strongest supporters to say *"ughhh."* But if the lessons of effective communication are followed, and the examples in this chapter tell us anything, it's that words that don't work *can* be avoided. Political figures don't have to die a cold, lonely public death thanks to their tongues. The trick is to approach every communication opportunity from the perspective of the audience—and always be armed with one really good sound bite. If labels are important in politics because they help us categorize and remember, sound bites are essential because they can actually change minds. Americans vote based on short bursts of political communication that are typically seven to ten seconds in length and squeezed in between a car chase and the latest panda birth on the local news—not from marathon viewing sessions of *Road to the White House* on C-SPAN. Out of a thousand voters we surveyed on election night 2000, not one of them had read both party platforms that year.

Almost every presidential debate is won or lost not on substance, or even style, but on a single phrase or statement that catches the public's ear and is replayed again and again. In 1976, Gerald Ford's statement during his debate against challenger Jimmy Carter that Poland wasn't under Soviet domination stalled his accelerating campaign and probably cost him the election. In 1980 it was Reagan's *"There you go again"* refrain against Carter that captured the public's imagination and diminished

---

*The same argument could be made from the right about John McCain when compared to George W. Bush. McCain has a maverick reputation, and his well-known support for campaign finance reform and anti-tobacco legislation made him a darling of the Left. But on an issue-by-issue basis, from opposition to federal spending to support for additional troops in Iraq, a case could be made that McCain was and is actually more conservative than Bush.

Carter's relentless attacks. In 1984, it was Reagan once again who delivered the perfectly timed sound-bite jab against opponent Walter Mondale, *"I will not make age an issue in this campaign. I am not going to exploit, for political purposes, my opponent's youth and inexperience,"* that helped shore up an otherwise lackluster debate performance.

But perhaps the most famous of all debate sound bites wasn't delivered by a presidential candidate. Lloyd Bentsen, the 1988 Democrat vice-presidential nominee, provided a seemingly ad-libbed attack line for the ages against opponent Dan Quayle that will forever be taught not just in history classes but in communication courses as well: *"Senator, I served with Jack Kennedy. I knew Jack Kennedy. Jack Kennedy was a friend of mine. Senator, you're no Jack Kennedy."* Quayle's non-response response sealed his political image and his fate. As one comedian joked, *"What did Marilyn Monroe say to Dan Quayle after making love? 'You're no Jack Kennedy.' "**

As we've seen in this chapter, the power of poignant language is immense, but the destructive power of an ill-thought sound bite is unending and unforgiving. Successful, effective messages—words and language that have been presented in the proper context—all have something in common. They stick in our brains and never leave, like riding a bicycle or tying our shoelaces. Not only do they communicate and educate, not only do they allow us to share ideas—they also move people to action. Words that work are catalysts. They spur us to get up off the couch, to leave the house, to *do something*. When communicators pay attention to what people hear rather than to what they are trying to say, they manage not merely to catch people's attention, but to hold it.

---

*Tom Brokaw had asked Quayle to explain what he would do if, as vice president, he had to assume the duties of president. Quayle's response was to emphasize correctly that he had "as much experience in the Congress as Jack Kennedy did when he sought the presidency." Bentsen's quick response sounded like it was ad-libbed, but according to political journalists Jack Germond and Jules Witcover in their outstanding text "Whose Broad Stripes and Bright Stars," Bentsen had actually tried a similar line in a debate rehearsal: "You're no Jack Kennedy and George Bush is no Ronald Reagan."

# VII

## Corporate Case Studies

*"My language was meant to be transparent and clear. If there was a theme, it was always to simplify, simplify, simplify, to make them feel it in their blood, get it into their skin. You have to reach people in their soul so that they internalize your message. Too many messages are just internal gobbledygook."*[1]
—JACK WELCH

Jack Welch understood the power of words that work better than anyone in corporate America. True, he had his critics who complained that he was unnecessarily blunt and occasionally too aggressive, but he was universally appreciated for his candor and applauded for his results. *"I used my words to give our people a more outward focus on the customer so that they would always try to satisfy that customer,"* he told me emphatically. *"That's why I said again and again: 'Companies don't give job security. Only satisfied customers do.'"* I asked him why, if language is so important in motivating employees to please customers, corporations and CEOs so often get the words so wrong. He pointedly refused to criticize his former colleagues, but he did have a message for every employee reading this book:

"I used to have coffee with the assistants and the staff once a month when we were restructuring the company, and they would ask me whether they'd still have a job after we were done downsizing staff functions. I'd tell them to look at their phone logs. If they were primarily filled with calls coming *from* the field with customers wanting to buy something, that's a good sign of job security.

But if the calls were coming from the corporate office *to* the field just to get data for me, their days may be numbered. The message I was sending was clear: their job was not to kiss our fannies. Their job is to make things, sell things and do things. I communicated quite plainly that you'd have job security if you were customer focused, and you wouldn't if you weren't."

Words that work in business don't merely inject themselves into memory and compel you to act; at times they actually mean the difference between millions of dollars and billions of dollars. The following stories are ripped straight from the corporate world, and I was an active participant in most of them. For those of you who define success in terms of revenues and profits and like to keep score via bank accounts, 401(k)s, and the Dow Jones Industrial Average, this chapter is for you.

The one component that virtually all successful corporate communication efforts have in common is the decision to take a proactive approach. In today's anti-corporate, deeply distrustful, and highly politicized environment, there's a simple linguistic equation: *"Silence = Guilt."* Two graphic examples I am personally acquainted with:

- For years, Wal-Mart did not respond to an increasingly serious set of public, community, legal, and governmental challenges, and now it finds itself on the defensive in neighborhoods where it wishes to locate or expand, and at open war with public interest groups that once hailed the company for low prices and job opportunities.
- Vons, the Southern California division of supermarket giant Safeway, consciously made the decision to encourage its store directors *not* to talk to employees or customers about labor issues in the run-up to the terribly destructive strike in 2004, and it paid the price in employee agitation and an angry consumer marketplace during and even after the strike.
- Halliburton, the defense contractor, ignored the public outcry over its suspect accounting and billing procedures, despite efforts by public relations experts to step in and coordinate an explanation and response. Their silence may have been driven by concern that any public statement would reflect poorly on former CEO Dick Cheney.

Regardless of the facts, even if it's unfair to do so, it's only human nature for audiences to regard silence as a tacit admission of wrongdoing. Every attack that is not met with a clear and *immediate* response will be assumed to be true.

This may seem obvious, but an examination of the public behavior of public companies suggests otherwise. Whether in the midst of an employee strike, corporate scandal, or just a bad quarterly financial report, a company's communication with the public must be proactive, consistent, and ongoing. Whether a difficult event is about to take place—or a crisis has just landed in your lap—the rules are the same. The key word is *more: more conversation* with the affected community rather than less, *more information* rather than less, and *more details* rather than fewer. If the words are right, there is no such thing as overkill.

So let's take a look at what has happened when the principles of simplicity, brevity, credibility, consistency, novelty, alliteration, aspiration, visualization, questioning, and context—the ten rules of communication—have been applied to real-world communication challenges. Let's see what happens when communication professionals have truly embraced the theme of this book: *It's not what you say, it's what they hear. . . .*

## WORDS THAT WORK CASE STUDY:
## FROM "GAMBLING" TO "GAMING"

One of the best examples of an industry tackling its greatest image weakness and turning it into its most beneficial strength just by changing a single solitary word (two letters, really) is the *"gaming"* industry—formerly known as the *"gambling"* industry. After a long tenure as Chairman of the Republican National Committee, Frank Fahrenkopf took his well-honed political and communication skills into the corporate arena as president of the American Gaming Association. Turning gambling into gaming wasn't his idea; the strategy had been implemented years earlier.* But Fahrenkopf intensified the effort in a seemingly simplistic

---

*In the 1970s, Wall Street began to recognize the linguistic reform by renaming the industry. By the late 1980s, the media began to accept the terminology without snickering. By the mid-1990s, only the Washington politicos still called it gambling.

yet revolutionary re-branding strategy for the entire industry; with one single, powerful word, a new context was set for all that goes on in Las Vegas, Atlantic City, the Mississippi Gulf Coast, and at all the commercial and Indian casinos in a majority of states across America. *"Gaming"* changed everything.

What's important to understand is that the underlying products and services changed not a whit. Same slot machines. Same deck of cards. Same dice. Same casino advantage. But the switch from *"gambling"* to *"gaming"* in describing one's behavior contributed to a fundamental change in how Americans see the gambling industry.

Here's where the communication principle of visualization plays such a major role in the perception transformation. All of the old, unsavory associations (e.g., organized crime, pawnshops, addiction, foolishly losing one's fortune) gave way to a lighter, brighter image of good clean fun. *"Gambling"* looks like what an old man with a crumpled racing form does at the track, or sounds like the pleas of a desperate degenerate trying to talk a pawnshop punter into paying a little more for his wedding ring, or feels like the services provided by some seedy back-alley bookie in some smoke-filled room. *"Gaming"* is what families do together at the Hollywood-themed MGM Grand, New York, New York, or one of the other "family-friendly resorts" in Las Vegas. *"Gambling"* is a vice. *"Gaming"* is a choice. *"Gambling"* is taking a chance, engaging in risky behavior. *"Gaming"* is as simple as playing a game with cards or dice or a little ball that goes round and round and round.

This linguistic swap coincided with a genuine image makeover right in the heart of the world's gaming Mecca. For a time in the 1990s, Las Vegas sold itself as family friendly, a sort of Disneyland suitable for kids and parents alike—a theme park full of shows and attractions, with *"gaming"* only one diversion among many. Instead of the spinning teacups there were spinning roulette wheels. Instead of the pinball machine or the arcade games lighting up, it was the slot machine that rang and jingled. True, the child-themed Circus Circus hotel had been around for ages, but now the Circus Circus model was being applied up and down the Strip (otherwise known as Las Vegas Boulevard, when the kids were around), from Treasure Island with its pirate ship battle to the Excalibur and its nightly jousting performances.

And for a while, it worked.

But like veteran Vegas performers Paul Anka and Tom Jones, as well as some of America's most successful cities, Las Vegas is constantly engaged in the act of revitalization and rejuvenation. The family-friendly Vegas didn't last, but thanks in part to the more innocuous *"gaming"* label, the city was able to return to an older, more adult incarnation without all the bad connotations. Today, the performances in Las Vegas are more risqué than ever, even at mainstream, family-oriented hotels such as the MGM Grand, where nobody under eighteen can get into *La Femme,* a topless French review. If the 1990s were the family decade in Las Vegas, the first decade of the twenty-first century is the *"What happens in Vegas stays in Vegas"* decade (perhaps the best city promotion since *"I Love New York"* in the 1970s).* It has become, once again, an outlaw town, a place where average Americans can cut loose without the neighbors watching, even if just for a long weekend, because the normal rules don't apply. But the family interlude was a crucial stage in the evolution of the city—and the industry as a whole. That evolution, and the reinvention that came along with it, would not have been imaginable without the shift from *"gambling"* to *"gaming"*: *a word that worked.*

## WORDS THAT WORK CASE STUDY:
## FROM *"LIQUOR"* TO *"SPIRITS"*

The revival of the term *"spirits"* is analogous to the coining of *"gaming."* While I did not participate in this effort, it deserves a mention because of its essential role in changing the entire image of an industry of beverages that had been struggling to stay mainstream, relevant, and fashionable. *"Spirits"* refers to alcoholic beverages that were more commonly called *"hard liquor"* or just *"liquor."* *"Spirits"* is an older term, chiefly British, that's been popularized in the United States in recent years. It comes from the Latin word *spirare,* "to breathe."

*"Spirits"* and *"liquor"* currently carry quite different associations. *"Liquor"* has many negative implications; it calls to mind "liquored up,"

---

*In 1975, New York City was on the verge of financial insolvency. Desperately hoping to generate tourism income, the New York Commerce Commission hired ad agency Wells, Rich, Greene to develop a campaign that would promote New York City and state as a desirable tourist destination. The slogan they came up with: *I Love New York.* When the ads came out in 1977, they featured noted New York celebrities including Frank Sinatra, Liza Minnelli, and Yul Brynner. Those ads continued to air long after the city had climbed out of the economic Dumpster, earning their place in American culture. Even today, three decades later, you can still hear an occasional tourist singing that simple jingle.

alcoholism, and winos carrying paper bags with bottles of fortified wine inside. *"Spirits,"* on the other hand, calls to mind the clink of glasses raised in a toast, and that sound itself evokes pleasant, warm images and feelings—an unspoken but all-knowing affirmation and connection between people. When you touch glasses with another person across the table, you are in good company, and the clink itself signifies a certain elegance and sophistication, as well as the pleasant promise of camaraderie. Even more than the alcohol itself, the clink puts people in the right frame of mind because it emotionally transports them where they want to go. When people raise a glass, they simultaneously raise their spirit (or spirits in this case).

Spirits have one more advantage of late: novelty. In the past, when people thought of liquor, a limited number of predictable drinks came to mind: scotch, bourbon, whiskey, vodka, gin, and a few others—but the choices were limited. Sure, certain brands attempted to liven up the options, most notably Captain Morgan and several of the Seagram's brands. But as part of the switch from *"liquor"* to *"spirits,"* companies began offering new colors, new flavors, new mixers, and exotic new tastes.

And so what was once a tired, predictable, and downscale beverage had become new and exciting—and that has sent shivers of concern throughout the beer industry. Watch for a new lexicon, new visuals, and a more aspirational marketing approach from your favorite beer company as a result.

## WORDS THAT WORK CASE STUDY:
## *"BANKS" VERSUS "CREDIT UNIONS"*

Here is an example where the language effort was focused on enhancing an image rather than choosing between words. The state and local credit unions have two small trade associations to represent them in Washington, and both of them hired my firm in the mid-1990s to take on the hard-charging, big-spending, politically pushy banking lobby and help credit unions promote a more favorable regulatory climate. This was a challenge I was destined to lose. The banks had all the money. The banks had all the political contacts. The banks had every advantage but one: language.

While I wouldn't quite go so far as to say that the word *"bank"* has a stigma, it does have many strongly negative connotations—and many of them are visual and location-centered. Just say the name and people visualize high ceilings, marble lobbies, expansive wooden desks, and a fancy décor that customers have to pay for through all the hidden fees. It's one reason why you rarely see the inside of a bank in their advertising, and when you do, it's always a close-up of a pleasant teller and not the bank president's opulent office. Sure, visualize is communication rule eight, but that assumes the picture is a pleasant one. For *"banks,"* it's not.

*"Credit unions,"* on the other hand, are to *"banks"* what the TV show *Cheers* was to the local neighborhood bar—an idealistic setting and place to do business that you hoped existed somewhere other than inside your television set. I didn't create this analogy: Thirty credit union members themselves in Cleveland and St. Louis created it for me in focus groups we conducted a few years ago. *"Credit union"* creates the perception of being small, intimate, kind, and caring—where you actually know the teller and the teller knows you. Whereas *"bank"* conjures up visions of concrete buildings and robber barons with vast unattainable wealth, *"credit union"* evokes the friendly people who work inside—for you. Banks are Mr. Potter from *It's a Wonderful Life*. Credit unions are the Building and Loan Community.

Also important in the credit union advantage is the idea of *membership*. Being a *"member"* rather than a *"customer"* sounds much more inclusive, participatory, and friendly. Returning to the *Cheers* analogy, *"credit unions"* are places where "everybody knows your name, and they're always glad you came." In fact, if I were the head of one of the national credit union associations, I'd hire Sam Malone, Norm Peterson, or Woody Boyd as my national spokesman. No matter what he said, it's the image he'd conjure up that matters.

Sure enough, the credit unions were able to pass legislation favorable to their expansion over the cries and very public pressure from the banking establishment. The banks eventually spent hundreds of thousands of dollars in a futile effort to fight back, but with every contribution and expenditure, they only reminded members of Congress why their constituents loved their little credit unions and hated their dreaded banks.

Ahhh, the power of visualization.

## WORDS THAT WORK CASE STUDY:
## FROM *"LE RÊVE"* TO *"WYNN RESORTS"*

While the best language has a musical sound to it much like an opera or orchestra, for words to have a real impact, the public, at an absolute minimum, has to know what they mean—and how to say them and repeat them. If they don't, or can't, it is hardly the recipe for success. Such was the situation for *"Le Rêve,"* the original name for Steve Wynn's newest hotel in Las Vegas. It means "the dream" in French, and in theory it would have been a perfect name for the most beautiful, innovative hotel in Las Vegas.

As I discovered in my research, however, not only did people have no idea of what *"Le Rêve"* meant, they also had no clue how to pronounce it. Put twenty people in a room and only about half would say it correctly. This was clearly a problem.

But my market research revealed that Steve Wynn already had access to a far stronger and more widely identified word—a word that had simplicity, brevity, credibility, and relevance to Vegas patrons from across the globe: his own last name. In fact, *"Steve Wynn"* was so widely recognized and popular within the gaming and Vegas community that people were willing to pay a fair bit more for a product, a service, or a hotel stay if it had a direct association with his name. So *"Le Rêve"* became *"Wynn Resorts,"* creating a brand that has proven to be a smashing success. As Wynn himself has said, "Branding this property was the smartest thing we've done. Whenever I walk through the casino, people come up and ask to take a picture with me or sign something. That's never happened to me before. Not after Bellagio. Not after the Mirage. Not even during the days when Sinatra was promoting my Golden Nugget. It's the name. It's the name."

*"Wynn"* is one of the few names from the business world that evokes an immediate and favorable image. We recognize it right away (30 percent of us do), and it stands for certified, guaranteed quality. The same could be said of names such as *"Welch," "Jobs," "Gates," "Iacocca,"* and *"Murdoch."* It's very rare for a CEO to transcend the product he or she provides, but when they do, their own name is often the word that works best. It doesn't hurt that "Wynn" sounds like "win"—which is an important advantage in a gaming town.

If Steve Wynn had not been a creator of spectacular hotels, he would most certainly have been an award-winning advertising executive. His vocabulary rivals that of an Ivy League English professor, and he thinks visually rather than verbally. He tells a great story about the ad copy he had crafted for his original casino in Atlantic City, the Golden Nugget. The would-be star: Diana Ross. But it never got made because of what Strother Martin's character in *Cool Hand Luke* would have called a failure to communicate. Says Wynn:

> "I write a spot for Diana myself, where she walks into the chairman's apartment in Atlantic City with a lot of bags like Elizabeth Taylor. I introduce myself. 'Hi, Ms. Ross. I'm Steve Wynn. I run this place.' And she says, 'Make sure someone takes care of my bags,' like I'm the bellman or something. But she gets this face like 'Oh I couldn't do that Steve, it'll make me look stupid—like I don't know who you are.' So I say, 'No, Diana, [you assuming that I'm the bellman is] a joke,' but she thought [the ad] would make her look stupid like she was disrespecting me. I look at her and realized I'm beating a dead horse here, so I said 'forget about it, we'll do something else.' "

## WORDS THAT WORK CASE STUDY: FROM *"HONEST DATA"* TO *"ACCURATE DATA"*—AND THEN SOME . . .

In the wake of the Enron scandal, the accounting profession in the United States faced the biggest public relations crisis in decades. With the indictment and dissolution of Arthur Andersen, the Big Five swiftly became the Big Four—and the remaining public accounting firms faced the enormous challenge of defending their integrity, their business practices, and their very right to continue doing business. In the spring of 2002, when pressure on the industry had reached its highest intensity, I undertook a language project for PricewaterhouseCoopers—a research-based effort to discover and define the lexicon of corporate accountability and the role of the accounting profession in achieving it.

The tough times called for a true crisis communications lexicon. Listening to accounting professionals across the country and, more importantly, their accounting clients—including the CFOs of many of the most powerful companies in the world—it was painfully clear that PwC's old, pre-Enron language had to go. There had to be a complete reshaping of their messaging to match the changing priorities and responsibilities of the profession. After three months of extensive research, we offered PwC a complete revision of the way they defined themselves, their profession, and the services they provide:

| THE LANGUAGE OF CFOS AND CORPORATE ACCOUNTABILITY | |
|---|---|
| **DON'T SAY . . .** | **DO SAY . . .** |
| Honest/credible/truthful data | Accurate data |
| Interpretation | Analysis |
| Responsibility/professionalism | Accountability |
| Capital markets | Investors/The public interest |
| Innovative approaches | Principles and rules |
| Attested to | Certified |
| Experienced | Independent |
| Breadth of services | Back to basics |
| Codes of conduct | Internal controls and accountability procedures |
| Comprehensive | Easy to understand |

Some of these words transcend the accounting profession and have become essential descriptive terminology in the post-Enron corporate scandal environment:

*"Accurate"* data is more important than honest, credible, or truthful data because it is a statement of fact rather than someone's explanation. For similar reasons, *"facts"* and *"fact-based"* are more powerful descriptors in the legal world than *"evidence."* It may seem like a distinction without a difference but it really does matter. Facts are indisputable. Evidence is open to interpretation.

*"Responsibility"* and *"professionalism"* are obviously important, but *"accountability"* trumps them because it implies enforcement and perhaps even punishment for failure. We want all our institutions and all our leaders to suffer if, in some way, they have made us suffer or let us down. We truly live in unforgiving times.

*"Attested to"* is far less effective than *"certified"* because the former is perceived to be about human judgment and the latter suggests a specific process or procedure followed, along with a guarantee.

The phrase *"back to basics"* appeals because it represents a change in focus and a shift in priorities to those things that matter most. A *"back to basics"* approach is particularly popular in times of economic instability or personal anxiety.

## WORDS THAT WORK CASE STUDY: FROM *"CELL PHONES"* TO *"INTEGRATED ENTERTAINMENT"*

In rare cases, applying words that work is about focusing on people's fears rather than appealing to their hopes and dreams. Today's digital, portable, cellular, interactive world is the perfect illustration. Not long ago we were hired by a cell phone company that was in the process of buying up one of its rivals. They wanted to use the purchase to reshape their public image not just as a simple provider of cell service but as an *"innovative twenty-first-century deliverer"* of *"comprehensive integrated entertainment"* that people could *"always count on."* And yes, each of those words matters individually as well as collectively.

*"Innovative twenty-first-century"* language is both visual and aspirational, encouraging consumers to imagine the digital benefits of the future rather than accepting the analog limitations of the present.

*"Deliverer"* is seen by consumers as more active and aggressive than *"provider,"* enhancing the company's credibility and differentiating them from their less consumer-friendly competitors.

The words *"comprehensive"* and *"integrated"* come right from the mouths of consumers themselves. The second biggest complaint of personal portable device users is that the various components, including even the service itself, do not function together easily. The idea that each and every component would work seamlessly together addressed one of the two fear factors of cellular use.

*"Entertainment"* is the novelty component. No longer will consumers see their cell phones as merely tools to make calls. From text messaging to listening to music to taking photos to watching live television broadcasts and even movies, their cell phones will soon be able to do it all—and do it well.

*"Always count on"* is the foundation upon which everything else is built because it addresses the single biggest complaint as well as the primary aspiration of all cell phone users worldwide—that they actually work. Consumers aren't demanding all the new bells and whistles, even

if they do appreciate them. They just want their phones to work—always—or in their words, "I don't want to think about it."

And that's exactly the language customers want and expect to hear from their service provider. Residential customers want to know that their handheld device gives them a *"lifeline"* to the outside world. Small business owners want to know that their provider will deliver *"hassle-free technology"* so they have the freedom to focus on the other aspects of their business. And the people who are responsible for all the technology at America's largest businesses want to know that if something bad happens, *"I'm protected"* so that it won't cost their company too much time or money, and it won't cost them their job.

So instead of telling the cell phone customer all the myriad of positive things the device can do, the wiser and more effective approach is to remind the customer of all the bad things it won't. Additional words that best address these inherent fears:

- *"The Power of ONE."* Consumers want the entire process simplified. ONE-stop shopping, ONE bill to pay, ONE single point of contact if and when something goes wrong, ONE person to hold accountable.
- *"We deliver."* That phrase, and *"Anything, anywhere, anytime, on any device . . ."* both project a robust concept of reliability that goes well beyond mere connectivity.

These case studies offer a wider message for those in the business community. To be blunt, while you are focused on the language of sales and service, you simply do not recognize or care to accept that your own corporate language is contributing to the anxiety Americans now have about the economy in general and corporate America in particular. Since the fall of the Iron Curtain and the spread of elections worldwide, we have collectively concluded that democracy is the only true, legitimate, fair, and representative form of government (though as this book goes to print, the situation in Iraq, as well as the Palestinian success of Hamas, have the potential to undermine that conclusion), but we have yet to award that endorsement on our economic institutions or their structure.

On the contrary, a sizeable minority of Americans reject "capitalism" for its perceived winners-and-losers outcome and for its constant competitive nature. In a poll I conducted in the late 1990s, fully one-quarter of the electorate had a negative opinion of capitalism—and the primary reason was the perceived behavior of corporate America. Since then, thanks to Enron, WorldCom, Tyco, the arrogance of CEOs like Martha Stewart and Richard Grasso, as well as the burst of the Internet bubble, insider trading scandals, and corporate credibility crusader Elliot Spitzer (formerly New York's hyperactive attorney general and now its hyperactive governor) public faith and confidence in capitalism has deteriorated even more. That may be a long sentence for a short book, but that's still not the exhaustive list of complaints by Americans up and down the economic ladder. If you ask the average shareholder what they don't like about corporate America and big business, be prepared to wait at least five minutes for them to finish, and get ready to wipe the saliva off your eyeglasses: Americans are spitting mad right now.* And when seemingly distant and unaware CEOs—the public face of the capitalistic culture—talk over or around the heads of most Americans, you have all the makings of a crisis in corporate credibility.

Linguistically, the first step for corporate America is to stop selling *"capitalism."* True, if you happen to be targeting the big winners on Wall Street, that word does have an attractive and positive allure, hence *Forbes*'s *"Capitalist tool"* successful tagline to promote the business magazine. But for tens of millions of Americans who either identify with or personify the economic losers in society, the *"free market system"* has a much less harsh connotation and is much more accessible.

The second step is to drop the word *"private"* from the corporate lexicon. To most Americans, hearing about *"private"* markets and *"private"* offerings conjures up images of private clubs they cannot join, private schools they cannot afford, private jokes they do not get, and private communities that keep them out. Individual consumer privacy is a good thing. Private markets are not.

As with the word *"capitalism,"* there is a well-defined segment of society that not only appreciates the notion of *"private"* but will pay more for it. But when it comes to communicating corporate citizenship or enhancing corporate reputation, again the *"free market system"* wins out. For example,

---

*I call this the *"spitting principle"* of market research. When people get so angry that they actually spit out their words, it tells you about the intensity of their opinions. It happened in the 1992–94 period when the public was angry with Washington, and it began again in 2006 when the topic turned to corporate America.

in a poll I took for the pharmaceutical profession (notice I didn't call it an "industry") by a two to one ratio, Americans would rather receive their health care from a free market system than a private system. Just a simple shift in a single phrase can and does account for a huge shift in public perception.

And this brings me to two final corporate communication case studies that struck right at the heart of the American economic system. The first had an impact on the millions of unionized service workers that continues to reverberate today. And the second had an impact on tens of millions of shareholders—including most of the readers of this book.


## WORDS THAT WORK CASE STUDY: FROM
## *"EMPLOYEE STRIKE"* TO *"EMPLOYEE SATISFACTION"*

Much of my work has been on the corporate side of labor disputes, and it often has involved the service industry. From a supermarket chain that offered its workers a salary plus health care and other benefits that far exceeded nonunion Wal-Mart but still had to endure a lock-out (a phrase that even employees of the company didn't understand), to the hotel and hospitality industry, which has to suffer through local strikes that are often vicious and occasionally violent, the best strategy to deal with a strike is to utilize the rules of effective communication to prevent it.

Companies need to recognize that the words they use to communicate with their employees in strike situations can be almost as important as the contract provisions themselves. In looming strike situations, silence is death. If you want to know which side is most likely to win public approval, the answer is almost always the side that is communicating more often to the workforce and more frequently through the media. When it comes to labor issues, quantity is almost as important as quality.

The first language lesson is to set the context and accept the fact that most employees start with an anti-company, pro-union bias. Therefore, the corporate side needs to be the first to provide employees with answers to their questions—*preferably in writing*. Employees tend to accept the arguments of the side that made them first, particularly when they are made with a personal and passionate tone, and a written presentation has more credibility than verbal.

In the strike against the Southern Californian subsidiaries of the supermarket giants Kroger, Safeway, and Albertson's, the unions dominated the messaging because management made the incredibly stupid assumption that silence was a good communication strategy. When we showed up midway through the strike to help with communication, we were stunned to learn that the employees had absolutely no idea of management's position. In particular, employees had been convinced by the union that they were losing their free health care when in fact they were only being asked to pay a tiny portion of their premiums. Worse yet, since management at the three supermarket chains had agreed to a communication policy of no communication, they'd turned not just the employees against them but the surrounding community as well. Because of that silence, employees had every right to assume that management "wanted" the strike to "punish" the union, and shoppers had every right to shop elsewhere to punish the striking companies for punishing their employees. Again, for corporations in the midst of controversy, silence = guilt.

True, some companies in some states may find themselves somewhat hamstrung by federal and state labor negotiation laws, but that makes context-setting that much more important. Unions have the initial advantage of "representing" the workforce, and unfettered access to say and do almost anything, but companies can level the playing field by reminding employees that they not only have the power of the paycheck, but they also pay all the benefits that the union takes credit for.

The second language lesson of strike prevention and strike management is to acknowledge that communication goes on twenty-four hours a day, seven days a week, and that establishing credibility is a never-ending process. *Never, never, never* let any union communication go without an immediate rebuttal. A charge made is a charge believed unless and until refuted.

In a looming strike situation with a Denver supermarket chain, the local union boss (who earned that title with his dictatorial behavior) was constantly threatening management not just privately but in the press as well. Behind the scenes, however, management was communicating with the rank and file at a store-by-store and even individual level, responding to every attack with an immediate response. In some cases, the response was so quick and spread so effectively that employees actually found management more credible and responsive to their questions and concerns than their own official union representatives.

A third language lesson is to exceed expectations. Message timing is important. Few things are worse for employee morale than being left in the dark with regard to job-related turmoil. Management should aim for a twenty-four-hour turnaround on personal, one-on-one questions from employees and a forty-eight-hour turnaround to produce written responses to written union communications. Employees expect management to react slowly and deliberately to any union attack or assertion. Exceeding expectations by improving communication turnaround time immediately establishes credibility.

Our work in strike situations allowed us to develop a specific lexicon, a *"words that work"* dictionary. Companies facing labor action need to keep employees informed by putting out a *weekly "Tough Questions: Real Answers"* document. Why that title above all others? Since employees assume management will duck the substance, a company that is responsive to the *"tough questions"* has an advantage. And the *"real answers"* component is exactly what they want to hear and is more credible than management claiming simple *"honesty."*

But written communication is still no substitute for direct dialogue. Some companies call them *"roundtables."* We recommend *"conversations"* because the term suggests a more informal and interactive environment where the *"facts"* of the dispute can be openly discussed. If you examine some of the major strikes and labor disputes of the past decade, you rarely see management laying out the *"facts"* behind the conflict. Instead, you hear comments like *"what we're offering is more than fair,"* which is not only unpersuasive—it risks coming across as downright arrogant, even obnoxious. No employee who's on the verge of striking wants to hear that kind of editorializing. It will only harden opposition.

Employing the words-that-work principles, corporations need to communicate with employees in concrete, objective, back-to-basics terms. When talking about health-care benefits, for example, *humanize* and *personalize* what the company proposes to spend on each employee by using real statistics from everyday life (for example, comparing the five dollars a week for health care premiums to the cost of two dozen eggs, two gallons of gas, or a single latte at Starbucks) rather than making abstract economic arguments that are harder for individuals or employees to relate to. Similarly, in this era of rising health-care premiums, it is essential for companies to emphasize what they pay for their employees—not just what the employees are required to pay for themselves.

Another mistake companies make is to bash the union leadership when a softer touch would be more effective. We learned early on that beating up on the *"union bosses,"* even if justified, will quickly turn employees against management. In fact, just that phrase alone says to employees that you fear, disrespect, or are intimidated by the union. That language won't work in a political campaign, and it will certainly fail in a labor context.

If it does become necessary to go on the attack, it's crucial for management to draw a bright-line distinction between union *"leadership"* and union *"members."* Unless this distinction is extremely clear, corporate communications will prove counterproductive, offending the people they are trying to influence.

There are three essential statements in labor disputes that allow management to set the tone—and they offer the simplicity and brevity of good communication. The first is aspirational:

*"We're pro-employee and we're pro-union."*

The second applies the rule of questioning to the discourse, playing on employee doubts and anxieties about what exactly their union is up to and where it's headed:

*"Are you getting value for the dues you're paying? What do your dues actually pay for? Is your union paying attention to YOUR needs and YOUR priorities?"*

And the third applies the rule of personal relevance while undermining labor's credibility:

*"No one wins in a strike . . . but union leaders continue to get paid. Is that really fair to you?"*

This is even more persuasive if the union leaders make astronomical salaries in comparison to union members—which most of them do. The final language lesson, in a word, is *more*. To win over your employees, emphasize the need for *more* information, *more* facts, and a *more* honest approach.

Applying the results of extensive union opinion research to the ten rules of effective communication, what follows is the appropriate lexicon and the dos and don'ts of management communication to their workforce. Using these words early and often can turn a looming employee strike into employee satisfaction.

---

## PERFECT LABOR DISPUTE LANGUAGE FOR COMPANIES

"There are great union reps out there who are committed to our employees and have long, successful relationships with them. We don't always agree on policy, but we will always listen to each other. But union leaders who use confrontational tactics are usually advancing their own standing at the cost of employees suffering. There is a better way.

"Employees deserve representation that will not jeopardize their job stability or ignore the long-term impact of these important decisions. We respect the union leaders' desire for tough negotiations. But they should also communicate openly and honestly with us and with their employees. After all, your union leaders are paid to do just that.

"We are ready to sit at the table with our local union partners today to find a solution that is fair to our employees and fair to the company as well. We come to this discussion in good faith. We ask only that the union does the same."

---

The following linguistic contract negotiation checklist outlines the dos and don'ts of specific words and phrases. This analysis is based on interviews with close to 5,000 union members over the past three years from various economic sectors, but the words will also apply to most employees in most fields. You'll notice throughout that the language that worked well twenty or thirty years ago has a better alternative today:

## THE LANGUAGE OF CONTRACT NEGOTIATIONS

| DON'T TALK ABOUT . . . | DO TALK ABOUT . . . |
| --- | --- |
| Peace of mind | Security |
| Being rewarded | Being valued |
| Compassion | Fairness |

| | |
|---|---|
| Commitment | Respect, responsibility |
| Listening to employees | Keeping promises, respecting employees |
| Finding common ground | Negotiating in good faith |
| Comprehensive contract | Long-term contract |
| Balance | Fairness, common sense |

| DON'T SAY . . . | DO SAY . . . |
|---|---|
| The union is biased. | Full disclosure/ You have a right to hear all sides. |
| Objective | Accurate |
| Union leaders should not hold local employees hostage over national issues. | Local problems require local solutions. |
| When a union strikes against a company, it isn't just hurting the company. | No one wins in a strike. |
| If the union chooses to strike, have a legitimate right to stay open. | We will do whatever we can to avoid a strike. |
| It is the union's fault, not ours, if the workers have to walk a picket line. | If there is a strike, we will do whatever we can to fulfill our responsibilities to our customers. |

Some of this language is absolutely essential, and a few of the words above do conflict with the recommendations in other chapters for important reasons:

*Peace of mind* is one of the most powerful phrases in the public mind today, but in today's environment of economic and job anxiety, we put even greater emphasis on *security*. With employment duration decreasing every year and the media focus on American jobs being outsourced to foreign countries, *peace of mind* is simply not tangible and explicit enough for the workforce. We want the *security* of knowing that our job, our paycheck, and our benefits will be there when we need it.

Being *rewarded* is about financial compensation, and that is obviously important. But being *valued* transcends dollars and cents. *Value* is about an employer saying thank you, a colleague expressing appreciation for a job well done, a sense of purpose and belonging. Being *valued* is a throwback to the days when employees (don't call them workers any more—a worker is a lower valued job) had a sense of loyalty to their employers because their employers had a sense of responsibility to them.

*"Full disclosure"* and *"you have a right to hear all sides,"* and *"we want you to read the fine print"* are all about giving people all the information they need to make the right decision about their job, their employer, their union, and their contract. Ask employees what they hate most about the period just before a strike vote and they'll tell you the lack of accurate, unbiased information. The smartest strategic communication decision we've seen in the recent history of contract negotiations was when several companies linked their own Web sites right to the union's Web site. Imagine the surprise, and positive impact, when employers said that their people had the right to see both sides of the contract debate, side-by-side. Companies have learned that if they are willing to provide more information in a more timely fashion than the union—and include what the union is saying in an unbiased manner—employees will come to the company first. And when they see the company is providing more information than the union, it makes them more likely to support the company position.

## WORDS THAT WORK CASE STUDY: FROM "CORPORATE ACCOUNTABILITY" TO "CORPORATE RESPONSIBILITY"

How does a corporation kill "reform?" While Americans are natural reformers who deeply believe and respond to appeals for positive change or, in the words of Robert Redford's character in *The Candidate,* "a better way," the best counter is by defining change as worse than doing nothing. If the forces of change have descended on your doorstep and you find yourself having to defend the status quo, the phrase that pays is *"do no harm."*

I learned this principle while working for a *Fortune* 100 health care company that was interested in stalling or perhaps even blocking SEC efforts to promote reforms to corporate governance rules in the name of the ever-popular *"shareholder democracy"* principle. Since I assumed that the concept of *"shareholder democracy,"* a term (and policy) that has no real definition and yet satisfies at least half of the ten rules for effective communication, would be so popular that no language, no matter how polished or reasoned, would achieve this task, I passed the job off to a colleague, Buckley Carlson. His approach was remarkably creative and a perfect case study of what to do when the language challenge seems insurmountable: Determine all the individual values that define *"corporate democracy"* and then linguistically undermine each one:

- True, under the SEC definition of *"shareholder democracy,"* individual investors would technically have more opportunities to be heard. But shareholders also believed it would slow a company's reflexes and make it more difficult to react swiftly to the competition or a change in the marketplace. Words that work in response: *"loss of flexibility," "delayed reaction,"* and *"unnecessarily tying the hands of management."*
- True, *"shareholder democracy"* would make it easier to challenge the decisions of the Board of Directors, particularly in regard to compensation for corporate officers, and that would make individuals and the entire board more accountable. But shareholders feared it would aid outsiders or dissidents in wreaking havoc on corporate governance by challenging *every* decision the board made. Words that work in response: *"increased instability"* and *"creating corporate chaos."*
- True, *"shareholder democracy"* would allow a smaller minority of shareholders to participate more actively in company affairs. But shareholders knew it would increase the potential for professional raiders to move in and break up the company, just as Michael Douglas did to Blue Star in Oliver Stone's blockbuster movie *Wall Street*—turning a quick profit for themselves at the expense of employees, customers, and long-term shareholders. Words that work in response: the overarching and most influential language in the ongoing debate, the *"principle of corporate responsibility."*

*"Shareholder democracy"* looked good on paper and in a vacuum, but when the consequences were examined, alternative outcomes probed, and a lexicon created to respond, the bloom came off the rose. And so the reply to *"shareholder democracy"* became *"corporate responsibility,"* and the language and examples referenced above were utilized successfully by a coalition of *Fortune* 500 companies in reversing the SEC efforts.

The successful result of this case study is living proof that the principle of *do no harm* still resonates on both Wall Street and Capitol Hill. Similarly, the language of "unintended consequences" is also an effective argument for defending the status quo—particularly among more sophisticated audiences. Of course, if you should ever find yourself in this situation, don't make the mistake of actually saying that you're defending the status quo. To make that explicit would be to tell listeners that you're *"inflexible"* instead of *"dynamic,"* *"backward looking"* instead of *"innovative,"* and *"defensive"* instead of *"bold."*

Those are just a small sample of the corporate case studies where words that work were applied to reshape products, companies, and even public policy. They all have one thing in common: usage of the essential communication rules and a clear focus on the target audience—the customer. It is incredible just how a simple change of words, phrases, positioning, or context can alleviate public pressure, restore consumer confidence, and refresh a product or brand. And yet as easy as it sounds, application of smart language is still more the exception rather than the rule in corporate America.

# VIII

## Political Case Studies

*"Our major obligation is not to mistake slogans for solutions."*
— EDWARD R. MURROW[1]

*"When the Contract with America takes down a few of our candidates, which it will inevitably be blamed for, everybody is going to lay the blame at the feet of the person who created it: Frank Luntz."*
— TONY FABRIZIO*
REPUBLICAN POLLSTER, OCTOBER 28, 1994[2]

The *death tax."*
*"Energy exploration."*
*"Opportunity scholarships."*
*"Save, strengthen, and simplify Medicare."*
*"Personalizing,"* not *"privatizing,"* Social Security.

The truth is, I didn't create some of those phrases, though I certainly took an active role popularizing them not just in Washington but nationwide. But there is one language project I was involved with that stands out above the rest. To this day, I'm best known as the pollster for the Contract with America, and the question I'm asked most often is "Why did you call it a contract?" The real answer is that every other option was out.

A *"plan"* wouldn't have sounded sufficiently binding, plus we all know what happens to the best-laid plans.

---

*I never took personal credit for creating the contract. It was clearly a team effort led by Newt Gingrich. But Fabrizio and several other establishment GOP pollsters' vocal opposition to the strategy the contract embodied, his assumption that the GOP would fail as a result, and his very public attempt to wrap the contract around my neck prior to the election ended up working to my benefit after the landslide victory earned Republicans their first congressional majority in forty years.

*"Promises"* are made to be broken, especially when politicians make them.

*"Pledges"* go unfulfilled.

*"Platforms"* are too political.

*"Oaths"* have legal connotations.

*"Covenants"* have religious overtones (and Bill Clinton had used the *"New Covenant"* motif in his 1992 presidential nomination speech).

So why a contract? The catalyst was the House Republican annual retreat held in Salisbury, Maryland, in early 1994. I was one of only two non-Member "outsiders" invited to present to the 110 members of Congress in attendance, and my charge was to really shake them up to the reality that while their criticisms of President Clinton's first year in office had brought down his popularity, they had also made Republicans even more unpopular. My staff had been tasked with producing a video and charts to demonstrate statistically that the GOP was in real trouble, but an ice storm that afternoon had closed off all the roads leading to the town—so it was just me and the members. Without visuals to soften my presentation, I took after them the way a cat corners a mouse. For nearly an hour, I took them apart for failing to understand, connect with, empathize with, and listen to the American people. The mood was ugly, and so were my comments. When I finished, absolute silence. Later, I was advised by several members to apologize to a Texas Congressman named Tom DeLay whom I had publicly and vehemently disagreed with over strategy (DeLay would later become an advocate for my language efforts), and was given a *"Way to go, kid"* punch in the shoulder by a freshman California Representative named Randy "Duke" Cunningham.

But what I remember most was the brisk ten-minute early-morning walk with Newt Gingrich the next day to complain that the Republicans had no agenda to appeal to the majority of Americans, that we had become so cynical toward politics and politicians that all the traditional words and labels would fail the credibility test. I asserted that any overarching platform had to look, sound, and actually *be* different from anything that had come before. After listening and essentially agreeing, he turned to me and asked, *"Okay, so what if this year we did it differently? What if we offered Americans a platform that clearly highlighted not just our principles but a plan to get it done?"* The following week, Kerry Knott, a communication-savvy senior Republican leadership aide, coined the phrase *"Contract"* to describe Newt's vision, and the rest became history.

That was the genesis of the Contract with America—a simple document signed by virtually every House Republican nominee that led to the election of a Republican majority for the first time in four decades. The Contract became the message during the crucial weeks leading up to Election Day, and it was articulated in such a way that anyone who became aware of it ended up supporting it—and it created a rising tide that lifted all Republican boats. Gingrich understood what campaign professionals at the time could not fathom—give the American electorate the dream of a positive agenda on issues that they care about and the sense of accountability that it will actually get done, and they'll vote for it. He knew instinctively that Americans vote for dreamers because they themselves like to dream.

Understanding how the language for the Contract was created, and why, will illustrate how words that work are crafted in the political realm.

First, the title. In early concept testing, the actual name of the document was *"The Republican Contract with America."* I personally asked Gingrich to drop the word *Republican* from the title, against the wishes of my GOP polling colleagues, because I could tell from public opinion research that millions of independents and conservative Democrats could be swayed to the GOP if—and only if—the pitch was ideological and philosophical rather than political and partisan. I knew that being perceived as a Republican document would detract from the contract's credibility. Indeed, since the 1980s, *"conservatism"* has been more popular than the Republican Party, and more Americans identify themselves as *"conservatives"* than as *"Republicans."** If it was a *"Republican Contract,"* I argued, millions of potential supporters wouldn't even read the first line. But if it was a *"Contract with the American People,"* they would keep an open mind.

The establishment pollsters within the GOP strongly disagreed—and even went so far as to undermine the image and its execution in the media. John McLaughlin—the pollster, not the *McLaughlin Group* host—who tends to work for conservative Republicans, complained that by not using *"Republican"* in the Contract title, it "allowed the Democrats

---

*On the other hand, there are far more *"Democrats"* than there are self-proclaimed *"liberals."* So Republicans are almost always better off downplaying their partisan affiliation and playing up their ideology, while Democrats are better off citing their party identity than they are their liberalism. The relative paucity of self-described *"liberals"* is one reason George Lakoff and others have argued so strongly for the re-branding of *"liberals"* as *"progressives."* *"Progressive"* not only lacks the negative baggage of *"liberal,"* but it also suggests *"progress"* and is therefore future-oriented.

to define this instead of us."[3] McLaughlin argued for an all-out attack on the Democrats' strategy that had been tried—and had failed—election after election. "We have been on the defensive because of the Contract," he said.[4] What he didn't understand, or at least didn't appreciate, was that while the Democrats were attacking the Contract loudly and relentlessly, their criticisms not only didn't stick but were actually backfiring. The public was fed up with all the negativity and partisanship of politics—and was searching for an alternative approach. Even though I made sure that the word *"Republican"* was sprinkled throughout the actual document and the advertising created to promote it, it was removed from the title.

And as for the *"Contract,"* we found early in the process that for a political document to have genuine credibility and truly represent a break from the past, it had to be legally binding—or at least have that feel. A *"contract"* makes it sound as if signatories, the elected officials themselves, would have to comply with it . . . or else. And as voters reminded me in the focus groups I conducted, by definition, every *"contract"* has an enforcement clause. And so I, hardly a lawyer, wrote one that appeared at the very bottom of the document: *"If we break this contract, throw us out. We mean it."* The untold story of this was the original enforcement clause I had created: *"If we break this contract,* **we will not seek re-election**.*"* Newt vetoed it because he felt members would never sign up for such a drastic commitment. He was right. Several members resented the fact that there was any reference to electoral punishment at all.*

Critics made a habit of getting the name wrong, calling it the Contract *for* America or, later, the Contract *on* America (as if the GOP had solicited a mob hit by Tony Soprano on the citizenry). The key word in the real document, *with*, connotes reciprocity, respect, and fair play. The Democrats knew what they were doing by intentionally (and often obnoxiously) mangling the name, but that didn't deter the Republicans from emphasizing that this document represented a partnership with the electorate that had never been tried before—a leveling of the playing field by raising the interests of the American people above that of the many special interest groups. The "with" in the *"Contract with America"* was a small but essential detail.

---

*I had also tried to insert another enforcement clause, publicly rejecting any pay increase for members of Congress until the budget was balanced. Newt rejected this as well, fearing an open revolt among members' spouses.

What follows is the actual wording of the document that all but two Republican congressional incumbents signed on September 27, 1994, just five weeks before that historic Election Day. You decide if this is an agenda you could support and vote for.

---

## THE CONTRACT WITH AMERICA

As Republican Members of the House of Representatives and as citizens seeking to join that body we propose not just to change its policies, but even more important, to restore the bonds of trust between the people and their elected representatives.

That is why, in this era of official evasion and posturing, we offer instead a detailed agenda for national renewal, a written commitment with no fine print.

This year's election offers the chance, after four decades of one-party control, to bring to the House a new majority that will transform the way Congress works. That historic change would be the end of government that is too big, too intrusive, and too easy with the public's money. It can be the beginning of a Congress that respects the values and shares the faith of the American family.

Like Lincoln, our first Republican president, we intend to act "with firmness in the right, as God gives us to see the right." To restore accountability to Congress. To end its cycle of scandal and disgrace. To make us all proud again of the way free people govern themselves.

On the first day of the 104th Congress, the new Republican majority will immediately pass the following major reforms, aimed at restoring the faith and trust of the American people in their government:

* **FIRST,** require all laws that apply to the rest of the country also apply equally to the Congress;

* **SECOND,** select a major, independent auditing firm to conduct a comprehensive audit of Congress for waste, fraud or abuse;

* **THIRD,** cut the number of House committees, and cut committee staff by one-third;

* **FOURTH,** limit the terms of all committee chairs;

* **FIFTH,** ban the casting of proxy votes in committee;

* **SIXTH,** require committee meetings to be open to the public;

* **SEVENTH,** require a three-fifths majority vote to pass a tax increase;

* **EIGHTH,** guarantee an honest accounting of our Federal Budget by implementing zero base-line budgeting.

Thereafter, within the first 100 days of the 104th Congress, we shall bring to the House Floor the following bills, each to be given full and open debate, each to be given a clear and fair vote and each to be immediately available this day for public inspection and scrutiny.

**1. THE FISCAL RESPONSIBILITY ACT:** A balanced budget/tax limitation amendment and a legislative line-item veto to restore fiscal responsibility to an out-of-control Congress, requiring them to live under the same budget constraints as families and businesses.

**2. THE TAKING BACK OUR STREETS ACT:** An anti-crime package including stronger truth-in-sentencing, "good faith" exclusionary rule exemptions, effective death penalty provisions, and cuts in social spending from this summer's "crime" bill to fund prison construction and additional law enforcement to keep people secure in their neighborhoods and kids safe in their schools.

**3. THE PERSONAL RESPONSIBILITY ACT:** Discourage illegitimacy and teen pregnancy by prohibiting welfare to minor mothers and denying increased AFDC for additional children while on welfare, cut spending for welfare programs, and enact a tough two-years-and-out provision with work requirements to promote individual responsibility.

**4. THE FAMILY REINFORCEMENT ACT:** Child support enforcement, tax incentives for adoption, strengthening rights of parents in their children's education, stronger child pornography laws, and an elderly dependent care tax credit to reinforce the central role of families in American society.

**5.  THE AMERICAN DREAM RESTORATION ACT:** A $500 per child tax credit, begin repeal of the marriage tax penalty, and creation of American Dream Savings Accounts to provide middle-class tax relief.

**6.  THE NATIONAL SECURITY RESTORATION ACT:** No U.S. troops under U.N. command and restoration of the essential parts of our national security funding to strengthen our national defense and maintain our credibility around the world.

**7.  THE SENIOR CITIZENS FAIRNESS ACT:** Raise the Social Security earnings limit which currently forces seniors out of the work force, repeal the 1993 tax hikes on Social Security benefits and provide tax incentives for private long-term care insurance to let Older Americans keep more of what they have earned over the years.

**8.  THE JOB CREATION AND WAGE ENHANCEMENT ACT:** Small business incentives, capital gains cut and indexation, neutral cost recovery, risk assessment/cost-benefit analysis, strengthening the Regulatory Flexibility Act and unfunded mandate reform to create jobs and raise worker wages.

**9.  THE COMMON SENSE LEGAL REFORM ACT:** "Loser pays" laws, reasonable limits on punitive damages and reform of product liability laws to stem the endless tide of litigation.

**10.  THE CITIZEN LEGISLATURE ACT:** A first-ever vote on term limits to replace career politicians with citizen legislators.

Further, we will instruct the House Budget Committee to report to the floor and we will work to enact additional budget savings, beyond the budget cuts specifically included in the legislation described above, to ensure that the federal budget deficit will be less than it would have been without the enactment of these bills.

Respecting the judgment of our fellow citizens as we seek their mandate for reform, we hereby pledge our names to this Contract with America.

Let's break this document down a bit. First, why ten items? Because people are accustomed to seeing things in lists of ten: the Ten Commandments, the top ten records on the Billboard charts, David Letterman's top ten lists, and so on. Sure, three examples lend credibility to an argument—and storytellers and stand-up comedians have long known the so-called "rule of threes"—but a list of ten items is long enough to be substantial and comprehensive.

The Contract pledged action on Day One with the eye-catching promise to *"require all the laws that apply to the rest of the country to apply equally to the Congress."* That led off the document because so many Americans were visibly shocked and annoyed when they learned that this wasn't already the case. The Contract also promised to make a host of additional internal, procedural reforms of Congress on the very first day of the new session, and that initial flurry of activity meant the public would see an immediate change.

But why one hundred days for the remaining ten items on the agenda? Two reasons: First, it was a measurable, limited amount of time for the electors (the American people) to hold the elected accountable, and two, it forced the elected (Republicans) to get the job done quickly and efficiently to prove to the electorate that they had made the right decision. The hundred-day pledge created a sort of countdown. Of course, Newt Gingrich, ever the historian, was also thinking of Franklin Roosevelt's famous first one hundred days in office. Gingrich knew that an initial burst of frenzied activity would get GOP control off to a productive start. He also knew, unlike anyone else involved in the project, that the media would appreciate the historical parallels, raising the Contract's importance in their coverage.*

Since I knew that many people would only read the first and last items in the document, I asked that the Contract begin and end with the two highest-priority proposals in the eyes of the voters: a balanced budget amendment and term limits. And in one case—tax cuts—I actively sought to blur the substance. The so-called *"tax cuts for American families"* plank, known as the "American Dream Restoration Act" in the actual Contract, did not publicly specify that it was actually a $500-per-child

*Sure enough, Gingrich was the first speaker of the House to address the American people live on a prime-time network broadcast. For that first one hundred days, he was surely more significant and influential than even President Clinton, and more cameras followed his every move than the President's. Unfortunately, that coverage was not all that favorable, and it actually sowed the seeds of his fall from power less than four years later.

tax credit in the *TV Guide* advertisement because we found it did not have much of an impact on voter sentiment. In fact, it made some voters angry because they thought it wasn't large enough. The way we resolved it was to tell candidates to tell voters that it was a tax credit of $1,000 for *a family of four.*\*

Less than twenty-four hours before the Contract with America was to go to press, the Republican leadership asked me to come in and edit the final text. To my chagrin, it still contained four mentions of Bill Clinton. I removed all of them. Not only did the final version of the contract never mention Bill Clinton by name, it also made no mention of the Democratic Party. Finally, a political party would be defined by what it stood *for,* not by what it was against.

There were other important language lessons and essential symbols attached to the Contract:

- The actual advertising for the Contract appeared in *TV Guide,* a million-dollar proposition but with equally powerful rewards. It was the only magazine that people kept in their homes for an entire week and opened up on a daily basis—seven unique opportunities to communicate the Contract and all it represented.
- The ad could be easily removed from the magazine. Readers were encouraged to cut it out and tack it up on their refrigerators as a way to demonstrate how serious Republicans were about accountability.
- An actual checklist was provided down the entire left side of the document that encouraged voters to keep tabs on the Republican progress.
- The language of the ad was carefully crafted to include phrases to demonstrate that they were listening and were ready to take immediate action, like *"we hear you loud and clear,"* and that Republican candidates *"have pledged, in writing, to vote on these 10 common-sense reforms."*

The initial Democrat reaction was surprise, which quickly degenerated into hostility. Tony Coelho, a genuine sage of electoral politics

---

\*Comedian Bill Maher is an occasional critic of my language efforts, particularly regarding tax policy. In my interview, he complained that *"tax relief"* was *"very misleading"* because *"relief makes you think of loosening your belt after a long, full Thanksgiving meal."* I would hope that tax relief has more positive powers the other 364 days of the year.

who a few years earlier had been the House Democrat majority whip, said the Republicans had made a big mistake with the Contract because it gave the Democrats something concrete to attack. He and his Democrat colleagues didn't realize how fed up the public was with the status quo.

Newt Gingrich knew from the outset that the media would be hostile toward the Contract, but like a black belt performing a judo move, he figured out how to use the power and weight of the media to his advantage. He understood that most major newspapers would run stories cynical and critical of the Contract . . . but he also realized that they would also reprint the Contract itself, often in a sidebar or a box right next to the more critical news piece. And Newt realized that more people would read the easy-to-digest, eye-catching, ten-point list than the long gray paragraphs of the news story. Every journalistic effort to debunk the Contract that included the text itself would end up being a free advertisement for it.

The influence of the Contract with America was felt around the world. In 2001, I advised Silvio Berlusconi on an Italian version. The Italians loved the idea of a contract with the Italian people, and Berlusconi went further than the House Republicans by including an enforcement clause that promised he wouldn't run for reelection if he didn't enact at least four of the five items in his contract. And he wasn't just promising to bring these items up for a vote; he was promising success (in the United States, House Republicans brought each item in the Contract with America up for a vote, but some failed to become law). He signed the document himself, forty-eight hours before Election Day, and when he won, he held up the contract and waved it triumphantly in the air.

But despite his promises and pronouncements, Berlusconi didn't fulfill the terms of his contract with the Italian people. The Italians agreed: He was turned out of office in 2006.

Despite Berlusconi's failure to follow through, the Italian contract's political success in his 2001 campaign demonstrated that good language and powerful symbolism know no international bounds. There was a Contract with Mongolia, a Contract with Romania, and there was even interest in creating a contract for the Ukrainian elections in 2005. The reason is simple: communication rule four, credibility (in this case, the lack of it). Politicians not keeping their promises is a problem the world over, and voters' lack of faith in them can be found anywhere you go.

Because of this worldwide cynicism, the word *promise* should simply not be part of the vocabulary of any elected official.

About ten days after Republicans won the House in 1994, Newt Gingrich convened a private Saturday afternoon meeting in the Capitol with about twenty insiders to discuss how to talk about and pass the ten items in the Contract. During this discussion, Newt maintained that the GOP had to replace the Democrats as the party of compassion, and he used the example of how "every American" would support the funding of emergency room care even for illegal immigrants. I replied that Americans might not *deny* them care, but they wouldn't necessarily *give* it. Newt trivialized the distinction, and on the underlying policy and real-life result he was correct—but rhetorically there is an enormous difference between *not giving* and *denying*. I tested the issue, and sure enough, while only 38 percent of Americans would *deny* emergency room care to illegal aliens, fully 55 percent would *not give* it.

While Newt eventually acknowledged that the words used to articulate immigration policy can be as influential as the policy itself, it was too late to prevent his disastrous discussion of several other highly emotional issues, most notably the societal value and benefit of *"orphanages"* as a better alternative for abused and neglected children than *"foster homes."* As a matter of policy, he is of course correct, but the political ramifications were something completely different. He chose an inopportune time of year—Christmas—for a full-fledged debate about how best to raise kids who come from unstable or nonexistent homes, triggering an avalanche of hostile, unflattering cartoons comparing him to Scrooge and, even worse, The Grinch. He never recovered from that poorly timed and clumsily articulated policy discussion.

What follows are other notable, but for the most part unknown, examples of how the rules of communication have played a role in public policy and how words that work—and a few that don't—have been applied to almost every political issue raised in Washington today.

The most contentious debate of the 1995–96 congressional session was the reform of Medicare. The language in question: Is slowing the planned rate of spending growth in the program a "cut" or not? The answer mattered. In polling I conducted in 1995, I found that Americans opposed *"cutting spending"* on Medicare by a sizeable three to one. Yet by a still significant ratio of five to three, the public supported *"increasing* *spending but at a slower rate"*—just what the Republicans were advocating. And so that became the official way to talk about Medicare.*

I also tested three different ways of describing how Medicare spending would increase under the Republican plan:

**1.** Medicare spending would increase from $178 billion to $250 billion over six years (what I called the *"billions to billions"* approach).

**2.** Medicare spending would increase by 6.4 percent a year, every year, for six years (the *"year over year"* strategy).

**3.** Medicare spending would increase from $4,700 per person per year to $6,200 per person per year (the *"personalized"* approach).

All three statements were true, and all three statements represented the exact same underlying mathematical reality. But the personalized approach was by far the most popular. The billions to billions strategy only works if you're Bill Gates or Ross Perot, and while math majors or M.I.T. graduates may appreciate a discussion about percentages, no one else does. They're too abstract. But by zooming in to the personal level, you encourage people to relate the numbers to their own lives and learn exactly what the benefit means to them. Numbers with the smallest denominators and applied *per individual* are therefore almost always the most effective. And by increasing people's understanding of what government programs cost and what they pay out, I would argue that you're being informative, not manipulative.

Setting context, creating language that is clear, simple, and aspirational, helping voters visualize the future—none of this is new. The 1952 presidential election of Dwight Eisenhower was the first to make use of the new medium of television by adopting many of the techniques of commercial advertising and applying pithy Madison Avenue language to the electoral contest. His opponent, the overly academic Adlai Stevenson, used much of his television time to air entire speeches—in a sense nothing more than putting a picture to a radio broadcast. But Eisenhower's

---

*Newt was never more effective than when explaining the importance of and details about Medicare reform. He even developed specific hand gestures that he taught his colleagues to better illustrate how Republicans were not cutting Medicare, as the Democrats claimed, but in fact increasing spending. Republicans still lost the public relations battle, but they kept control of Congress and therefore won the political war.

media consultant Rosser Reeves—who had come up with successful campaigns for M&M's ("Melts in your mouth, not in your hand"), Anacin pain reliever, and Colgate toothpaste—found that audiences didn't remember much after listening to one of Eisenhower's speeches because Ike was just not an engaging speaker.

A different approach was called for. Working with pollster George Gallup, Reeves determined Americans' chief concerns and then developed the ad campaign *"Eisenhower Answers America,"* which featured the general taking short questions from ordinary Americans and providing simple, succinct answers—the birth of the sound bite. Instead of trying to compete with Stevenson's intellectual brilliance (which was so far above the intellectual level of the average voter that some found it sleep-provoking), Eisenhower shifted to a different arena and redefined the battlefield. Gone were the lengthy, expansive, bone-dry performances. In their place came single, simple ideas nicely packaged in small, manageable, memorable bites. And so, the thirty-second political "spot" was born, and political communication would never be the same again.

There was a strategic philosophy behind this revolutionary change in communication. Reeves believed that each TV spot should focus on a product's "unique selling proposition": the one thing that made it stand out from the competition. Each Eisenhower ad, therefore, consisted of the candidate answering a single voter question. It was all scripted and staged, of course. Eisenhower and the questioners never met; Reeves edited the footage together later. The questioners looked up as they asked their questions, as if the general were on a pedestal, and Eisenhower was shot from a low angle to make him appear more formidable. In some of the spots, you can even see Eisenhower's eyes moving—he's reading (badly) from cue cards without his glasses. Still, *"Eisenhower Answers America"* said in three words what the competing candidate couldn't say in three thousand. It was something new, and it worked. [5]

Each subsequent presidential campaign would rely on an increasingly sophisticated commercial-style catchphrase or slogan to define the persona of its candidate, attempt to set the terms and framework of debate, and establish the stakes of the election. A few of these slogans were never spoken or authorized by the candidates themselves, but they became associated with the candidate during the election. This is only a fraction of what the campaigns have used:[6]

## THE LANGUAGE OF POLITICAL CAMPAIGNS

| | | |
|---|---|---|
| 1952 | Dwight Eisenhower | I Like Ike |
| 1952 | Democratic Party | You Never Had It So Good |
| 1956 | Dwight Eisenhower | I Still Like Ike<br>Peace and Prosperity |
| 1960 | Richard Nixon | For the Future |
| 1960 | John F. Kennedy | A Time for Greatness |
| 1964 | Barry Goldwater | In Your Heart, You Know He's Right<br>A Choice, Not an Echo |
| 1964 | Lyndon Johnson | The Stakes Are Too High for You to<br>    Stay at Home<br>All the Way with LBJ<br>Vote, As If Your Whole World<br>    Depended on It |
| 1968 | Richard Nixon | Nixon's the One |
| 1972 | George McGovern | Come Home, America |
| 1972 | Richard Nixon | Now More than Ever<br>Acid, Amnesty, and Abortion<br>    [against McGovern] |
| 1976 | Gerald Ford | He's Making Us Proud Again |
| 1976 | Jimmy Carter | A Leader, for a Change |
| 1980 | Ronald Reagan | Are You Better Off Than You Were<br>    Four Years Ago? |
| 1984 | Ronald Reagan | It's Morning Again in America |
| 1984 | Walter Mondale | America Needs a Change |
| 1988 | George Bush | A Kinder, Gentler Nation |
| 1992 | Bill Clinton | Putting People First<br>It's the Economy, Stupid |
| 1992 | Ross Perot | United We Stand<br>Ross for Boss |

| 1996 | Bill Clinton | Building a Bridge to the Twenty-first Century |
|------|--------------|-----------------------------------------------|
| 1996 | Bob Dole | The Better Man for a Better America |
| 2000 | Al Gore | Prosperity and Progress<br>Prosperity for America's Families |
| 2000 | George W. Bush | Compassionate Conservatism<br>A Uniter, Not a Divider<br>A Reformer with Results |
| 2004 | John Kerry | Bring It On<br>Stronger at Home, More Respected in the World |
| 2004 | George W. Bush | Steady Leadership in Times of Change |

Most of those are forgettable, as are most of the campaigns and even some of the candidates. Virtually all of them applied communication rule seven (aspiration)—but they most often fell short either because they broke rule three (credibility) or rule ten (context).

To focus just on presidential campaigns would ignore the language development that goes on in the rest of the political world. Consider the committee in the House of Representatives that deals with our nation's tax collection system. Is it called the *"Committee on Taxation"*? Of course not. No politician in his right mind would dare attach such a negative concept to his work. Instead, members of Congress serve on the *"Ways and Means Committee"*—a body whose name obscures its unpopular area of responsibility. After all, would you reelect a representative to Congress who sits on the "Confiscating Your Hard-Earned Income Committee"?

What follows are several issue case studies of words that worked—and one notable exception where the words did not. In addition to addressing contentious issues and a polarized electorate, they all have one thing in common: a commitment to the principle that *it's not what you say, it's what people hear.* . . .

## Words That Worked Case Study:
## Changing the *"Estate Tax"* to the *"Death Tax"*

Other than the Contract with America, my most significant political work has been working to remove the elitist sounding *"estate tax"* from the political lexicon and replacing it with the more emotional, more personal *"death tax."* It's tough to admit that when I first tackled the *"death tax"* challenge, I was neither a believer nor a supporter. At the time, I thought Republicans advocating the elimination of a tax on the heirs of millionaires would play badly with the electorate. But over time, not only did my opinions change, but so did America's.

A clear but somewhat narrow majority of Americans today support eliminating the so-called *"estate tax,"* and a slightly higher percentage would back the elimination of the *"inheritance tax,"* but more than 70 percent would abolish the *"death tax."* Sure, some object that the term *"death tax"* is inflammatory, but think about it. What was the event that triggered its collection? You pay a sales tax when you are involved with a sale. You pay an income tax when you earn income. And when you die, if you've been financially successful—and forgotten to hire really smart and expensive accountants—you may also pay a tax. So what else would you call that, if not a *"death tax"*?

The notion that the phrase *"death tax"* is euphemistic or Orwellian does not withstand scrutiny. For one thing, it supposes that *"estate tax"* and *"inheritance tax"* are purely neutral terms. But that's ridiculous. *"Estate"* conjures up images of rolling green hills and vast real estate holdings, of J. R. Ewing and Donald Trump rubbing their hands together and cackling like corporate villains or toasting with champagne glasses—not a mom-and-pop hardware store that may have to close its doors or a family farm that may have to liquidate the very land upon which it depends to pay a tax of nearly half its value. *"Inheritance"* evokes images of celebrity debutantes like Paris Hilton squandering the fruits of their parents' labor while the huddled, deserving poor tremble in the shadows—not a small business owner hoping to pass on to his children the savings he has wrung from a lifetime of toil.

## "THE DEATH TAX DESERVES TO DIE"

The language for killing the death tax has evolved over time. From *"taxing the American Dream"* to *"you shouldn't have to visit the undertaker and the taxman on the same day,"* the language of death tax repeal is easy for working and retired Americans to understand and appreciate.

---

### WORDS THAT WORK

"Benjamin Franklin, perhaps the wisest of our founding fathers, said there were two certainties in life: death and taxes. But I do not believe even Franklin could have foreseen that today, both would occur at the same time."

---

When Congress began to debate reduction and elimination of this tax in 2001, I prepared a language document for death tax repeal advocates that contained four essential "common-sense" communication principles. Each one was related to the ten rules of effective communication:

First, the death tax is the wrong tax. It accounts for just 1 percent of the nation's revenues. Dollar for dollar, it costs more to collect than any other federal tax. While not put in the form of a question, this encouraged listeners to challenge the value of such a tax.

Second, it comes at the wrong time. A core principle behind repealing the death tax is that people should not be further burdened at the most difficult times of their lives. Mourning families have enough grief when their loved ones die. The IRS doesn't need to pile on. People could actually visualize having to search through boxes and boxes of junk trying to find some slip of paper to get the IRS off their backs at the very moment they were so deeply suffering the loss of a parent.

Third, it hurts the wrong people. If you saved for the future, put away money for your children, built a small business, ran a family farm, or achieved the American Dream in other ways, the death tax punishes you by preventing you from sharing the fruits of your hard work with your loved ones. This was a direct attack at the credibility of the tax—why would anyone want to tax success?*

---

*I give credit to those who fashioned the response, "You tax success for the same reason Jesse James robbed banks—it's where the money is. Would you rather tax failure?"

Four, it helps the wrong people. The only people helped by the estate tax are the fancy lawyers, pricey accountants, and ravenous IRS agents. And this became the *context*—that the tax was simply the wrong way to raise revenues for the government.

This effort came to fruition in late 2001 when Congress voted to reduce the death tax every year through 2010, and then actually eliminate it in 2011. Ten years ago, eliminating the *"estate tax"* would have been a political non-starter. Today, there is broad support for killing the *"death tax"* permanently. Change the name and you change the fortunes.

---

## Words That Worked Case Study:
### Changing *"Drilling for Oil"* to *"Exploring for Energy,"* from *"Domestic"* to *"American"*

Back in 1995, Newt Gingrich came to me asking not only how I could help make Republicans sound more environmentally friendly, but also whether I could create a vocabulary that would actually encourage Republicans to *be* more environmentally friendly. And so for more than a decade, I have conducted dozens of dial sessions and surveys that explore the relationship between the environment, energy, and the role of language in communicating a common-sense policy to the American people.

The ultimate result of Newt's language request in 1995 was the tagline *"A cleaner, safer, healthier environment,"* which was meant to embrace the varying priorities in the fifty states, establish a proactive context, and explicitly reject the status quo. Read the phrase carefully: *"cleaner, safer, healthier"* takes all the elements of the environment into account. It asserts the need for progress. And it doesn't get bogged down in process or blame. In every public opinion survey we have completed, Americans not only expect the environment to be cleaner next year than this year—they demand it. And they don't really care how it's done as long as it gets done.

There's a consumer perspective to this as well. Companies have taken to the idea of *"environmentally friendly"* packaging and production, but that has limited appeal. In order to get people to act more environmentally responsible, it can't just be about the environment. Other needs must be met—and communicated. People wouldn't be paying top dollar and enduring waiting lists for Prius automobiles if they didn't perform as well as a regular car or meet a status need or aspiration. Nobody wants to buy a recycled paper product if it falls apart or doesn't feel just like the less environmentally sound version.

One reason why the Democrats have been so unsuccessful in turning a significant perception advantage over Republicans on most environmental issues into measurable electoral gains is because their environmental language is so reactive and reactionary. Just look at the *"Healthy Forest"* debate in 2003–04. Republican *"conservationists"* advocated clearing dead trees, leaves, and detritus out of the forests that naturally produce them and turning at-risk forests into . . . you got it . . . Healthy Forests. Conversely, Democratic *"environmentalists"* (their chosen label) resist doing so . . . and then lose the entire forest to rampaging forest fires, stoked by the very trees, leaves, and detritus they were determined to "preserve."

There are two specific phrases that entered the dialogue because of my work. The first came about because of my effort to explain why a tiny sliver of Alaska known as ANWR, the Arctic National Wildlife Refuge, should be opened up for careful exploration of energy. And that is the phrase that has triggered so much consternation within the environmental community. I would assert that *"responsible exploration for energy,"* which includes the search for clean natural gas, is a different and more productive activity than haphazardly plunking down a well and *"drilling for oil."* The problem was, while the politicians adopted the new and improved language, the energy companies (again, not oil) did not.

In so many ways, America's energy producers have been their own worst enemies—adopting communication strategies that undermine their image, or even choosing not to communicate at all. For as long I can remember, everyone affiliated with the industry—and their political supporters on Capitol Hill—has used the phrases *"drilling for oil"* and *"domestic"* sources of energy. Here's the problem: "oil drilling" reminds people of Jed Clampett shooting at the ground, conjuring images of liquid black goo gushing into the sky, and "domestic" is too much of a financial accounting term.

At almost every turn the context set by the energy companies was always financial and seemingly anti-environmental rather than patriotic and responsible. It's not that their words lacked visualization—they caused the *wrong* visualization and discouraged any sort of aspiration. Drilling for oil is ugly, and domestic production is economic, so for

Americans, never eager to pay more than is absolutely necessary for the energy they need, the words coming from the industry were only making difficult conditions even worse.

But today, many of America's energy-producing companies have switched their terminology to *"exploring for energy"* and have adopted a more *American*-centric approach to their messaging. These changes may not seem significant on the surface, but they have had considerable impact on public opinion. The best example: support for exploration for energy in ANWR is 10 percent more popular than *"drilling for oil."* Similarly, "American energy sources" has a more patriotic feel to it. Increasing exploration for American energy resources sounds energy-independent, self-reliant and efficient—all important aspirational attributes and values in twenty-first-century American life.

In fact, a sure applause line for anyone in the energy industry is to talk about *"American oil, American energy, American fuel, American innovation, American exploration—and American energy policy for a twenty-first-century American economy."* Redundant? Sure. Words that work? Absolutely. With this language, Americans could finally visualize an important industry at the cutting edge rather than lagging behind. And with fear and loathing of "Arab oil" at a post-Iranian-hostage high, anything that suggested American oil as its replacement was going to be received favorably.

Under the banner *"Working with you to use energy wisely,"* the following thirty-second ad from the American oil and natural gas industry contains almost a dozen smart linguistic articulations:

---

### AMERICA'S OIL AND NATURAL GAS INDUSTRY (:30)

Every day you look for ways to stretch your energy dollar, just as we are looking for new fuel solutions.

As you use energy wisely, our industry is searching for new supplies, maximizing efficiency with advanced technology.

Working together—consumers, government, industry—we'll insure diverse, reliable energy to live our lives and keep America going strong.

A message from America's oil and natural gas industry.

---

Examine this single thirty-second ad word by word, line by line, and you see the rules of effective communication in practice:

*"Every day you look for ways to stretch your energy dollar"* is exactly how Americans behave every time gas prices climb to a new level. It's a day-to-day struggle for millions of Americans, and an energy company that recognizes this is at least demonstrating that they are listening.

*"Just as we are looking for new fuel solutions . . . our industry is searching for new supplies, maximizing efficiency with advanced technology"* is about the aspiration of solving the energy problem once and for all. It focuses attention not on the present but on the future and the search for something better. Even the individual choice of words—*"maximizing efficiency with advanced technology"*—communicates a simple but effective message that a new approach will bring better results. We have also found that Americans would prefer greater energy efficiency to increased conservation because *"efficiency"* suggests getting more for less while *"conservation"* has a tone of sacrifice to it. For that same reason, *"renewable"* energy is more popular than *"alternative"* energy.

*"Working together, consumers, government, industry, we'll insure diverse, reliable energy to live our lives and keep America going strong"* offers the novel suggestion that we're all in this together and that we will all benefit if America's energy companies are successful. Morevoer, Americans equate *"diversity"* and *"reliability"* of energy with security of energy supplies.

---

## Words That Work Case Study:
## From *"Social Security"* to *"Retirement Security"*

It would be neither fair nor accurate to include only case studies that succeeded. Barely hours after John Kerry's concession speech, a relieved and confident George W. Bush announced to the American people that he now had "political capital" and that he planned on spending it to strengthen Social Security. Personally, creating the language for Social Security reform has been a part of my political tool kit for almost a decade, and I looked forward to the challenge of teaching Congress how to talk about the issue. I would have been more successful if I had started with the president.

The whole debate revolved around rule ten of effective communication: context and personal relevance. *"Retirement,"* as it was once defined, no longer exists. Or rather, it now means different things to different people. For many, what once were considered the *"golden years"* are now very much the working years: Almost half of all Americans plan to continue working in some capacity after age sixty-five, and nearly one in three say they will still be at work after age seventy, health permitting. Some still aspire to a "traditional" retirement, but many of them doubt they will ever reach it. Others define *retirement* as nothing more than a chance to change jobs or careers. They will continue to work, by choice or necessity, until the day their health gives out. And there are those, too, who love what they do and wouldn't dream of giving it up.

How people look and feel at sixty-five today is remarkably different than just a generation ago, and the choices now available to senior citizens and all working Americans should have been the prism through which Republicans entered the Social Security reform debate. That debate could have reflected these new possibilities. But it didn't.

Critics of President Bush's approach effectively charged that it amounted to *"privatizing"* America's commitment to retirees—a big no-no for a majority of Americans. As with every other political hot button issue, *those who define the debate will determine the outcome,* and the opponents of Social Security reform got the *"privatization"* label to stick, and therefore sunk Social Security.

For those who will be tasked with renewing the reform effort, the first step is to counter such inaccuracies by talking about how individual investment accounts *"personalize"* Social Security. When you *personalize* something—whether it's a pair of monogrammed towels, your Yahoo! home page, or Social Security—you enhance ownership by putting your mark on it and tailoring it to your needs. *"Personalizing"* Social Security implies partial ownership of our retirement dollars. Instead of Washington making all the decisions, each citizen would personally determine how a portion of his or her retirement savings would be invested.

From a polling perspective, *"personalizing"* Social Security has a 17 percent advantage over *"privatizing"* it. Fifty-one percent of Americans believe *"personalizing"* the program is a good idea, while only 34 percent believe *"privatizing"* it is. Using the term *"personalizing"* conveys to voters that you're on their side, fighting to help them get control of their retirement security.

The next step is to articulate the *"guarantee"* to current recipients and future beneficiaries. Never underestimate the personal bond between Americans and their Social Security checks. Republicans talking about *"strengthening Social Security"* (which is a more popular objective than promoting *"Social Security reform"*) should emphasize their commitment to 1) maintaining the promises the federal government has made to protect and care for current Social Security recipients; and 2) simultaneously strengthening the long-term health of the system to guarantee benefits for future retirees. Notice the enumeration? By splitting up the objectives and listing them out numerically, they are much more likely to be remembered.

Step three is about *"you and your future."* Republican communications will continue to come up short as long as the GOP fails to convince Americans that their proposals to reform Social Security have at their core Americans investing, controlling, and securing their own futures. Voters continue to trust the Democratic Party to handle Social Security, because they think Republicans lack the compassion and concern to find an equitable solution that benefits everyone.

That's why the debate should have been and must eventually be about *"retirement security,"* not *"Social Security."* And that leads me to a serious Bush error: creating a high-profile commission to *"reform Social Security"* rather than address the broader issue of *"retirement security."* Today, only a quarter of Americans rely on Social Security as the primary financial vehicle for their retirement—and every year that percentage shrinks. Social Security is a government program, and by definition, Democrats are seen as more likely to defend and expand government programs. Conversely, *"retirement security"* involves more traditionally Republican territory: 401(k)s, IRAs, private pension plans, and other nongovernment programs. Republicans would have been much better off focusing on expanding financial retirement choices rather than altering the most popular government program in modern history.

Another mistake was the focus on the program itself rather than the individual recipients. Moving from the current system to personal retirement accounts requires a shift in focus from the macro, eagle's eye view to a micro, individual view: The problem with Social Security is not the trillions of dollars in revenue shortfalls or the unsustainable worker-to-retiree ratios; the problem is that Social Security may not be there when *you* need it—and that fact alone undermines your retirement security. Republicans should have then explained how personal retirement accounts will improve each *individual's* retirement security, giving retirees three essential benefits that Social Security does not: *"ownership, control, and freedom."*

The final step should have been to educate Americans to the role Washington has played in spending their precious Social Security dollars. Social Security may be collected by the government, administered by the government, and undermined because of the government . . . but to America's seniors, *Social Security* and *government* are two totally unrelated things. It is therefore not surprising that the most popular signs at the various anti-reform rallies read "Hands off my Social Security," as though Washington was suddenly trying to take control. Americans fundamentally reject the notion that the government should have dominion over how they save or invest. People want a sense of control over their 401(k) plans, their pensions, and their other retirement vehicles—and Washington should be careful not to limit, restrict, or regulate anyone's retirement nest egg in a way that seems arbitrary or wasteful.

## ILLEGAL IMMIGRATION

Americans are not only ready for an overhaul of illegal immigration policy, they are demanding it. It has become such an important issue that many voters are willing to cast ballots against their traditional party if they disagree with their own candidate's position on immigration reform. In the fall of 2005, I was asked to create a Language Dictionary to help Republicans channel the anger on the ground into a lexicon to help them pass tough enforcement legislation without provoking a Latino backlash.

I failed. First, the words I provided often went unused. Second, there was no legislative consensus upon which to apply the words. The conservative political activists, along with millions of typical concerned citizens, felt that Republican efforts weren't strong enough, tough enough, or effective enough. Conversely, Latinos nationwide came together, organized, marched, and condemned the GOP for being anti-immigrant. It was the worst of all worlds.

But the language itself is still a solid example of how to apply the rules of effective communication to a controversial and often divisive political issue. So let's go step by step through the rules and how they could have been applied to the immigration debate. The quotes that follow come directly from the twenty-four-page confidential memo I drafted for members of Congress.

## Rule One
## Use Small Words

In the first paragraph of the memo, I laid out the entire immigration message in a single sentence that highlighted the four essential words that work:

*"Linguistically, as you enter the debate, there are four key themes that must represent the core of your message:* **prevention, protection, accountability**, *and* **compassion***."*

All four words represent basic universal principles and values, which made them universally acceptable. All four words would be understood by high school dropouts and Ph.D.s. And three of the four words have similar construction, making them easy on the ears and easy to memorize.

## Rule Two
## Brevity—Use Short Sentences

This is a simple task for President George W. Bush but very difficult for almost every other politician. In debates where emotions are high, the shorter the sentences, the better the audience response.

---

### WORDS THAT WORK

"This is about the overcrowding of YOUR schools. This is about emergency room chaos in YOUR hospitals. This is about the increase in YOUR taxes. This is about the crime in YOUR communities."

---

No, this is not beautiful language, but the politicians who used it reported heads nodding and hands clapping. The sentences were simple, straightforward, and to the point—and there were no commas to break up the flow. If your sentence has more than two commas, you have too many.

## Rule Three
## Credibility Is As Important As Philosophy

In the illegal immigration debate, an expression of *"compassion"* was the best way to establish instant credibility.

---

## WORDS THAT WORK

"Compassion is the component lacking in much of the Republican messaging on illegal immigration thus far. You are quick to condemn the problem, as you should be, but no one hears your sympathy for ALL of the innocent victims."

"A child brought here by an illegal immigrant is a victim, but so are the children of legal immigrants and citizens who pay for it in taxes and fewer services themselves. We cannot deny care to an illegal immigrant, but it is unfair for the rest of us to pick up the tab. The best way to show compassion for illegal immigration is to END illegal immigration."

---

Notice the use of the word *"victim"* and how it is tied to the children of illegal immigrants. It directly acknowledges the arguments put forward by the opponents of stricter immigration laws. But by accepting what we all know to be true, it earns the speaker credibility that can then be applied to the principle of fairness and eventually to ending illegal immigration altogether.

### Rule Four
### Consistency Matters

Rules aren't just for kids and books. To keep members of Congress focused, consistent, and repetitive, you have to tell them that there are specific rules to follow. Otherwise, they won't follow them. In the immigration debate, the public opinion research uncovered five specific rules:

1. *Always differentiate LEGAL from illegal immigration;*
2. *Always refer to people crossing the border illegally as "illegal immigrants"—NOT as "illegals";*
3. *Always focus on those who are hurt most by illegal immigration—American citizens and immigrants who came here legally and played by the rules;*
4. *Don't argue whether illegal immigration is a crisis, a major problem, or a national challenge. Describe the problem, quantify it, but don't measure it; and*
5. *If it sounds like amnesty, it will fail.*

## Rule Five
## Novelty—Offer Something New

In this case, something new was an endorsement of LEGAL immigration. *"Legal immigration is an important component of America's economy and social fabric. At one point or another, all of us are children of immigrants. We are a compassionate country—and we are eager to provide the opportunities of freedom and the American Dream to those who come here legally."* Republicans were warned that the lack of distinction between legal and illegal immigrants, coupled with occasionally overheated rhetoric, sent the wrong signals to the Hispanic, Asian, and other important immigrant communities. This was definitely one rule Republicans didn't follow.

## Rule Six
## Sound and Texture Matter

The words *prevention, protection,* and *compassion* are memorable not just to those who say them but those who hear them, and they helps align the rhythm of the speaker and the audience.

## Rule Seven
## Speak Aspirationally

The language of hope and opportunity works with everyone. Most of us believe in the American Dream. Most of us believe that immigrants who work hard, who have families here, who contribute to the economy by doing tough jobs that other Americans don't want to do, deserve a second chance. Most of us believe they should give them the opportunity to contribute to our society, our economy, and our culture . . . legally.

---

### WORDS THAT WORK

"In addition to being a land of opportunity, America is also a land of compassion. We believe that everyone deserves a second chance. If an illegal immigrant working here would like to re-enter the country as a guest worker and as a legal immigrant, they should be given that chance.

"This is a generous offer that allows immigrants who are here illegally to start over and apply for citizenship. And that's fair—illegal aliens are entitled to a clean slate—IF they follow the proper rules and procedures. There are second chances for citizenship—but there are no shortcuts. If they're willing to earn citizenship, legally, they should get a second chance. That's the American Way."

### Rule Eight
### Visualize

In some ways the *"visualization"* rule was the catalyst for the national outcry on both sides. Among proponents of stricter laws, watching televised images of dozens of people dashing across the border night after night drove an already agitated population to the breaking point. The mere reminder of this videotaped footage was enough to set off a heated discussion—and so that became the language lesson.

### WORDS THAT WORK

"There is something wrong with our borders, our enforcement, and our laws when NBC, ABC, and CBS can show us hundreds or thousands of illegal immigrants racing across the border every night and the federal government can't find them, catch them, and send them back."

In this case, it wasn't necessary to craft language that would generate a personal vision. A simple reference to something they had already seen with their own eyes triggered the emotion I was seeking.

### Rule Nine
### Ask a Question

The best messages intellectually invite audience participation. In this case, it was essential that the speaker used questions that triggered thoughts not just about the present but also about a troubling future if the status quo was allowed to stand:

## WORDS THAT WORK

"I know that there are some who would say that the illegal immigrants are here already so let them stay, let them work, and let them enjoy all the benefits of American citizenship. I don't agree. What message would that send to LEGAL immigrants who have played by the rules, waiting years for the chance to live and work here? What message does that send to law-abiding American citizens who work hard to pay their taxes—only to see those tax dollars go to lawbreakers? What message would that send to every would-be ILLEGAL immigrant? Just get yourself across the border and you're home free? Those are messages I don't want to send any longer."

### Rule Ten
### Provide Context and Explain Relevance

For some issues, context and relevance are the same. In the illegal immigration debate, they were distinct and needed to be addressed individually. I tested dozens of words, phrases, principles, and concepts to determine the most universally acceptable context. The one that came out on top was all of three words: **rule of law**. Here's how I told Republicans how to explain it.

"Respect for the Rule of Law is a core fundamental American principle. A nation that either cannot or will not enforce its laws—including immigration law—is inviting abuse of ALL of its laws."

## WORDS THAT WORK

"By allowing illegal immigrants to get away with crossing the border illegally, we have encouraged an entire culture whereby America's laws are optional—to be obeyed or disobeyed depending on what's convenient.

"It's time to treat America's laws like laws—not like guidelines to be followed or ignored depending on one's choice or country of birth. There is a right way and a wrong way to enter this country. If you do it the wrong way, there should be consequences. In America, when you break the law, you should be held accountable for your behavior."

## Words That Worked Case Study:
### From *"Crime"* and *"Criminals"* to *"Public Safety"*

Back in 1993, when I was working for Rudy Giuliani in his first successful campaign for mayor of New York, I pressed for him to talk about *"public safety"* rather than *"crime"* and *"criminals."* For twenty-five years, since the election of Richard Nixon in 1968, Republicans had emphasized their *"anti-crime"* agenda with a good degree of success. But in the polling I did with the voters of New York, I discovered that the public placed a higher priority on *"personal and public safety"* than on *"fighting crime"* or even *"getting tough on criminals."*

While crime and public safety may be integrally related and in some cases identical, there is an important distinction. *"Fighting crime"* is procedural and *"getting tough on criminals"* is punitive—and that's certainly important. But *"safety,"* although somewhat abstract, is definitely personal, and most of all aspirational—the ultimate value and the desired result of an effort to fight crime. And so Rudy Giuliani adopted not just an anti-crime message but a pro–public-safety agenda—and his success in New York City led to the reframing of the way Americans think about crime, criminals, and a safe, civil society.

These case studies all have one thing in common: a desire to fundamentally change public opinion. Words that work don't just happen. They are uncovered and utilized only in cases where someone cares enough to apply the principles of effective communication to an issue or cause. Politicians may have a greater need to communicate than almost every other profession, but that doesn't mean they're good at it.

# IX

## Myths and Realities About Language and People

*"Americans have different ways of saying things. They say 'el-evator.' We say 'lift.' They say 'President.' We say 'stupid, psy-chopathic git.'"*     —ALEXAI SAYLE, BRITISH ENTERTAINER

In February 1974, Norman Lear launched a new comedy ironically called *Good Times* about a lower-middle-class black family living in a high-rise ghetto on the South Side of Chicago. Lear and the two lead ac-tors, Esther Rolle and John Amos, were determined to provide audi-ences with an accurate portrayal of what life was really like for an economically struggling but close-knit urban black family.

"I remember sitting around a table with *Good Times* and listening to the cast, like in the second year, arguing about whether their sixteen-year-old daughter Thelma would think about sleeping with this boy, not necessarily doing it, but thinking about it," Lear recalls. "They were all fighting because everybody had a different point of view. Finally, I said, 'This has to stop. You guys can be responsible for the patina because you know so much more the language in which she would say a lot of things, but I'm a father, I'm a son, I'm a person, I'm all of the things represented around this table. And if there has to be a decision, the buck will stop with me.' I didn't feel the least bit concerned about it. We were all in that sense the same people."[1]

What Lear was saying, and what most social scientists have concluded, is that there is so much more that unites us as people than divides us by race, income, gender, and any other demographic attribute. Audiences may look very different on the outside, but they will respond to the same hopes and fears internally and emotionally.

One reason why there is so little successful communication in this country is that so many of our communicators don't truly understand something as basic as who their audience is. In this chapter, I explore and explode a number of all-too-common myths about America, Americans, and what we really think and believe.

So let's start with what should be an essential tool in the communication kit: the profile of an average American. Whether you deal with people on a day-to-day basis in any way, or if you just want to know where you personally stand versus the other three hundred million Americans, this up-to-date profile provides a vital examination of mainstream America. With this knowledge in hand, you'll steer clear of some of the most common linguistic pitfalls.

## THE AVERAGE AMERICAN: MEET JENNIFER SMITH[2]

In 1996, using a wealth of census data, statistical abstracts, and national surveys, I wrote an article profiling the average American. At the time, her name was Jennifer Smith. She was a thirty-two-year-old white female with a husband, a high school diploma, and a firm belief in God. During the weekday, Jennifer would leave her suburban St. Louis home (the closest major city to America's geographic population center), get into her American car, and drive to her sales and customer service job, anxious about her future but still striving to attain the American Dream.

Jennifer, more so than her husband, Michael, was concerned about crime and the economy. With little confidence in the federal government, she only voted once every four years. Closer to home, Jennifer was more of an optimist. She felt that her local community was headed in the right direction, and she believed that her personal condition would improve, albeit slowly.

More than a decade has passed since I completed that study, and while the technology available to us today has evolved significantly, the average

American has not. Those few things that have changed have done so in large part due to the country's streak of economic prosperity and an aging population. In short: Jennifer Smith (and that's still her name) is still alive and well, just a little bit older, working at a slightly better job, and making a bit more money.

And today, Jennifer, our ubiquitous white female of European (most likely German or Irish) descent, is married with two children and lives in a three-bedroom house in the suburbs that she and her husband, Michael, moved into about four or five years ago. The commute to and from work is longer than it used to be because her current home is farther from the city center, but she passes the time listening to the radio and making at least one cell phone call. She's now a full-time employee working five days a week, and her day-to-day responsibilities involve more interaction with computers than customers. Fortunately for the family, her weekly paycheck has increased considerably since she first entered the workforce, allowing them to take several extended weekend trips together and even a week-long summer vacation—but she still has barely $2,000 in savings in the bank.

Jennifer spends an hour less at work than her husband, Michael, but spends an hour more than John doing various household activities before and after she picks up the kids from school. Even though Michael makes the major expenditure decisions, Jennifer runs the family budget, clips the coupons, and does virtually all of the shopping. She's also responsible for the health care decisions, not just of their immediate family but for at least one of her parents—and one of his as well. During her extremely limited leisure time, Jennifer and Michael watch about 2.5 hours of television together per day. And as for her activity in the bedroom at night . . . she's not telling.

From the time Jennifer wakes up, until the time she goes to sleep, the life she leads today isn't much different than the life of the average American in 1990. What we *do* is virtually the same, it's just the *how* that has changed. In 1990, Jennifer had a VCR. Now it's a DVD player. Jennifer still subscribes to cable, but the twenty-something-inch TV in the family room in 1990 has grown to more than thirty inches today—and it's attached to a sound system.

But the biggest difference between the average American in 1990 and the average American today is the age. Back in 1990, the average Jennifer was 32.7 years old; now she's 36.4 years old. Jennifer's aging is indicative of an aging population, but it's not just that people are living longer. It's also a fact that the birthrate has not kept pace with the decrease in mortality. When Jennifer first entered into this world, her parents were at the leading edge of the baby boom generation and of the counterculture of the late 1960s—and smaller families were part of that rebellion. Today, her parents are roughly sixty years old and they can expect to live a full decade longer than *their* parents did. In fact, at least one of the Smith parents will live long enough to see their great-grandchildren born (and as a result, a whole new line of Hallmark cards will be created in nearby Kansas City, where Hallmark is headquartered).

So how do you apply this basic demographic, behavioral, and attitudinal information to the creation of words that work? Let's go back to the ten rules of effective communication.

*Simplicity* is important because the average American like Jennifer hasn't graduated from a four-year college.

*Brevity* is important because Jennifer or her husband don't have time to think about what you're saying. They need to be able to sort it out immediately.

*Credibility* is important because Jennifer Smith has been misinformed too many times to trust what products and politicians promise her.

*Consistency* is important because she won't hear you the first, second, or even third time you speak to her. You'll have to give your message again and again and again.

*Novelty* is important because you need to stand out. "Been there, done that" is Jennifer's creed. If you aren't different, you'll get lost. Say something that grabs her attention.

Sound (*alliteration*) is important in attracting her attention. She's already doing too many things at once. You need to break through the clutter.

*Aspiration* is important because you know that she has dreams for a better life. If she recognizes her dreams, sees your words in her dreams, she'll listen to you.

And *relevance* is important. The greater the impact you can demonstrate on her daily life, the more likely she is to pay attention to what you want to say.

All of the findings and assertions in this book are based on a scientific study of the population, with much of that derived from market research. So before I get to the specific myths of Americans, I feel the need to tell a story that most pollsters would probably keep secret. This, in essence, is the danger of using research to listen to real people, because sometimes they're actually not so real, and other times you *pray* they're not so real.

It was mid-summer in 1997 and New York Mayor Rudolph Giuliani was running for reelection. My firm was conducting a survey to see how the mayor was doing with his constituents. Now, in a typical political telephone poll, most questions are multiple choice, while a few are simple yes/no questions. But there is almost always a finite number of predetermined responses. However, a good survey often also includes one or two "open-ended" questions that give respondents the chance to say anything and everything on their minds. These responses are transcribed verbatim and can later be categorized—but they're often most interesting as impressionistic snapshots of what people are actually thinking—and how they articulate their thoughts.

In our New York City poll, we asked one of these open-ended questions: "If you had to name one positive accomplishment of Mayor Giuliani's first term in office, what would it be?"

A plurality of respondents cited the reduction in crime, followed by those who said the drop in welfare recipients. A handful mentioned Giuliani's battles with the bureaucracy and a few others addressed the cleanliness of the city. But there was one response that stood head and shoulders above the rest. Here it is, verbatim: *"When the chips were down, Mayor Giuliani stood up to the EPA and let the Ghostbusters do their job. He saved the city from Zul, and I really liked that about him."*[2]

Just some guy with an offbeat sense of humor? Perhaps. On the other hand, in a city the size of New York (or a country the size of the United States), the odds are pretty strong that there's *somebody* so confused and ill-informed that he'll give the real mayor of New York credit for the no-nonsense leadership shown by a fictional mayor in a *Ghostbusters* movie. As the lyrics in the movie theme song ask, "Who you gonna call?" In a telephone survey, you never know.

And so we finally arrive at the first of the *Ten Great Myths About Americans*.

## MYTH: AMERICANS ARE EDUCATED

False.

First, in the formal sense, fewer than half of us have graduated from college. In fact, only 29 percent of adults in the United States over the age of forty-five have a bachelor's degree or higher, and only 27 percent of adults over the age of twenty-five are college educated.[4]

And very, very few of those who did graduate from college have a "liberal education" in any traditional sense. Most higher education in the United States these days has taken on a distinctly vocational bent. Core curricula and "Great Books" programs have been abandoned most everywhere, even in the Ivy League and other high caliber institutions.

A warning to parents who are sending their kids to the Ivy League: You may want to skip this next paragraph. It cost a remarkable $41,675 in tuition, room, board, and fees to attend Harvard for just one year in 2006.[5] And yet Harvard's description of its own program of undergraduate study reveals a remarkably fuzzy, unfocused approach:

> *The Core differs from other programs of general education. It does not define intellectual breadth as the mastery of a set of Great Books, or the digestion of a specific quantum of information, or the surveying of current knowledge in certain fields. Rather, the program seeks to introduce students to the major approaches to knowledge in areas that the faculty considers indispensable to undergraduate education."* [Italics in original.][6]

Is it any wonder that even our best students have so little awareness of current events or key moments in American history, when even the premier institution of higher learning doesn't teach them, and actually finds the learning of "current knowledge" to be a lower priority than "approaches to knowledge." Almost no one learns Greek or Latin anymore—and few even read the ancient classics in translation. The classics are ignored. It's now actually possible to graduate from Harvard without ever having taken a course in American history or read a word of Shakespeare or studied Plato's *Republic*.[7] Incredible.

The upshot, in business and in political communications, is that complexity or intricacy of any degree *almost always fails*.

Most of us get our knowledge of history, politics, philosophy, sociology, economics, and so many other fields from some aspect of pop culture—

primarily TV and the movies. For those younger than age thirty, knowledge of politics comes from Leno, Letterman, and Jon Stewart. Many of us get our understanding of the legal system from Judge Judy and the second half-hour of *Law & Order.* Our perceptions of the American health care system are shaped by *Grey's Anatomy, House,* and the venerable *ER.* Our ideas of law enforcement come from the *CSI* franchise or the first half hour of *Law & Order.* (The good news: There were three *CSIs* and three *Law & Orders* at the time this passage was written.)

Case in point: Jay Leno's weekly "Jay Walking" segment on *The Tonight Show.* In this segment, he makes a joke out of how truly ignorant the "man on the street" is about American history and current events. The people Jay interviews are unable to answer basic questions such as "Who is the vice president?" "Which country was America fighting in the Revolutionary War?" and "How many United States Senators are there?" He broadcasts the most egregious examples, to be sure. Still, the people he finds aren't so different from the rest of us. The syndicated game show *Street Smarts* explores the same idea. From Beavis and Butt-Head in the 1990s to Bart Simpson, intelligence is mocked and ignorance is celebrated.

The problem begins in our elementary schools and high schools. My firm surveyed American teenagers aged thirteen through seventeen on their knowledge of U.S. history. Embarrassingly, in the words of singer Sam Cooke, they really "don't know much about history . . ."

- Only 23 percent of American teenagers know that there are one hundred U.S. Senators.
- Only 40 percent know that the first three words of the Constitution are "We the People."
- Twenty-four percent cannot name even *one* of the three branches of government. Only 42 percent of teens can name all three.
- Fewer than 10 percent know that the Supreme Court case that found separate but equal treatment of blacks and whites in public schools unconstitutional was *Brown v. Board of Education.*
- Only 25 percent know even one provision of the Fifth Amendment.
- Only 26 percent know that the Constitution was written in Philadelphia.[8]

And as bad as kids are with simple historic facts, their parents aren't much better. On election night in 2004, many *adult voters* found themselves woefully uninformed. Ten percent of voters—VOTERS—didn't know that the vice president for the past four years was Dick Cheney. Twelve percent didn't know that John Kerry's running mate was John Edwards. As for what they *did* know—only 18 percent could name the majority leader of the U.S. Senate (Bill Frist). These were the names of important people that had been in the news daily for months or, in some cases, years, and yet they didn't penetrate. Remember, this was not a poll of teenagers or American adults as a whole—these were *voters* on *election night*.[9]

When he left the White House in 1989, Ronald Reagan used his farewell address to the nation to warn Americans about the dangers of forgetting our history and heritage:

> Those of us who are over thirty-five or so years of age grew up in a different America. We were taught, very directly, what it means to be an American. And we absorbed, almost in the air, a love of country and an appreciation of its institutions. If you didn't get these things from your family you got them from the neighborhood, from the father down the street who fought in Korea or the family who lost someone at Anzio. Or you could get a sense of patriotism from school. And if all else failed you could get a sense of patriotism from the popular culture. The movies celebrated democratic values and implicitly reinforced the idea that America was special. . . . We've got to teach history based not on what's in fashion but what's important.[10]

The United States may not have some sinister Ministry of Truth that is *literally* erasing the past by dropping the things we used to know down the "memory hole" as in Orwell's *1984,* but if we as a people voluntarily forget our history, the effect is likely to be much the same.

Of course, our lack of knowledge isn't limited to history, politics, or public affairs. It extends to economics and finance, and even to specific topics of personal importance like disaster preparedness. In 2003, I conducted a survey for America Prepared, an organization founded by Steven Brill, a successful publisher and entrepreneur, in cooperation with the Department of Homeland Security, to educate people about civil defense in the aftermath of September 11.[11] As my poll demonstrated, Brill's organization had a lot of teaching to do.

Only 28 percent of Americans eighteen and older were able to answer correctly at least three of six questions related to the basics of emergency preparedness. For example, nearly half thought, incorrectly, that any disease that can become an epidemic is contagious. In fact, many diseases that could be used in a terrorist attack, such as anthrax, botulism, and salmonella, are *not* contagious. And 82 percent did not know that while it is always advisable to try to cover your nose and mouth with a dust mask or T-shirt in the event of a biological attack, a radiological attack, or any kind of explosion, it does *not* make sense to take the time to do so after a chemical attack.

Americans' lack of education also extends to the meanings of many words. After World War II, safety officials worried that people would erroneously think that the word *inflammable* meant "*un*-flammable" or "fireproof." So they campaigned for the use of *flammable* instead, a word that had been out of fashion for decades. These days, you rarely hear the word *inflammable* any more.[12] Once again, it all comes back to understanding the listener's *context*.

## MYTH: AMERICANS READ

False.

In all my years of conducting polls, dial sessions, and focus groups, I've found again and again that nobody reads.

Take newspapers. If their current decline in readership continues along the recent trend lines, the last daily newspaper reader in America will disappear in October 2044, according to University of North Carolina Professor Philip Meyer.[13] Consider the following:

- Home subscriptions are way down. In 1985, 67 percent of households subscribed to one or more newspapers. By 2001, only 43 percent of households received a newspaper. Home subscriptions dropped by a third in less than twenty years—and that accounts for the bankruptcy of dozens of newspapers all across the country.[14]
- There's a generational component at play. Back in 1985, almost two-thirds of twenty-five-to-thirty-five-year-olds said they had recently bought a newspaper; by 2005, only 37 percent of people in that age group read at least one newspaper a week.[15]
- The trend continues. In 1998, over 58 percent of adult Americans read a newspaper on an average weekday. Over a period of seven

years, that number has fallen to 51 percent. By the time you read this book, if you are the "average American," you will not be reading a newspaper on a daily basis.[16]

Now, it's true that some of the drop in circulation is from people getting their news online rather than in paper format. According to Nielsen//NetRatings, there were 39 million unique visitors to online newspaper Web sites in October 2005, with an annual growth rate of 11 percent. Among the online population who read a newspaper, an overwhelming 71 percent still prefer the print edition, but a sizeable and growing 22 percent choose the online version and 7 percent divide their time equally between the two sources.[17] So the precipitous collapse in newspaper readership is not as staggering as the print statistics would suggest. But that doesn't negate the fact that fewer people are reading their news with each successive year.

Magazine readership has also dropped precipitously. Only one in four Americans say they read a magazine yesterday, in 2005, versus one in three in 1994.[18] Even book readership has dropped 10 percent since 1982.[19] True, we may never have been a nation of voracious readers. But for many of us who once read a great deal, that experience has now been supplanted by television and the entertainment components of the Web; we're content to get our news and information in short bites from either the increasingly slender talking box or the silent screen on our desk.

There is one compelling counter-example, however: e-mail and the Internet. Over the past ten years or so, e-mail has done a great deal to raise the importance of the written word—even if typos, misspellings, and acronyms like LOL (laughing out loud) have replaced dramatic prose. Most professionals write and respond to dozens and sometimes hundreds of e-mails every day. Teenagers engage in endless instant message (IM) conversations and "text" each other all day long on their cell phones. BlackBerries and Treos will eventually become as ubiquitous as note cards and envelopes were a century ago.

But that in itself poses other problems. Students—and some of my own staff—have proven incapable of switching back and forth between IMing/texting their friends and writing something more formal, such as a paper for class or the first draft of a memo for my clients. This casual abbreviated language is no more effective or convincing than the political use of acronyms. It will creep into formal language if teachers and businesses aren't sufficiently strict about the rules and articulation of language. Despite all of its graphic elements and audio bells and whistles, the Internet is primarily a reading medium that encourages brevity, but often of the wrong sort. So there is hope for the written word; it's just that the future may be written in html. LOL.

| TEXT/INSTANT MESSAGE (IM) ABBREVIATIONS AND TRANSLATIONS ||
|---|---|
| **TEXT ABBREVIATION** | **TRANSLATION** |
| ATM | At the moment |
| BBL | Be back later |
| BFF | Best friends forever |
| BRB | Be right back |
| CYA | See you [later] |
| GR8 | Great |
| IM | Instant message |
| JK | Just kidding |
| LOL | Laughing out loud |
| MYOB | Mind your own business |
| NP | No problem |
| OMG | Oh my God |
| OTL | Out to lunch |
| PPL | People |
| PW | Parents watching |
| TAFN | That's all for now |
| TBD | To be determined |
| TTYL/TTYS | Talk to you later/soon |
| TNX | Thanks |
| TMI | Too much information |
| WB | Welcome back |
| WTG | Way to go |

Among those who still do read, layout matters almost as much as content. The fewer words on the page, the more likely they are to be read (even President Bush subscribes to this practice). And when it comes to newspaper advertising, often the only content consumed is at the very beginning and the very end. Unless something catches the eye or the imagination, everything else is likely to be skipped by a great many readers.

It is an interesting phenomenon to watch television audiences at live studio tapings in Hollywood or New York. Those older than fifty will inevitably watch the actual performance, even if the actors are somewhat far away and partially obscured by television cameras or lighting. But those younger than forty will watch the performance through the television monitors, even when the monitors are high above them and the actors nearby. Why? Because for younger audiences, it's what comes through the television itself, not the performance, that defines the meaning of *live*. You can see this at sporting events as well. Younger fans watch the action on the "jumbotron" monitor rather than focusing on the game itself.

## MYTH: AMERICAN WOMEN ALL RESPOND TO MESSAGES LIKE . . . WOMEN

False.

It is true that there are real differences in men's and women's policy priorities, and one great ideological divide: Women typically put more faith in government than men, so they are less hostile toward Washington.

Once you get beyond this one generalization, though, women are as different from one another as they are from men. Whether you are a Republican or a Democrat, a CEO or a salesperson, it's a profound mistake to treat women as a single, monolithic bloc. It should be so obvious as to go without saying that not all women are alike, but you'd be hard-pressed to find political strategists who recognize it and actually act on it.

*Lifestyle relevancy* is an important linguistic tool in creating language for women. Using several different statistical testing techniques, my firm determined the two demographic characteristics that best predict how a woman is likely to vote: family status and employment status.

Age, education, and income—the traditional demographic targets for women—are less important in determining how to speak and appeal to women than knowing whether they have kids at home and whether they work full-time outside the house. A forty-two-year-old stay-at-home mom is more likely to respond to the same language that appeals to a twenty-eight-year-old stay-at-home mom than to the language of a forty-two-year-old career woman without children.

Men are exactly the opposite. Family status and career barely matter, while age, income, and education matter considerably. Conversely, men don't have as wide a scale of opinions. A thirty-year-old man is far more likely to share attitudes and opinions with a fifty-year-old man than are two women with the same age spread.

Women are also much more fascinating to study as they move through life. Men's political and ideological opinions tend to change far less as they get older than their female counterparts'. An unmarried working woman in her twenties rarely has the same issue agenda, approach to life, consumption patterns, or behavioral tastes as a married woman in her forties who stays home to raise her children, or a woman in her late sixties who has just been widowed.

Politically and statistically, we know that younger women lean heavily toward the Democrats, while older women split their votes more evenly between the two parties. We also know that married women over thirty-five with children at home slightly favor the GOP, while single women, including those who are divorced or widowed, are solidly in the Democratic fold.

These demographic differences lead to behavioral differences as well. Women are making far more consumer decisions than ever before. In fact, the typical woman tends to make decisions not only for herself, but also for the man in her life, her parents (and if applicable, her husbands' parents), and, naturally, her children. That has important linguistic implications for the selling of both products and politicians. From deciding which house to buy, to choosing the location of the family's next vacation, to selecting the brand of beer in the fridge for her husband, women are making choices that affect far more people than just themselves. Women may still face a glass ceiling in the workplace, but they have more control over the family wallet than their male counterparts do.

## MYTH: AMERICANS DIVIDE NEATLY AND ACCURATELY INTO URBAN, SUBURBAN, AND RURAL POPULATIONS

False.

Over the past five years or so, we've seen the emergence of a fourth, wholly new category: affluent homeowners with growing bank accounts, growing families, bigger big-screen TVs, and a bigger outlook on life. They are moving far away from the country's urban areas, far away even from the conveniences of the suburbs. They come looking for quiet communities and open spaces. Suburbia was created by those who wanted to get away from the modern hassles of the twentieth-century city. Today, many people are looking to flee the modern hassles of twenty-first-century suburban life—the congestion and the sprawl of it all. They are sacrificing the ease of close-in conditions in favor of younger, slower communities, for the purpose of pursuing a version of the American Dream that more closely resembles the life of Ward and June Cleaver in what the suburbs used to be, rather than Al and Peg Bundy's suburban life today.

Welcome to *exurbia,* a marketer's dream. New homes, manicured lawns, smart people, high discretionary incomes, and all the trappings of upwardly mobile families. Exurbia is such a new phenomenon that its residents aren't yet fully aware of their own existence as a unique demographic group with a language all its own. If you're reading this book and you live in a housing development that is twenty to forty miles away from a city center and was built within the past twenty years—you too may be a resident of exurbia.

Peace and quiet . . . open spaces . . . a slower, more old-fashioned pace—these are the values to emphasize when communicating to exurban neighborhoods. Their communities have the look and the feel of a Pepperidge Farms cookie commercial from the 1970s or a Smuckers Jam commercial from the eighties. Exurban dwellers prefer the familiar to the foreign. They want serenity and security, not risks or revelations. To them, a Hallmark card is not a *"moment,"* it's a way of life.

Exurbia is small town, Main Street USA, even if it's not authentic and was only manufactured to look that way. It is neither rural nor suburban. Think of the exodus to the exurbs as a "return to normalcy"—upwardly mobile young families projecting themselves forward . . . into the past. They are not trying to live their parents' lives; they are trying to live their grandparents' lives. Their communities, their values, and their aspirations recall an older, idealized age that may never have really existed for most people outside of Norman Rockwell paintings and Frank Capra movies. Not since the 1950s has there been such a significant geographic revolution. More than anything else, it is a movement that started as a state of mind, but has gradually transformed into a true territorial reality.

Before you can reach out and communicate to exurbia, you have to know exactly what it is and where you can find it. Newer cities like Atlanta, Dallas, Denver, and older urban areas like Washington, D.C., and Chicago have burgeoning exurban communities. But exurbia does not exist everywhere in America. Urban areas in the Deep South are too small to yield exurban communities, and the Plains states are peppered with old small towns rather than new exurban communities. New York and Los Angeles, the two most populated metropolitan areas in America, are so populated and developed for miles beyond their borders that none of the surrounding communities meet the definition. They have all the trappings of traditional suburbs along with many of the curses of urban life.

There's a linguistic component to the exurban phenomenon. The word *sprawl* is a relatively new and super-negative way of describing urban development that has bled into suburban life. It's not a subjective term whose meaning is in the eyes of the beholder or the ears of the listener; everyone knows exactly what *sprawl* means—and it is always ugly. Like *strip mall, strip mining,* and *clear cutting, sprawl* is a word that developers themselves came up with—and they have regretted it ever since. It's the most deadly word—and weapon—in the arsenal of those who oppose construction. The surest way to kill a new development project is to attach the label *sprawl* to it. And people determined to get away from sprawl have found a haven in the aptly named *"smart growth"* communities of exurbia.

To be sure, exurbia is only available to those willing to give up a certain amount of convenience and who have the financial resources to afford to live there. For that reason, exurbanites share consistent demographic characteristics—starting with demographic homogeneity. When you've seen one exurbanite, you've seen them all. City dwellers come in all shapes, sizes, colors, ethnicities, accents, and the like. Traditional suburbanites may not exactly represent the Rainbow Coalition, but the difference in demographics between neighborhoods can still be rather stark.

Not so in exurbia. Most everyone is white, most everyone has a kid or two at home, and most everyone thinks and votes alike. Nowhere in

America are you more likely to see deep green, manicured lawns lined with Republican campaign signs and bumper stickers on their SUVs and BMWs. Ask a resident of exurbia and he'll tell you how diverse his neighborhood is. But it's not. To exurbanites, diversity means a family with a dog living side by side with a family that has a cat.

Exurbia is defined by the traditional American family. More than three-quarters (78 percent) of exurbanites live in a single-family home—far more than their urban and suburban cousins. And in a higher percentage of those homes than anywhere else, the husband commutes to work while the wife stays home. It's almost Ozzie and Harriet.

Pets also matter. Don't laugh. Pets are an important illustration of how exurbanites view their homes, their families, and their lives. Exurbanites think not in terms of individuals, but of the family—and their pets are as much a part of their families as the kids. In fact, in exurban focus groups I conducted across the country, as many people said they moved to more open places for their dogs as for their children.

Economically, exurbanites may not all be rich, but very few of them are poor. They spend and consume at or above the level of those with slightly higher incomes who live closer to urban areas. Their homes truly are their castles—and they spend as much time there as they possibly can. They have enough money to choose where to live, and this mind-set carries over into their shopping habits. If they will drive the extra distance to live where they want, they will go the extra mile for the right shopping experience as well. Exurbanites will respond to old-fashioned, even corny sentiments such as, *"Home is where the heart is,"* and *"There's no place like home."* Retailers will do well to understand the centrality of their homes in their lives. (Politically, exurbanites hate property taxes more than any other simply because, to them, it truly is a tax on the American Dream, and because their larger property means a bigger tax bill.) Therefore, it should not be surprising that they will stretch their housing dollars to get the extra square feet of lawn space, and a larger kitchen, and a basement, and a guest room, etc.

Being geographically twice removed from the urban center has led to a psychological break as well. Exurbanites turn inward, to their own communities, rather than outward, toward the city. That intellectual and emotional separation is important. While many suburbanites live to work, exurbanites work to live. They are willing to sacrifice components of their employment life, including taking on "the commute from hell," to gain freedom and control in the other spheres of their lives.

Time *is* money to exurbanites. How ironic that people willing to spend hours in their cars each week are the group that most values time over money. Their commute is just one of the sacrifices they are willing to make during the week to get the quality time they want at nights and on weekends. In fact, that commute provides the underlying structure of their daily lives. They are a prime audience for car companies, music companies, college courses on CD, newer ventures such as satellite radio, and anything else that can be accomplished in a car and make their commutes more productive and pleasant. This is a major chunk of their lives that we're talking about. Show them that their arduous commutes are not merely a sacrifice for their homes and families, the price necessary to live in exurbia—that they can also be opportunities for learning, self-improvement, personal enrichment, and entertainment.

Exurbanites who commute to work each day do not read the morning paper, often because they leave long before it even arrives. They get their news from the radio in the morning, the Internet during the day, and from television at night. In any other community, this socioeconomic strata would form the core of newspaper readership, but in giving up urban or suburban life, they also gave up their newspapers. Half of exurbanites don't subscribe to a daily newspaper at home or at work anymore—preferring instead the weekly community newspaper. What matters to them is what is happening where they live, not in the cities where they work. They want news about local schools, local events, local youth sports, local development, local crime, the weather—and coupons.

Exurbanites "think rural" but "act suburban." They love exurbia's closeness to nature and lack of noise pollution. They think of their current living conditions as, in their own words, a "refuge," and an "escape" from the suburbs. Yet they have not given up their suburban lifestyle of conspicuous consumption. Their TVs are really big, their sound systems are really loud, and their gadgets are cutting-edge high-tech. In many respects, they are the ideal consumers. But to get their exurban money, it's essential for companies to understand their suburban minds. At times, exurbanites may look and sound downright rural, yet they live like suburbanites, with the same toys (only bigger) and disposable income (only more).

Slogans and taglines like *"American made," "tried and tested"* and *"no surprises"* appeal to this segment. The phrase *"new and improved"* is not necessarily better in the minds of exurbanites. Product pedigree, legacy, and dependability are much more important. If you want to sell to them, make life easy for them. *"Hassle-free"* genuinely means something to these people. They value being able to push a single button on their television remotes to order the movie of their choice, or being able to park right by a mall entrance without having to stop and pay when they leave. They place a premium on service, which to them means speed, accuracy, and dependability.

Politically, exurbia is a Republican bastion. Overall, exurbia gave Bush a fifteen-point margin over Kerry—among the biggest spreads of any demographic, geographic, or psychographic subgroup. But these Bush voters were not the ones you heard a lot about; they are fiscal conservatives who are socially moderate or even progressive, with a commitment to family but not necessarily to so-called "family values" as we commonly define them.

And what of the suburban America that exurbanites left behind? The subtle political left turn that the suburbs are making is not so much a turn as it is a change of drivers. In other words, the suburbs are not becoming more liberal because residents are shifting their ideology to the left, but because conservative voters are fleeing for, quite literally, greener pastures. Remember the "white flight" to the suburbs in the 1960s and 1970s? What we are witnessing is a twenty-first-century "right flight" to the exurbs, a flight that is as much ideological as it is emotional.

## MYTH: AMERICAN CONSUMERS RESPOND WELL
## TO PATRIOTIC MESSAGES

Wrong, sort of. It's American *pride* that sells products. Pride in American workmanship and in "Made in the USA" labels are far more appealing to a broad swath of the public than other more direct or flamboyant evocations of patriotism.

There is an essential perceptual difference between "American patriotism" and "American pride." To some, *patriotism* connotes arrogant, obnoxious, xenophobic, red-white-and-blue, flag-waving, America-can-do-no-wrong jingoism. They see it as too in-your-face, over-the-top, and disrespectful of other nations and other cultures. Those most likely to hold these views are people younger than thirty, ideological liberals, blacks and non-Cuban Latinos, and residents from the Boston to Washington, D.C., Northeast corridor and the Seattle to Los Angeles Pacific

Coast corridor. Conversely, overtly patriotic commercial messages res-
onate most with people older than fifty, self-described conservatives,
whites from Southern, Midwestern, and Western states, and people who
drink a lot of beer. Seriously.

American *pride,* on the other hand, has a far more universal appeal. In
fact, sales messages involving the word *pride* beat straightforward appeals to *patriotism* by better than two to one.[20] It's one thing for a president to evoke patriotism in a speech about our young men and women
in uniform or institutions like NASA and the NIH (National Institutes
of Health) that are at the cutting edge of science, medicine, or
technology—but it's something else entirely for a for-profit company to
drape itself in the flag in an effort to sell mouthwash or spark plugs to
people in their twenties and thirties who may be proud to be Americans,
but are not always proud of everything America does. To younger consumers, American *"patriotism"* represents blind acceptance of the actions and behavior of the country—but American *"pride"* is a celebration
of its people. Communicators who don't distinguish between American
patriotism and American pride risk alienating a large and important segment of the population.

That's not to say that most Americans don't consider themselves patriotic. They do. On a scale of zero to ten, two-thirds of Americans
would rate their patriotism at a seven or more. However, the intensity of
patriotism varies greatly depending upon a variety of demographic and
geographic factors. The challenge for marketers is that patriotic appeals
have the least pull with the most important consumers: America's youth.
For example, when given the choice, fewer than half of the twenty-
something generation say they would buy a more expensive American
product, while a majority would pick a cheaper import (one reason why
the all-American Wal-Mart actually gets the vast majority of the products it sells from Asia). Part of that preference for the cheaper foreign
product is due to a greater price sensitivity among the young, but a
lower intensity of "America First" feeling among twenty-somethings is
also a factor.[21]

## MYTH: RETRO SELLS PRODUCTS AND POLITICIANS

Hardly a month goes by when some product that's been around for decades doesn't decide to dig up an old commercial, slogan, or tagline from

way, way back. And hardly another month passes before they realize that what sounded good in the pitch room did not play well in the living room. Billy Joel had it right when he sang that "the good old days weren't always good." Retro and nostalgia may attract attention, and people may have a longing for the past, but they won't pay for products from the 1950s or 1970s or 1990s when they can get a piece of the twenty-first century.

The political world is no different. Bob Dole learned this the hard way in 1996 when Jay Leno suggested that his campaign slogan was "Building a Bridge . . . to the sixteenth century" because of his focus on the World War II generation and days (and values) gone by. There's an important language lesson that is uniquely American: Always look forward, not back. History goes in cycles, and everything old is eventually made new again. If you want to propose an old idea, don't acknowledge that you're stealing from the past. Present it as something fresh: renewing a concept and revitalizing it.

## MYTH: AMERICANS VOTE ACCORDING TO A CANDIDATE'S STANDS ON THE ISSUES

Not true. The news media naturally tend to place great importance on policy prescriptions and legislative proposals because they are concrete, specific, and substantive. What ends up in the headlines are the sound bites and the horse race, but reporter questioning is primarily focused on what the candidate believes rather than who the candidate is. The unspoken reality, though, is that the vast majority of Americans don't vote based on particular issues at all. The fabled issue voter is a rare specimen indeed, and "agrees with me on the issues" is inevitably one of the least important candidate attributes in determining public support.

Americans, by and large, decide who to vote for based on the candidates' *attributes*—personality, image, authenticity, vibe. The media is still in denial about this, and every time I have advanced the notion at press events that issues don't matter that much, the print reporters who cover politics rush to defend a more intellectual perception of what elections are all about. To them, accepting the fact that image matters more than policy would be accepting the fact that what people see through their televisions matters more than what they read in the newspaper.

The reason why issues and ideology are less significant is simply that most Americans don't know the substance behind the issues, and even though we seem on the surface to be a divided nation, most Americans are not intensely ideological. Another reason is that we don't place a high priority on perceived intelligence. Ronald Reagan and George W. Bush were not considered intellectual giants, and they had substantial double-digit deficits against their opponents in public perceptions of their relative intelligence, but they still won twice on election day. In fact, Americans would rather have a candidate with genuine common sense as their leader than almost any other attribute—including brains.*

## MYTH: AMERICANS ARE HAPPY

No we're not—not by a long shot. In fact, with each election season, the media seems to anoint a particular group as emblematic of mounting discontent, the key to an accurate understanding of what's going on in America. In the late 1960s, it was the "silent majority." Then in the 1970s it was the "forgotten middle class." In the eighties it was the "angry white males," replaced by "Perovians" (followers of Ross Perot) in the early 1990s, "soccer moms" later in the decade, and "security moms" and "NASCAR dads" in 2004.

During the past five years, a new attitude and a segment of American society has emerged—the *"Fed-Ups"*—along with a brand-new lexicon. In the past, the discontented constituted merely a slice of the population. Today, the Fed-Ups are nearing a majority of the population. In the past, the unifying emotion was anxiety. Today, it is frustration. In the past, the language expressed a mixture of fear and hope. Today, the lexicon is stark, dark, and bitter.

It doesn't matter what the issue is, the members of this group are fed up. Younger fed-ups idolize Howard Stern because he's uncontrollable and rips apart the establishment. Older fed-ups identify with Rush Limbaugh, Bill O'Reilly, and anyone else with a cranky attitude. These are the heirs of the Perot voters, the people who made Jesse Ventura the governor of Minnesota and voted in Arnold Schwarzenegger in California.

---

*In an *Economist* post-election poll, registered voters reported that they would rather have a cup of coffee or a beer with Bush than Kerry by a healthy 56 percent to 44 percent margin.

John McCain appeals to them. So does Rudy Giuliani. They're not ideo-logical. They just want their country to work again.

They are fed up with illegal immigration and the state of the war on terrorism. They tend to be nationalistic—you could even call them "America Firsters."

They are fed up with the loss of jobs to companies overseas—and, indeed, with free trade in general.

They are fed up with corporate America and with astronomical CEO salaries that seem to bear no relation whatsoever to the performance of their companies.

Fed up with traffic, congestion, and sitting forever to make a left turn at a crowded intersection.

Fed up with the decline of American culture—from sleazy television (that some do watch) to vulgar and out-of-control celebrities—including those they follow closely.

Fed up with the whole Hollywood mentality.

Fed up with the way they feel their kids' childhoods are being mort-gaged, or leveraged, or even outright stolen.

Fed up with the promises the federal government has made and broken.

Fed up with politicians and politics, lobbyists and special interest groups.

Fed up with oral sex in the eighth grade (and in the Oval Office!).

They are fed up with other countries, particularly our so-called allies France and Germany, and with what they regard as a toothless and anti-American United Nations. They are not swayed by idealistic arguments about spreading democracy and freedom or ending tyranny elsewhere in the world. They want to bomb the enemy back to the Stone Age and then come home to their gated communities.

The *"new and improved"* corporate lexicon doesn't appeal to them, and the political approach of promising to do things *"better"* won't work, either. They didn't like the original to begin with—and they don't want a Band-Aid for what they see as a gaping hole in American society.

Fed up, fed up, fed up.

## MYTH: AMERICANS PREFER BIG ORGANIZATIONS

Wrong. In fact, Americans distrust anything big. Many Americans re-sent large corporations and feel entitled to strike back at them in any way they can. From consumer boycotts to the slash-and-burn Web sites, corporations are faced with more hostility than ever, more ways for that anger to be expressed, and a greater need to communicate what they do and how they do it well.

The music industry is one of the greatest victims of consumer anger. Much of the illegal music downloading that takes places isn't done just because the music is free but rather because stealing music costs "the suits" money. In research we did for the entertainment industry, it became clear that music fans resent company executives for making too much money for themselves, too much profit for the corporations, and pampering and overpaying the "talent," and the way they express this anger is to download illegally to punish the industry. The same holds true for the piracy of movies, software, and other products.

Younger Americans are also motivated to steal music and movies precisely because they're told they can't or shouldn't. The entertainment industry made things worse initially by ignoring the problem and then responding ineffectively with words that certainly didn't work—not to mention the whole idea of prosecuting twelve-year-olds. The most egregious example was the seventy-two-second ad created by 20th Century Fox in 2003 to be shown in theaters across the country featuring Ben Affleck, who had recently come off a string of movie flops and an on-again, off-again laughable romp with actress Jennifer Lopez. The purpose of the ad, according to the Fox press release, was "to put a human face on the effects of piracy" and that "piracy costs real people real jobs." Fox executives refused to test the ad before delivering it to movie theaters. And not surprisingly, it was met with an outpouring of derision and flying popcorn by movie audiences offended that a "talentless actor would ask us to pay for movies that suck when he makes $20 million a film." (Their words, not mine.) Fox quickly had to pull the ad when they realized it was actually triggering the very behavior they sought to prevent. Apparently they were unaware of the mantra, *It's not what you say but what people hear that matters.*

Our nation's historically deep rooted anti-big, anti-authoritarian streak is alive and well in the MySpace generation of consumers. Simply put, Americans hate hearing the word *no*. That simple, two-letter word carries more meaning than anything else in the English language. As children, it was the word we dreaded most, and as ours increasingly becomes a society of perpetual adolescents, it's no surprise that, at any age, we don't take well to being told what we cannot do.

Capital One shrewdly picked up on this anti-no sentiment and made it the centerpiece of a series of TV commercials starring David Spade. The ads, a takeoff on a character Spade played in the 1990s on *Saturday Night Live,* may be annoying and juvenile, but they have fixed the association between the word *no* and all the competitors to Capital One in viewers' minds. Capital One *owns* the antithesis of the word *no*—and if we're annoyed by hearing David Spade repeat it again and again in those ads, so much the better—we'll be more likely to consider doing business with Capital One so that we *don't* have to hear it from the other credit card suppliers. That's effective communication.

But not all attributes of a large institution are necessarily rejected. In fact, of all the taglines lines we have tested for *Fortune* 500 companies over the past few years, none has done better than *"Big enough to deliver; small enough to care"* created for a cell phone provider in 2005. (Note to CEOs: The slogan is still available, and I guarantee it will work for you if you can deliver the promise.) Attentive and personal customer service is paramount in today's highly sought-after "hassle-free" lifestyle. There is a definite competitive advantage not just to *owning* customer service but also being large enough to deliver it.

For the rapidly merging cell phone companies, it means becoming *"a communications company that actually communicates,"* a tagline that no one has picked up yet. Again, another opportunity just waiting for a smart CEO.

For the large airlines it's about *"fly the friendly skies,"* a tagline United dropped years ago but which applies today, even when the wait at the metal detector seems forever and the flight is overbooked and understaffed—which also defines United.

And most importantly, for automotive companies at least, it's a simple five-word pledge: *"We stand behind our cars."* Yes, Americans want reliable, dependable cars, but when things go wrong, as they inevitably do, the automaker that articulates that five-word commitment and then delivers on the promise will earn a higher level of customer loyalty—no matter what their size.

## MYTH: AMERICANS HAVE FINALLY GOTTEN OVER 9/11

Unfortunately, wrong. September 11, 2001, changed everything. It rocked our confidence, undermined our beliefs, changed our expectations, and altered the language landscape forever. FOREVER.

For a time in the days and weeks following 9/11, Americans forgot about or relinquished the drive for the more material aspects of life in favor of the more spiritual—particularly in regard to faith and family. In speeches I delivered across the country, I would ask the audience whether they were less focused on their work life and spending more time with their families and at church, synagogue, or mosque. The answer was inevitably yes.

However, starting just after the first-year anniversary of the attacks, things began to change, and the real impact of 9/11 began to unfold. Thanks to the televised images of the Twin Towers' collapse that we all saw again and again and again and again, it was truly the first nationally shared experience of the twenty-first century. It wasn't simply New York and Washington, D.C., that were attacked. We all were. Watching scores of funerals, of brave police officers and fire fighters laid to rest, turned an entire country into mourners. We grieved together, and in our sorrow we were truly a united people.

But a more insidious emotion was also lurking just underneath the surface—the shared loss of national confidence. In a sense we were mourning the end of our collective security—that we would never again feel confident and protected because an ocean separated us from those who would do us harm. An anxiety began to take hold, the old habits of division began to return, and the unity of purpose and spirit began to dissipate. And the old-fashioned chest-pounding American bravado that had worked before simply stopped working now.

First, the United States went into Afghanistan to get the mastermind of 9/11, Osama bin Laden—and couldn't. A cave-dweller in a backward land was able to elude the most powerful military force the world has ever known. At the time, President Bush's "We'll smoke him out" Texas tough talk sat well, but as the weeks and months passed, a certain anxiety came to replace that bravado—at least among the public.

Then the United States went in to topple Saddam Hussein, but after the first dramatic blush of success, it became apparent that while some Iraqis supported our efforts, we were not to be "greeted as liberators" as Vice President Cheney had promised. Nor was the insurgency in Iraq in its "last throes" as both Cheney and Defense Secretary Donald Rumsfeld asserted in the summer of 2005.

Though the intensity of the personal feelings we felt in the months after 9/11 has diminished, all of us remain forever changed. The long-term consequences of the terrorist attacks are now much clearer. We no longer live in a country where we can take our personal security for granted. We now board planes with a wary eye toward the passenger sitting next to us, and we look up at the planes flying overhead and think back to That Day when the dream of human flight became the nightmare of human missiles of destruction.


If, as I've been arguing, it's not what you say that matters, but what they hear, then understanding the nature of your audience becomes vitally important. You can't anticipate what an audience is going to hear if you don't know who they are. And, unfortunately, many communicators don't. In this chapter, we've spent some time exploding some prevalent myths about who Americans really are. Yet this is only part of the challenge. In the next chapter, we'll take a look at the emotional side of Americans—their fears, their hopes, their dreams—as it is reflected in the political language they like to hear.

# X

## *What We REALLY Care About*

*"Advertising is the art of convincing people to spend money they don't have for something they don't need."*
— WILL ROGERS

Don't call Anthony "Tony" Robbins a motivational speaker. Sure, he created the self-help industry and has "motivated" more people in his three decades than anyone else in his field, but he hates that label with the same kind of intense passion with which he embraces life. What you see in his infomercials is exactly who he is, what he represents, and the product he sells. Whether he's speaking to 20,000 people in an arena or sitting behind a one-way mirror watching would-be consumers react to his message, there is a sense of passion to everything he says and does. Passion for understanding. Passion for communication. Passion for success. In my two decades of moderating focus groups, this was the first and only time where the real action was happening behind the focus group mirror, not in front.

Getting Tony Robbins to sit still and listen to an instant-response focus group for three hours was much easier than I expected. Encouraging him to leave the comfort and safety of the back room to engage the thirty-two participants in a one-on-one conversation was a breeze. Asking Tony to stop that conversation at the appointed hour so that people could get home to their TVs and families—well, that proved to be impossible. At 209 minutes, it was the longest dial session I had ever moderated. But the words Tony used that night to describe the power of language had an immediate and lasting impact. His amusing linguistic examples turned a group of skeptics into true believers:

> Words change our emotions, whether we know it or not, so I teach people what I call transformational vocabulary—the words you use to change your emotions. I don't mean looking in the mirror and saying "I am good enough, I am strong enough, and by golly people love me." I'm not talking about that crap.
>
> I am talking about a one word change. If I say to you, "We are going to have a break and we are going to have some **nutritious** food, **nutritious** snacks . . ." look at your faces [*the participants shake their heads, frowning*], but if I say they are delicious . . . [*laughter*] . . . a very different reaction.
>
> Or if you come to me and say, "Hey Tony, you know a lot of people. I'm single and I'm looking for someone, and I say to you I know this person and they are . . . 'nice.'" [*Group responds in unison: "Nooooo."*]

Words not only can determine how we feel. They can also determine what we achieve. And what we hear often defines exactly what we want.

Words that work are powerful because they connect ideas, emotions, hopes, and (unfortunately) fears. You are now familiar with the lexicon and the connectivity of effective communication, but there is still one piece missing: a definition of what really matters. How do Americans feel about their world? What do they care about? This chapter identifies more than a dozen priorities, principles and preferences that matter to all of us, no matter what our political leanings. Taken together, these elements comprise the semantic terrain we all share, and their importance extends well beyond politics. No matter what communicators are selling, those who establish the correct tone by presenting their ideas in terms of these three keys of American thought and behavior will arrive at the right words.

## PRINCIPLES

Americans know *what* they believe, even if they don't know or can't explain why they believe it or give you any evidence to prove it. For

Americans to trust you—whether "you" are a candidate for office, a product for sale, or a service for offer—they need to know that you believe. If you tell them it's just what you "think," it won't carry weight. Thoughts or feelings are random, inconsequential, and often not particularly important or relevant. But *principles,* much like *values,* represent deeply held convictions—they don't change overnight, or sometimes ever.

Politicians have generated such a low degree of trust that they actually have to say the phrase *"as a matter of principle"* before any statement of belief before voters will even begin to trust them. Products don't carry as much baggage. Remember several decades ago when Orson Welles told viewers in that breathy deep rasp of his that *"Paul Masson will sell no wine until its time."* He didn't say that the product sales strategy was a matter of principle, but viewers thought they heard that aging fine wine was a matter of principle for serious winemakers, and therefore if Paul Masson aged its wine, it must be a serious winemaker. Principles are rigorous, examined, serious. They have weight. If *your* principles match *their* values, the details won't matter.

### OPPORTUNITY (MORE THAN FAIRNESS)

In the years since 9/11, the word *"freedom"* has been politicized. President Bush has used it so often and so consistently that Americans have come to think of it as a Republican euphemism for his foreign policy. In my dial sessions, when an elected official uses the word *"freedom,"* the participants immediately assume he's a Republican. This change in the connotations of freedom has been very recent and may not be permanent, but in the current historical moment, *"freedom"* has, remarkably, become a polarizing term.

On the flip side ideologically, *"fairness"* has always been a core component of the Democratic lexicon. From FDR's New Deal through Lyndon Johnson's Great Society to the modern-day Democratic Party, almost every presidential, senatorial, and congressional nominee has run on a platform that somewhere, somehow, included the words *"fair"* or *"fairness."* When you hear the word spoken, you know the party affiliation of the speaker.

One word that bridges the partisan divide is *"opportunity."* It is more unifying, alienates fewer people, and gives out a less philosophical, more practical impression. Politicians who pepper their speeches with the word *"opportunity"* aren't guaranteed success, but their use of the word will underscore a larger message about where they want to take the country and what life will be like when they get there. Democrats tend to win when they define a process or procedure as having unequal opportunity or providing an unfair advantage—the "level playing field" argument. Americans do not expect everyone to end up equal—they just want to start that way.

Republicans, on the other hand, tend to win when they are able to define fairness as *"equality of opportunity."* In a recent poll for the U.S. Chamber of Commerce, my firm gave Americans three definitions of fairness and asked them to choose the one they agreed with the most. The number one answer was: *"Fairness means that every American has the chance to succeed even if the ultimate outcomes may vary."* Americans clearly believe in equal opportunity, even as they reject programs that mandate equal outcomes.

*"Opportunity"* is linguistically valuable because it is a principle that Americans want made available to all. It's expansive and limitless. Political leaders who show a real, genuine commitment to equal opportunity— a commitment backed by specific examples (enterprise zones, parental choice in education, etc.)—will hit on what Americans from all backgrounds hold most dear.

## OPPORTUNITY (MORE THAN OWNERSHIP)

The administration of George W. Bush initially chose to present its second-term legislative agenda around the theme of *"ownership."* This was a mistake. It did provide a larger context for the individual policy goals, but it failed to account for a significant segment of society that sees ownership as opportunity for others but denied to them.

Some will argue that the principle of ownership is at once aspirational and essential to the free market system, and they are correct. The private sector relies on the same aspirational concept. That's why the mortgage industry created interest-free loans to entice buyers into buying homes they really couldn't afford. And credit card companies encourage people to buy and own all kinds of things with sharply reduced introductory interest rates that come back to kick them in the teeth six months or a year later.

However, one just had to watch the aftermath of Hurricane Katrina to realize that there are tens of millions of Americans who fall outside the *"ownership society,"* no matter how desperate they are to be included. There are too many Americans who know they will never own a business, own their home clear of debt, or own investments like stocks or bonds. The ownership society is for the "haves" of America—and while there are tens of millions of them, there are almost as many who would classify themselves as *"have nots."* For them, and for those who sympathize with the underclass, opportunity means more than ownership. Actual ownership is limited and limiting, but the *"opportunity of ownership"* is limitless.

## "COMMUNITY"

The notion of *"community"* has always had an appeal for most Americans, but the desire to associate, affiliate, and belong is even greater in the post 9/11 world. We relate to smaller institutions and subsets of society much better than we relate to large and remote entities such as Big Business, Big Media, and Big Government. Aristotle said that the family is the foundation and model for all government—and the closer to the family level and scale it is, the more real an institution or organization seems to Americans. More than two centuries ago, Edmund Burke talked about the *"little platoons"* of society as the primary recipients of the people's loyalty and affection, and that concept still holds true today, but emerging technology has thoroughly revolutionized the definition of *"community."* The Internet allows us to communicate with people halfway across the globe instantly, and the borderless chat rooms today are for teens and twenty somethings what casual neighborhood get-togethers are for older adults.

Geographically, as Americans move to exurbia, as they organize themselves more and more into small communities of the like-minded, they are looking for politics and politicians that acknowledge their new reality. There's a power in community relationships that politicians are only now beginning to discover.

Behavioral communities are also part of the twenty-first-century American psyche. From Internet chat rooms about favorite rock bands to e-mail listservs about esoteric topics, Americans are building their own virtual communities and spontaneous new social structures that would be inconceivable absent the new technologies of the digital age. Bloggers formed *"alliances"* and banded together to bring down Dan Rather in 2004 and Supreme Court nominee Harriet Miers in 2005. There's no such thing any more as *"broadcasting."* It's all *narrowcasting* now, and the implications for our politics are clear. Instead of one *"American conversation,"* there are dozens and dozens of individual community conversations going on at all times. Each virtual community has its own buzzwords, its own pet peeves, its own special demands. To ignore them or to refuse to afford them community status simply because they do not share a Zip code is to ignore what's happening in America, and around the world.

## COMMON SENSE

Ask Americans what one principle or value is most missing in Washington today and they'll say *"common sense"* more than any other answer. All Americans assume they themselves are blessed with common sense, and they respect it in others—indeed, they consider it a legitimate expression of intelligence. And yet, common sense is the quality they believe to be most lacking in Washington, D.C., and in many of the state capitals across the country.

But the value and appreciation of common sense in day-to-day life transcends our opinion of government and is at the core not just of who we are but of what we want to be about as people and as a nation. The public understanding of common sense dates back to the mid-1700s, and it has been an ongoing part of the American heritage for 250 years.

Because the definition is in the eyes of the definer, trying to define *"common sense"* is almost as difficult as defining pornography, but as Justice Potter Stewart once said, you'll know it when you see it. What Americans know today is that displays of common sense in the political world are much too uncommon. Americans believe their government is far too ideological, political, overcomplicated, and bureaucratic. Ross Perot's idea that it's possible to just *"pop the hood"* and fix this country's problems like you would a bad carburetor, without having to make any painful trade-offs or compromises, still has widespread appeal. It's a very populist, democratic idea: identify the problem, solve it, and everybody wins. True, life (and government) doesn't work that way, but that's what Americans still want and expect. In their view, with just a little common sense, some of our most intractable political problems would just solve themselves. *"Common sense"* doesn't require any fancy theories; it is *self-evidently* correct, like the truths of the Declaration of Independence.

When President George W. Bush is at his best, as he was in the weeks after September 11, 2001, his message embodied simple and direct common sense: The terrorists knocked these buildings down . . . so now we're going to go knock the terrorists down. When John Kerry was at his worst, he got so tangled up in abstract concepts like the *"global test"* of our foreign policy that he seemed to be lecturing in a college seminar rather than expressing the common sense of the real world.

In 2006, the Democrats adopted a campaign slogan, *"America Can Do Better."* This was a very *common sense* slogan, making a simple populist appeal. Instead of starting with a lot of detail or theory about what the GOP was doing wrong or delineating what the Democrats would do differently, the *"America Can Do Better"* message basically stated the obvious: things aren't as good as they could be. But they could have done even better than that. *"Common sense, common values"* was the most popular tagline we tested in 2006, even ahead of the official Democratic verbiage.* In fact, if you think back to every presidential election since the age of television, it can be argued that the candidate who best demonstrated *"common sense"* always won.

*"Common sense"* is also the best context (rule ten) to sell an issue. Social Security should be reformed because it's just plain common sense to have a pay-as-you-go system and because the current program will collapse if we don't do something—*not* for any theoretical free-market reason. Health care should be nationalized (if you're Hillary Rodham Clinton) because it's only common sense that the richest country in the world shouldn't have forty-odd million people with no medical care—not because of some economic theory about the pooling of risk and the problems of premiums, and so on. We need to kill the terrorists over there so they can't kill us over here, because that's simply *"common sense."*

*"Common sense"* is not just the best argument for almost any policy prescription you might propose—it's essential. If you win and occupy the rhetorical territory owned by *"common sense,"* your position will be virtually unassailable.

---

*Republicans never came up with a slogan, tagline, or organizing statement for 2006—the first time since 1994 that they had none. Not coincidentally, they fared poorly at the polls.

## GETTING "VALUE" FROM GOVERNMENT

Conservatives will be unhappy with the following research finding, but *"getting value for government"* is a preferable outcome to *"limited government"* among a majority of Americans. *"Limited government"* is structural and process-oriented—and it does not, by definition, guarantee better government. Because it is such a nebulous term, it is open to interpretation—and what is limited government for some is too little or too much government for others.

By comparison, *"value"* is more outcome-focused and measurable. President Bush's 2004 Republican National Convention address marked the return of his 2000 campaign effort to redefine what Americans thought of conservatism. But he added a twist—a definition of the role of government as both positive and limited:

---

### BUSH WORDS THAT WORK

"I am running for president with a clear and positive plan to build a safer world and a more hopeful America. I am running with a compassionate conservative philosophy: that government should help people improve their lives, not try to run their lives."

---

Democrats are correct: Americans accept some positive role for government in making things better. But Republicans are correct that Americans don't want to give up their personal freedom or the right to choose their own path to tomorrow. And the crucial intersection between the two partisan philosophies is this: Americans wanted *limited* but *effective* government that delivers *value* for their tax dollars. Those things that Americans believe government ought to be doing, they want government to do them more effectively.

Republicans err when they talk only about the negative aspects of government—particularly local government. What is closest to us we tend to accept and appreciate more—particularly when we can see and feel the impact. People are more likely to know their local government representatives personally, and that kind of familiarity breeds trust. But Democrats are on the wrong side of the government debate as well when they argue for national solutions that the public believes can best be handled on the local level.

From the consumer perspective, the challenge for marketers is in the shifting definition of *"value"* and how best to explain it. With efficiency a high priority in today's economy and in our day-to-day lives, *"value"* is a measurement of result rather than overall cost. The *"value"* equation is defined by how much more do you get out of it than you put into it. We no longer want the simple value proposition of the 1950s: *"You get what you paid for."* We want more. In my focus groups and other research I have done over the years, the value of *"value"* is most often articulated by older women—but we can all relate.

One business, Wausau Insurance, puts a friendly face on an industry that is often seen as anything but. Welcoming customers to a world where *"price does not equal cost,"* Wausau gives consumers the impression that they, as opposed to their money, are most important. This utilization of the word shows that value is just as applicable to business as it is to the customer. *"Value"* is a relative term. Just as in the corporate context, in politics, *"value"* is not absolute, but contingent—judged as a ratio of what you pay versus what you get. In plain English, it is the answer to the question: "Are you getting your money's worth?"

### "CONVENIENCE"

*"Time is money"* is a phrase still heard from the boardrooms to the bedrooms of America. But the twenty-first-century linguistic definition of time is, in a word, *"convenience."* This is not a political term in the conventional sense, but it certainly is a high priority in America today—and it will have an increasing impact on the free market economy and how we do business as the years go by.

The perception of convenience is the most important component of the *hassle-free* experience—but it is only just a component. *"Convenience"* has less to do with how we relate to the product itself or with what the product says about our own self-image; rather, *"convenience"* is about process, about what we have to go through to make a purchase, about how we shop. In concrete terms, *"convenience"* is directly proportional to time: the more time it takes, the less convenient it becomes. The more convenient you make the experience, the more time you return to the consumer. And the more time you return to the consumer, the more likely they are to spend that additional time utilizing more of what you have to offer.

For example, many grocery stores have begun installing self-checkout stations, where shoppers can scan the bar codes of their own groceries. These self-scanners are intended to make grocery shopping much more convenient by cutting down on the need to stand in long lines, and they save the store real money in reduced payroll costs. More and more movie theaters are also installing automated, ATM-style check-ins, and hardly anyone uses the full service airport check-in line any more since the automated check-in kiosks are just so, well, *convenient.*

Another example of innovation breeding convenience can be seen in the growth of the instant access vehicle industry. Companies like Flex-car, which allow consumers to rent a car for as little as an hour or as much as several days, provide much-needed convenient transportation to those living in big cities, where it might not be practical to own a car but renting is not economical. Some of the initial home-delivery companies in New York, Chicago, and Los Angeles went bust in the late 1990s because they couldn't make their business models work, but more and more companies are finding ways to bring their products and services right to your home. Having groceries delivered is gaining in popularity, for example.

Online shopping at companies like Amazon and online payment systems like Paypal are driving the mega-malls crazy because they take this aversion to standing in line a step further; with a few mouse clicks, your purchase arrives at your door without you ever having to interact with another human being at all. Of course, the downside of this lack of human interaction is the frustrating difficulty of getting a live person on the line when you need that human touch. Tradeoffs like this are inevitable, but this opens a brand-new potential advantage for companies that invest in live *"help-now"* operators rather than an automated machine to respond to complaints.

Personalization and individualization are all important elements of *"convenience."* For decades we've been a Fast-Food Nation, but these days we are most definitely becoming a Self-Service Nation as well. The first sign of this may have been the advent of self-service gas stations in the 1970s, but the trend is accelerating. And corporate, fiscal reasons for eliminating personnel are secondary; the greatest factor driving this trend is customer *"convenience."* We may never reach a day when we stop interacting with clerks and salespeople altogether and the world is staffed by polite robots—but it certainly might seem that way to a time traveler from the 1940s.

### "MAIN STREET, NOT WALL STREET"

Americans have an ongoing love-hate relationship with corporate America. From pulling for the underdog to the proverbial *"good things come in small packages,"* American culture is much more attuned to the challenges facing Main Street small business than their Wall Street big business cousins. To work for a small company—or, even better, to work for yourself, be your own boss, create your own life (or *lifestyle*)—this is what so many of us still hold up as the ideal. The mom-and-pop store on the corner may have disappeared from most American neighborhoods, but we still think it's the epitome of America, a wonderful example of what we hold dear (personal service, community, hard work, independence). We may no longer be a nation of family farmers and shopkeepers, but we still appreciate—and venerate—those who are.

Therefore, the more convincingly you can present your company as personal, relatable, down-to-earth, and in touch—the virtues of a small business—the better you will weather large-scale growth. *"Big enough to deliver; small enough to care"* is the best bridge for consumers who despise the impersonal nature of mega-giant corporations while simultaneously relishing all the innovations in speed, service, and capabilities they provide.

Symbolism is very important in this regard. To take just one example, even as Hewlett-Packard became a multibillion dollar company, it always gave great prominence and paid great deference and respect to the story of its genesis, symbolized by the tiny Palo Alto garage in which the founders first began to build their small business. The symbolism of *Main Street* is and will always be *All-American.*

Another example of this symbolism is found with HSBC Bank. With branches all over the world, stretching from Brazil to Hong Kong, it might be difficult to equate a truly multinational bank to the bank on the corner. Yet with a slogan like *"The World's Local Bank,"* Main Street is the impression HSBC is trying to project, and it resonates in an industry where automated voices have replaced actual people.

But whereas *"Main Street"* is sunny, warm, personal, and approachable,

*"Wall Street,"* by contrast, is seen as global and cold, with sterile glass structures and office cubicles filled with number crunchers concerned more about profits than people. The old slanders against the robber barons of the Gilded Age never really lost their currency in America. We remain suspicious of great concentrations of old wealth that still symbolize Wall Street today, though we don't begrudge Bill Gates, Steve Jobs, and the Google guys their billions, because they started small and grew in front of our eyes.*

The message *"Main Street, not Wall Street"* is really a message of customer service, customer caring, genuine attentiveness, and that interaction between business and consumer that used to be the norm in America. It's taking the political communication concepts of *individualizing, personalizing, empathizing,* and *humanizing* and applying them to products, services, marketing, and customer relationships.

Politically, our self-image as a nation is of the *"Main Street"* of a small town, not the urban lifestyle of Manhattan. At our founding, this was a nation of farmers, even if Jefferson's agrarian republic was always more of an ideal than a reality. Our westward expansion as a country, our national narrative of conquering and settling a hostile wilderness, ties us emotionally to the land. And many people still associate cities with crime, crowds, and concrete. The American myth is of open skies and far horizons, a land of milk and honey—a manicured lawn, not the corrupted urban jungle.

So talk about *"Main Street"* values and a *"Main Street"* approach, and you will evoke all of these subconscious associations. *"Wall Street"* is about profit. *"Main Street"* is about people. *"Wall Street"* is about greed. *"Main Street"* is about green. *"Wall Street"* is about buyouts and takeovers. *"Main Street"* is about family.

This stark contrast was used brilliantly by some Democrats across the country in 2002 during the height of the corporate accountability scandals. The Voter Reform Project, a group dedicated to *"holding politicians accountable,"* attacked incumbent Arkansas Senator Tim Hutchinson for working for Wall Street rather than his state's citizens. Ads were run claiming that Wall Street firms "invested $135,000 in his campaign." By linking *"Wall Street,"* the ubiquitous symbol of greed and corruption in

---

*During my death tax language research, I would ask middle-class and working-class Americans whether people like Gates should be taxed more. The answer: No! For all of his accomplishments and all he has done to modernize American life, American's don't begrudge his many billions. Donald Trump? That's a different story.

the minds of many, and investment, the Voter Reform Project was able to suggest that Hutchinson would make a return on that investment, spending more time and effort appeasing his Wall Street financiers than your neighbors on Main Street. While Republicans made gains in other races, Hutchinson lost.

## FAMILY VALUES

Americans want and expect to see *"family values"* exhibited by their political leaders. Napoleon once derogatorily labeled Britain a nation of shopkeepers. But as far back as de Tocqueville, America has been a nation organized around families. We respect the life experiences of our parents and see things through the eyes of our children—and when the family unit is challenged in whatever way for whatever reason, we sit up and take notice. And that's why the term *"family values"* (45 percent) tests better than *"traditional values"* (18 percent), *"American values"* (17 percent), or *"community values"* (11 percent).[1]

And contrary to the writings of left-leaning columnists, Americans do not define the term *values* in a strictly religious context. The night after the 2004 Presidential election, my firm polled one thousand voters and asked them to define what *"moral values"* meant to them. A clear plurality (32 percent) said "the personal beliefs and character of the candidate," followed by "the abortion issue" (24 percent), "the gay marriage issue" (18 percent), "topics such as religion and spirituality" (14 percent), and "the way the war in Iraq is being waged" (10 percent). *"Moral values"* are more about who you are and how you behave than about how you worship or where you stand on social issues.

Sensing a hostility among voters in what a Democratic political pundit derogatorily referred to as the "fly-over" states—the part of America that is often forgotten by the Harvard faculty and the Hollywood elite—some Democrats have attempted to redefine *"values"* and *"faith,"* moving in a broader, more secular direction. Several speakers at the Democratic National Convention in 2004 talked about the value and importance of faith . . . but without overt religious or spiritual appeals. In fact, they specifically accused the GOP of inserting religion into the public square and defining values only from a religious perspective. For the majority of "swing voters" who do not attend church weekly, this appeal was, well, appealing. Democrat vice-presidential candidate

John Edwards took an even more direct route, linking values to personal behavior, and it ended up being one of the most popular sound bites in his speech.[2]

---

**DEMOCRAT WORDS THAT WORK**

"Where I come from, you don't judge someone's values based on how they use that word in a political ad. You judge their values based upon what they've spent their life doing. So when a man volunteers to serve his country, and puts his life on the line for others—that's a man who represents real American values."

—John Edwards

---

There is a caveat to this, however. Values—at least in the political context—are not for everyone. In taking a close linguistic look at the likely 2008 Democratic presidential candidates, I heard something from grassroots, rank-and-file primary voting Democrats that startled me. Whenever a candidate began to talk about *"values," "faith," "religion,"* or an explicit reference to Jesus, the reaction was immediately and almost universally negative. When I asked why, the response was unanimous: *"We're just as concerned about values as the Republicans. The difference is, we don't like it when politicians try to define it."* In other words, *"If we wanted our elected officials to talk about values, we wouldn't be Democrats. We'd be Republicans."*

The best way to communicate values that will transcend partisan divisions is to use words and phrases that no Coke-drinking, apple pie–eating, GM-driving American could disagree with. *"Family." "Freedom." "Opportunity." "Responsibility." "Community." "Sacrifice."*

One of the best articulations of the values debate came from Ralph Reed, the former director of the Christian Coalition. It is quite ironic that he formulated these words when the American economy was arguably its strongest ever—and even more ironic considering his subsequent involvement in the Washington lobbying scandal involving Jack Abramoff.

---

# WORDS THAT WORK

"The greatness of America has never been measured by the Dow Jones Industrial Average, the gross national product, or the combined value of our individual and corporate checkbooks. The strength of America, the true greatness of America, is in the moral fiber of her people, in the integrity of her leaders, and in how we treat those who are least and most vulnerable in our midst. That is the greatness of America."

—Ralph Reed

---

There is one set of "values" that no one should want to endorse or promote: *"Hollywood values."* In the 2004 campaign, Dick Cheney was particularly effective labeling John Kerry a *"Hollywood liberal,"* and it didn't help Kerry that every time his Hollywood friends got together to say something political, it always sounded rude, vulgar, or insulting to the millions of centrist Main Street Americans. Comparing the president and vice-president to various parts of the human anatomy at a fundraising concert in Madison Square Garden will never qualify as words that work.

## THE FUTURE (NOT THE PAST)

We Americans perpetually have our feet on the gas pedal. We're staring straight ahead through the windshield, never pausing to glance back in the rearview mirror. As a culture and a people, America fundamentally rejects the status quo—even in times of peace and prosperity. We are a nation of change agents, or, as Bill Clinton called his campaign effort, *"Agents of Change."* We always want something better. This was a key component of President Bush's reelection victory in 2004. Every presidential candidate seeks to position themselves squarely in favor of a better tomorrow. But George W. Bush did it better than most.

---

## BUSH WORDS THAT WORK

"This changed world can be a time of great opportunity for all Americans to earn a better living, support your family, and have a rewarding career. And government must take your side. Many of our most fundamental systems— the tax code, health coverage, pension plans, worker training—were created for the world of yesterday, not tomorrow. We will transform these systems so that all citizens are equipped, prepared—and thus truly free—to make your own choices and pursue your own dreams."

---

### POSITIVE MESSAGES

As all elected officials know, you need to be *for* something rather than merely *against* something. Unfortunately, American political campaigns have gotten steadily more negative and bitter, ever more focused on why the opponent deserves to lose than on justifying their own candidacy.

---

## WORDS THAT WORK: THE APPEAL OF HOPE AND OPTIMISM

Here's a sampling of wisdom on the subject from some historical giants who knew of what they spoke:

- Martin Luther King, Jr.: *"Even if I knew that tomorrow the world would go to pieces, I would still plant my apple tree."*
- Winston Churchill: *"I am an optimist. It does not seem too much use to be anything else."* [3]
- Harry Truman: *"A pessimist is one who makes difficulties of his opportunities and an optimist is one who makes opportunities of his difficulties."*
- Dwight Eisenhower: *"Pessimism never won any battle."*
- Robert Kennedy: *"All of us might wish at times that we lived in a more*

> tranquil world, but we don't. And if our times are difficult and perplex-
> ing, so are they challenging and filled with opportunity."
> - Ronald Reagan: "There are no great limits to growth because there are
>   no limits of human intelligence, imagination, and wonder."
> - Franklin Roosevelt: "The only limit to our realization of tomorrow will be
>   our doubts of today. Let us move forward with strong and active faith."
> - John McCain: "We are taught to understand, correctly, that courage is
>   not the absence of fear, but the capacity for action despite our fears."
> - Margaret Thatcher: "I am in politics because of the struggle between
>   good and evil. I believe that in the end good will triumph."

Until 9/11, Americans had always been a fundamentally optimistic people, and this was deeply rooted in our national fabric and culture. You'd
*have to be* an optimist to leave your homeland behind, brave a perilous
ocean crossing, and attempt to carve a new civilization out of the harsh
wilderness of an unknown continent (unless, of course, you were brought
here on slave ships against your will). America wasn't built by people who
stayed put. We are the descendants of restless adventurers who set their
sights on strange lands, not those placid souls who were content to stay
behind—and this holds true whether your ancestors signed the Mayflower
Compact, your grandparents were processed at Ellis Island, or whether
you snuck across the Mexican border last month. All the clichés are true.
We are a nation of pilgrims and pioneers, immigrants and dreamers.
America's first immigrant generations came here hoping to found a new
Atlantis, a second Jerusalem, a shining city on a hill that would be a light
for the entire world. That visionary spirit of exploration animates us still.

It's no great surprise, then, that we prefer as our politicians those who
see the proverbial glass as half-full rather than half-empty. A cramped,
sour, negative outlook on life comes across as downright un-American.
Both Al Gore and John Kerry learned that lesson the hard way.

A philosophical cousin to the optimism attribute is a focus on the future. One key to Bill Clinton's natural appeal was that he always seemed
relatively sunny and upbeat, even at his most self-indulgent or when
wallowing in self-pity. His *"building a bridge to the twenty-first century"*
theme articulated perfectly a long-term perspective that was firmly
focused on the world of tomorrow.

By contrast, his opponent for reelection in 1996, Bob Dole, seemed to want to build a bridge to the sixteenth century. His rhetoric and frame of reference was firmly rooted in the past and called to mind the pinched-faced old lady at the orphanage who forces the kids to drink their castor oil in *The Little Rascals*. Even his name carries gloomy import; *dole* means sorrow or "mourning," and indeed Dole did run a "grief-inducing" campaign (ironic considering what a witty man he is—and yet his wit is mordant, edgy, and occasionally bitter).[4]

By common consensus, Dole gave a masterful acceptance speech at the Republican National Convention in 1996. In fact, it was the only time in the entire campaign where he pulled even with Clinton in the polls. Yet the narrative of that speech, beautifully written by novelist and *Wall Street Journal* contributor Mark Helprin, was at heart an account of American decline. In fact, this was the narrative thread of Dole's campaign as a whole. Things used to be better, Dole remembered, because he was there. He was an old man telling the kids about the lost world of his childhood, when the sun shone a little brighter and the sea sparkled a little bluer.

Maybe Dole was right. Maybe America *was* in decline. But if so, we certainly didn't want to hear about it. It was joked at the time that Bob Dole was so old it took him an hour and a half to watch *60 Minutes,* and that his favorite painting was *The Last Supper* because he was in it. (Rim shot.) He actually knew who was buried in Grant's tomb—because he was at the funeral. And so on. But just as nostalgia doesn't sell consumer goods, it doesn't sell political candidates. This was the exact opposite of Reagan's "Morning in America" language, and it left Americans cold. Not since the *"Return to Normalcy"* campaign of Warren Harding in 1920 has a presidential candidate harkened back to the days gone by and won with that message.

Much more consistent with the American ethos was the conclusion of Ronald Reagan's farewell letter to the American people in 1994, in which he disclosed that he had Alzheimer's disease: *"I know that for America, there will always be a bright dawn ahead."*[5] Indomitable good cheer—*in a letter announcing that he was afflicted with a cruel, terminal illness.* THAT is the winning optimism Americans love.

True, like anything else, it is possible to take optimism too far. Famed gossip columnist Walter Winchell defined an optimist as "a man who gets treed by a lion but enjoys the scenery." Ambrose Bierce, author of the *Devil's Dictionary,* humorously described optimism as "the doctrine or belief that everything is beautiful, including what is ugly."

From a product perspective, women, in particular, don't respond well to gloom and doom. Some marketers have tried scare tactics: from insecurity about their appearance to anxiety about what others think of them, from concern about gaining weight to fear of aging. I disagree with such methods. Women are proactively looking to make themselves beautiful, not just looking to hide away the extra pounds or additional wrinkle. They are seeking health, not simply running away from illness. It is not fear of something bad that motivates them; it's the hope for something better. That's why every communication should include the message of limitless dreams, unending possibilities, and the promise of a better future.

*On April 4, 1968, Robert F. Kennedy delivered what was probably the best unscripted political speech of the modern era. Dr. Martin Luther King had been assassinated earlier in the evening, and it was left to Kennedy to deliver the horrible news to a mostly black audience in Indianapolis, Indiana. While his many well-crafted speeches have been overshadowed by the man he eulogized that night and by his brother the president, this impromptu address represents aspirational language at its very best because it was delivered from the heart, without notes, rather than from some scribe's pen.*

Ladies and Gentlemen: I'm only going to talk to you just for a minute or so this evening.

I have some very sad news for all of you, and I think sad news for all of our fellow citizens, and people who love peace all over the world, and that is that Martin Luther King was shot and was killed tonight in Memphis, Tennessee.

Martin Luther King dedicated his life to love and to justice between fellow human beings. He died in the cause of that effort. In this difficult day, in this difficult time for the United States, it's perhaps well to ask what kind of a nation we are and what direction we want to move in.

For those of you who are black—considering the evidence evidently is that there were white people who were responsible—you can be filled with bitterness, and with hatred, and a desire for revenge.

We can move in that direction as a country, in greater polarization—black people amongst blacks, and white amongst whites, filled with hatred toward one another. Or we can make an effort, as Martin Luther King did, to understand and to comprehend, and replace that violence, that stain of bloodshed that has spread across our land, with an effort to understand, compassion and love.

For those of you who are black and are tempted to be filled with hatred and mistrust of the injustice of such an act, against all white people, I would only say that I can also feel in my own heart the same kind of feeling. I had a member of my family killed, but he was killed by a white man.

But we have to make an effort in the United States, we have to make an effort to understand, to get beyond these rather difficult times.

My favorite poet was Aeschylus. He once wrote: "Even in our sleep, pain which cannot forget falls drop by drop upon the heart, until, in our own despair, against our will, comes wisdom through the awful grace of God."

What we need in the United States is not division; what we need in the United States is not hatred; what we need in the United States is not violence and lawlessness, but is love and wisdom, and compassion toward one another, and a feeling of justice toward those who still suffer within our country, whether they be white or whether they be black.

(Interrupted by applause)

So I ask you tonight to return home, to say a prayer for the family of Martin Luther King, yeah that's true, but more importantly to say a prayer for our own country, which all of us love—a prayer for understanding and that com-

passion of which I spoke. We can do well in this country. We will have difficult times. We've had difficult times in the past. And we will have difficult
times in the future. It is not the end of violence; it is not the end of lawlessness; and it's not the end of disorder.

But the vast majority of white people and the vast majority of black people
in this country want to live together, want to improve the quality of our life,
and want justice for all human beings that abide in our land.

(Interrupted by applause)

Let us dedicate ourselves to what the Greeks wrote so many years ago: to
tame the savageness of man and make gentle the life of this world.

Let us dedicate ourselves to that, and say a prayer for our country and for
our people.

## ACCOUNTABILITY

Skepticism of and cynicism toward the federal government is running
higher in 2006 than at any time since the Perot season of 1992–94.
Thanks to unmet expectations in Iraq, the dismal "heckuva job Brownie"
response to Hurricane Katrina, the scandals that have engulfed Congress, and the indictments of the House Republican leader and the vice
president's chief of staff, Americans have become suspicious not only of
the motives of Washington but its ability to lead and succeed.

In the past, the biggest fear of government was that it would overre-
act. Today, the biggest fear is that it can't react and won't take responsibility for its actions, or that it will react, but incorrectly. Accountability
is the attribute and action Americans most want from Washington, even
more than they want it to provide lower taxes or better services.

Accountability also matters when examining the record and worthi-
ness of political candidates. In fact, voters prize *"accountability"* above
other personal characteristics in their politicians. Asked "Which attribute
would make you feel best about a congressional candidate?" Americans

cited *"accountability"* (46 percent) over *"responsibility," "opportunity,"* *"prosperity,"* and *"community"* combined.[6]

---

### DEMOCRAT WORDS THAT WORK

"Members of Congress have a constitutional obligation and public responsibility to oversee the activities of the President and the executive branch. There are too many unasked and unanswered questions, and the American public deserves better. This is about honesty and accountability, and reforming our federal government."

—Senate Minority Leader Harry Reid[7]

---

### RESPECT

The word *"respect"* is most important not when talking to customers, but to employees. In fact, it's the single most important word related to how employees perceive their treatment and what they think of their employer. In the twenty-first-century economy, few people expect loyalty any more from their bosses—at least not in the sense that workers did in the 1950s. Americans know that they live in a much more dynamic, and therefore much less stable, business world. They change jobs frequently, from firm to firm, even from industry to industry, and profession to profession. The idea of a spending your entire adult life at a single company and then retiring with a gold watch and a pension is so ancient to most young people today that it might as well be feudalism. In fact, if you talk a person under age thirty and used the term "gold watch" in relation to retirement, they probably won't get the reference.

Nevertheless, while most of us don't expect a job for life, we do expect—no, we *demand*—to be respected in the jobs that we're in, so long as we're there, even if that's only a few months or a few years. Our corporate overlords need not be loyal or committed to us for the long haul, but they had better not *"dis"* us in the short run. If respect for employees is lacking—in addition to long-gone job security and stability—their reasons for contributing to the larger, collective effort of the whole will swiftly erode.

Companies that make a point to treat their employees with respect are often noted for it. The San Francisco–based Great Place to Work Institute annually publishes a list of the hundred best companies to work for. The list is compiled using a variety of factors, one of which is respect. Respect in this case is synonymous with employee involvement and development.

Genentech, a California biotechnology company, is the number-one ranked business in 2006. With 95 percent of employees owning shares in the company and an active community involvement program, Genentech gives their employees a sense of involvement, purpose, and respect. This serves not only to capture high rankings from groups like the Great Place to Work Institute, but in turn gives employees additional incentives for increased productivity—and the company's bottom line has improved as well.

The linguistic key to communicating respect is to talk about *"value:"*

- The value of serving and satisfying customers;
- The value of a good day's pay for a good day's work;
- The value of a simple "thank you" for a job well done.

If you say to your employees, your boss, or the people around you that you *"respect"* them, you probably don't. It's like a used-car salesman saying "trust me" or a dictator asserting that his country is democratic. *"Respect"* can certainly be articulated, but not by using the word itself. You need to use language to show it rather than say it.

## SOLUTIONS

Since the 1990s, many companies have posited a third category in addition to *"products"* and *"services"*—*"solutions,"* a loaded term if ever there was one. A *"solution"* implies a problem and therefore a need. Compared to dry, concrete, and factual *"products"* and *"services,"* the word *"solution"* is downright propagandistic. A product or service may be necessary or it may be superfluous, but if what's being sold is a *"solution,"* the problem or need it addresses moves seamlessly from hypothesis to reality.

Selling a service as a *"solution"* not only makes the service seem more valuable, it also subtly raises the status of the solution provider. Butlers and maids *serve.* Detectives *solve* problems. So the migration from *"service"* to *"solution"* is in part a matter of simply increasing the value of the product and the buyer's self-esteem.

The difference between selling *"services"* and selling *"solutions"* is substantial because the desired experiences of the two are at different levels. In today's world, everyone has a problem. A *"service"* helps you live with the problem. A *"solution"* alleviates the problem. From a thirst that needs to be quenched, to a car that never needs repairs, to a computer virus that needs to be contained and destroyed, we are in constant need of *"solutions"* to keep us up and running. Knowing this, companies have rallied to the cause, integrating *"solutions"* into the way do business and the way they talk about their business.

One example of this is Network Solutions, a company specializing in almost every aspect of the Internet. Network Solutions can assist an individual or a business in registering a domain name, creating a Web site, and marketing the Web site to consumers. Branding itself as a *"quick and easy way to establish an online identity,"* Network Solutions sells the hassle-free experience—a core component of solution-oriented language. For Network Solutions, it's not just a name, a product, or a service. The name is their primary selling point.

Another example of a company that uses solutions to sell its services is Siemens. The German company that makes everything from cell phones to ultrasound machines doesn't simply sell medical products, it provides *"medical solutions."* By selecting the solution terminology, Siemens moves the focus away from the product or process and toward the end result—accomplishment. So Siemens doesn't sell *"MRI machines."* It sells *"a faster and more accurate diagnosis of serious health problems."* Which would you rather buy?

As our world becomes ever more complex, and our problems become more difficult to solve on our own, the importance of products and services that offer solutions will become more evident, and the language used to sell them will become more widely used.


*It's not what you say, it's what they hear.* Looking to politics, this chapter has identified some of the key themes that influence how Americans perceive any message. Patriotism, opportunity, democracy, cooperation—these things matter to all of us, regardless of our political leanings. But what about when you don't want to convey some lofty idea? What about when you simply want to get out of a parking ticket or convince your boss to give you a raise? The next chapter provides some helpful tips on how you can use effective communication to get what you want in your everyday life.

# XI

# *Personal Language for Personal Scenarios*

*"Man invented language to satisfy his deep need to complain."*
LILY TOMLIN[1]

So we've studied the audience that most Americans address when we communicate (that is, other Americans). We've focused primarily on how people can best use language in political or business settings to achieve desired objectives. In this chapter, we take a brief look at some rhetorical techniques we can all use in our daily lives to help people better hear what we have to say.

## AT HOME:
## HOW DO YOU SAY I'M SORRY?

Men and women have radically different styles of communication. This is not a news flash; we all know about the Mars-Venus conflicts, and the battle of the sexes has raged since the beginning of time. But without getting mired in the debate over whether the differences between men and women are primarily biological in origin or constructed and conditioned by social institutions and culture, we can all observe and agree on the end result.

From years of research on gender attitudes and communication roles, for clients ranging from Coca-Cola to General Motors to the hotel and healthcare industries, I can offer one overarching communication fact: *Men want to speak; women want to be heard.*

As with all generalizations, there are always exceptions. But for the most part, when a couple has a disagreement over an issue that particularly upsets the male, he will do a majority of the talking. In fact, he'll do almost all of it. And at some point the woman will simply walk away. He'll keep yelling as she walks out the door. She'll walk down the driveway . . . he may follow, still yelling. She'll drive away; he'll still be yelling. She'll cross state lines . . . you get the picture. Once she's tuned him out, the woman won't hear any of it, but for him that's almost beside the point. Once he's said what he felt had to be said, he'll be content. The male focus is on self-expression, not on the other person's reaction to or understanding of what he's saying. I don't want to make men look dumb in their arguing technique, but sometimes they are, and this helps explain why women generally make better communicators.

Women are strikingly focused on the recipient of their message. In an argument, their primary desire is not to make all their points, as if following a checklist, but rather to be *heard*, understood, and validated. A woman will stop speaking mid-word to observe whether the man is truly listening to her and will *only* speak when she feels assured that he's paying attention. Otherwise, she will just remain silent. It's one reason why when women are in an argument, it's peppered with questions that demand a response, while men tend to follow assertions with more assertions.

Since men tend to lose more arguments than women—even ones they start—here's a solid piece of communication advice: When a guy says or does something wrong in a relationship and it comes time to apologize, one of the unquestionably best ways to say "I'm sorry" is to go beyond words and communicate it with flowers. Yes, it is true that I have worked for Jim McCann, CEO of 1-800-Flowers, but that's beside the point. You may think it's corny, old-fashioned, or even sexist, but you're wrong. For most women, receiving flowers fixes just about everything.

When I first stumbled upon their healing powers, it was inexplicable to me, but women see flowers as the ultimate demonstration of humility, regret, love, affection, sympathy, and apology. Flowers mean any and all of these things all at once, *as defined by the woman receiving them.* And because *she's* the one interpreting the flowers' symbolism, there's no more quibbling and hairsplitting, no more opportunity for linguistic annoyance or misunderstanding. Flowers communicate nonverbally, and so the verbal argument is immediately over as soon as she receives them. It takes the eloquence of a Jerry Maguire "You complete me" speech to match the power of a bouquet. Flowers are to relationships what penicillin is to illness. They are the miracle elixir.

Now let me acknowledge that a senior executive in my polling organization, Amy Kramer, read this section and then told me bluntly that she found it *"borderline offensive."* In her words, *"When someone's motives are so transparent that the flowers look to be just another manipulative gesture, I think it will backfire. In fact, I've seen it happen."* She's right—to a degree. Amy has spent more than a decade of her life in the various newsrooms across Washington, ground zero for manipulative characters, so she can spot them a mile away. But it is just as manipulative (and cheap) to say *"I'm sorry"* and not really mean it, and just as disappointing to apologize verbally to someone and have it rejected. What sets flowers above and beyond everything you could possibly say is the explicit visualization—rule eight. And a heartfelt "forgive me" certainly won't hurt. By the way, Amy's first job in high school was in a flower shop.

## AT THE OFFICE:
## HOW DO YOU ASK FOR A RAISE OR A PROMOTION?

Most of us are uncomfortable marching into our boss's office and demanding a raise or a promotion. I know it's one of the conversations my own employees hate the most. It's a situation that at once requires delicacy and diplomacy, strength and determination. Most importantly, you have to put yourself in the shoes of your boss. To him or her, your raise or promotion is not viewed as a reward for past performance. It's a speculative investment in your *future* performance. The question your boss will be answering for you is not "What have you done for me lately?" it's "What are you going to do for me tomorrow?"

Be prepared to explain how you've done your job well—but realize that demonstrating past and current value is only half of the message you need to deliver. You will be most effective if you emphasize what your boss is most concerned with: the future. The next client. Future contracts. The upcoming project. Employ the concept of (but not the actual word) *consequences.* I'm not suggesting you use threats or extortion. No one appreciates his or her back being put to the wall, and doing so makes it easier for those in authority to say no. Just realize that the pivot point of your boss's decision will not be that you *deserve* a raise, but that there are certain implied consequences of your not getting one. You have demonstrated value . . . and now your effort must to be to convince your boss to *imagine* what would happen if that value were no longer there.

"*Imagine if* . . ." are the two most effective words you can use in this situation. "*Imagine if* I hadn't been here to work on Project X." "*Imagine if* Contract Y hadn't been hammered out last week." By merely inviting your boss to do a little thought experiment, you prompt a subtle but clear vision of you being out of the picture if more money isn't in your future. And if you achieve the "*imagine if*" visualization by demonstrating your *future* value, chances are you'll end up getting that raise, bonus, or promotion. Some bosses use raises to reward past efforts. For those that don't, *imagine if* is the best elixir.

## ON THE ROAD:
## HOW TO AVOID A TICKET

Most of you reading this have never been arrested, but you've almost certainly been pulled over for speeding, running a red light, or some other minor traffic infraction. How do you apply the communication principles of this book to an encounter with law enforcement?

The first and most important thing you can do is to recognize the police officer's authority and superiority—immediately and totally. Over the years I've questioned hundreds of people who've been stopped for all manner of moving violations and their experience tells me that the number one way to avoid a ticket is to acknowledge your offense at the outset and beg for mercy. This may not be what you want to hear, and it may not be in your nature to do, but language laced with pity, sympathy, and a plea for leniency is the best strategy.

When you've been pulled over, the reality is that you *are* at the cop's mercy. You are not in a courtroom, you are not on trial, and you are not presumed innocent. The police officer is neither a judge nor a debating partner, and the worst thing you can do is to make his or her difficult day even harder. If you're determined to go to court and right the wrong, that's one thing. But if you know you were caught, acknowledging your guilt is the best way to be let off with just a warning. Realize that the cop is not plagued by self-doubt, agonizing over whether you really ran that stop sign or not. Right or wrong, the cop has already made up his or her mind. If this weren't the case, you wouldn't have been pulled over in the first place. So pulling an attitude will make the cop dig in, not back down.

Police have a life-threatening job. So indicate that you pose them no threat by turning off your engine promptly after you pull over, rolling down the window (don't make the cop tap on it like they do in the movies), and putting both hands on the wheel or the dashboard where the cop can see them, with your license and registration ready. And when the police officer reaches your window, look him or her straight in the eye and say, "I'm sorry, officer."

Many people don't know that it's often more of a hassle for a police officer to write you a ticket than it is to let you go. Cops don't like paperwork any more than you do. In towns that have speed traps and ticket quotas, there's not much you can do. But everywhere else, think of yourself as a shopkeeper and the police officer as your customer—and try to provide the officer with a "hassle-free experience." I can't promise that you won't still get a ticket—but if you do, at least you'll know that you did the best you could.

## AT THE AIRPORT:
## HOW DO YOU TALK YOUR WAY ONTO THE PLANE?

Sometimes it feels as if I spend most of my life in airports. LAX, Washington Dulles, Atlanta Hartsfield, and Chicago O'Hare are a lot like home to me—I spend more time there than I do in my own home. Seriously.

If you're a frequent business traveler, you know the feeling of cold panic that seizes you when you realize that you're likely to miss your flight for a meeting you must attend. As busy people, we all try to cram far too much activity into far too little time, and we never take into account contingencies that inevitably arise—traffic, airport lines, and that the time you have left before your flight leaves is invariably indirectly proportional to the length of the line at security and distance you have to walk to your gate: less time, more distance to walk.

Unfortunately, when the airport employees close that door to the jetway, it's almost impossible to get them to open it again (interestingly, *jetway* is a trademark in the United Kingdom; the original name of the portable path to an airplane is *air bridge*). Airlines have preboarding for children, the elderly, and those who need special assistance. They should add to that *post*boarding for manic businesspeople. But in the meantime, until some enterprising airline gets on board with that innovation, how do you talk your way onto an airplane that's about to depart?

Learn from the master.

The situation of the airline employee running the gate is exactly the opposite of a police officer's on a traffic stop. For the cop, writing you a ticket means paperwork and hassle—and deep down the cop would rather not. But opening the jetway door—even if it was only shut three seconds ago . . . as you watched from a hundred feet away . . . constitutes a major hassle. The paperwork is already complete. The passenger manifest is complete. Closing the door has sealed the deal for a technically, legally on-time departure. The job is done. Opening that door again requires effort, sacrifice, and even a potential reprimand.

So the status quo and the path of least resistance are for airline employees to tell us desperate travelers "No!" And every second that the door has been shut makes it much less likely that it will be reopened. Not only are the odds long, but the clock is running. There's no time to think—and yet you must choose your words carefully. Merely saying *"I need to get on that plane"* will not get the door open. *Demanding* to be let on the plane will definitely keep the door shut. An angry or insulted bureaucrat will stick strictly to procedure. At the same time, a passive, nondescriptive reason will not get the attendant to change the status quo, either. So what do you say?

Answer: You beg.

Grovel, plead, prostrate yourself. Make it clear that you understand you're at the employee's mercy, and ask for help. Tell a story that is compelling, and that will invest him or her in the outcome. Merely needing to get on the plane is meaningless. The impact of missing this flight has to have a *life-changing* impact on you—so that it has a behavioral impact on the gatekeeper. It could be a family emergency. It could impact a promotion (or firing) at work. But whatever the reason you need to be on that flight, it must be related to a major life event. Asking someone to endure a hassle to do you a major favor that will change your life is much more reasonable than asking the employee to merely swap his or her hassle for yours to save you the inconvenience.

The second component of persuading the airline agent to open that door is to mention your status with the airline. (If you happen to have the CEO's cell phone number in your BlackBerry, dial it.) If you're a frequent flyer or a longtime customer, don't be afraid to say this. *Do not* couch this as a threat or suggest that you're going to get the employee in trouble with the boss. Simply note that you're a good customer of this air-line who flies X-number of miles a year, and that may get you some extra consideration.

I've been told that a twenty-dollar bill on the counter can also make a difference—but I refuse to try it. I'm too afraid of rejection. Not to men-tion that anything that could be construed as putting the security of a plane (such as bribing your way onto it) in jeopardy is a surefire way to get the airline employee fired and you banned should you get caught. Anyway, the purpose of this book is the creation of the right language, not making the right bribe, so you're on your own with other, more un-orthodox methods. Be short and to the point. Make your case in no more than four sentences. Begin and end with *"please."* And when the airline employee opens that door, say, *"This will change my life"* and *"I will for-ever be grateful."* Then hope you don't run into the same employee the next time you're late for a flight.

## OUT TO EAT:
### HOW TO GET A TABLE AT A PACKED RESTAURANT

The line snakes out the front door. Just finding your way to the hostess's podium is like riding the Tokyo subway. It's Saturday night (or Valen-tine's Day, if you're a guy and a real cad), and you realize you forgot to make reservations. How do you get that perfect seat by the window . . . or at least a table in the back by the entrance to the kitchen?

You can get your bribery lessons from *Curb Your Enthusiasm* or *Sein-feld* reruns, but if you want to talk your way into a table, you need to tell the hostess an emotional hard-luck story. It should be personal, and it should involve a relationship that tugs at the heartstrings and makes you the bad guy or girl. It also needs humor. A funny story that explains, at your expense, why the table is so important can work wonders. If you can make the hostess laugh, she will certainly find a way to get you a table. Or at least she'll try.

As in the case of getting on an airplane—and unlike when you've been pulled over by a cop—your aim should be to create empathy, to make the person in power put him- or herself in your shoes. If the host-ess can see the situation from your perspective, she may consider the potential for karmic reciprocity—helping you out today means someone some day in a similar situation will do the same thing for her.

The important first step is to get the hostess talking. It's like flirting; as long as she continues to reply to your jokes and your story, she hasn't completely closed the door on you. Make her laugh, or feel genuinely sorry about the hazard to your love life, and chances are she'll say, "I'll see what I can do" and come back with a table.

## THE WRITTEN WORD:
## WRITING AN EFFECTIVE LETTER

It is shocking how many members of Congress, people whose professional success depends in large measure on their ability to communicate with constituents, send mail that is almost unintelligible to the average reader. I've seen senators (who only face their voters once every six years) send out letters with paragraphs twenty lines long. Harvard professors would have problems working through the text, not to mention the average constituent, with 20/40 vision, a junior college education, and a short attention span.

But this chapter consists of real-life scenarios for people with more common concerns than the omnibus reconciliation bill, the Davis-Bacon Act, or the ABM Treaty. Let's focus on what you need to do to get your letter read and acted upon. If you need to ask customer service for your money back because of a defective product or if you are applying for a brand-new job with an employer who doesn't know you, the communication rules are the same. Here's how to construct a letter that works:

First, start with a single authoritative statement. The best opening paragraph is just a single sentence. Whether verbal or in writing, your first words are by far the most important. Over time, we have become increasingly sophisticated linguistically, able to immediately decipher situations and figure out what's going on. You only have a few seconds—and a few words—to catch people's attention . . . and a few more to make your case. Every second after you begin speaking, the clock is ticking. You don't have the luxury of leisurely pacing or deliberative arguments; the reader could tune out at any moment. As the old expression goes, "Grab them by the throat and don't let go!" So seize your audience from the start. Remember, everything you *need* to say should be up front. All that you *want* to say can come later.

In my research into the effectiveness of direct mail, the single most-read portion after the opening paragraph is the postscript. The reason is easy to understand: The average reader looks to the P.S. to determine whether or not it is in fact a personal letter, and whether that letter has any relevance to his or her life. If it isn't, and if it doesn't, the average person won't read anything else. So make the postscript as human and emotional as possible.

Third, use enumeration and text that is **bold** and *italicized*. This is not a personal letter to a friend or family member; it's designed to get some stranger to do something that they might not necessarily want to do. Therefore, think of it as a jury trial; you are the accused and the reader is the judge. It needs to be organized in argument form, with each statement enumerated and each opening sentence bolded and under-lined. The reason? We don't read straight from top to bottom. The eye darts about, fixing on whatever catches its fancy—and it moves on if nothing stands out. The enumeration and different-looking type will definitely catch the eye, and therefore the attention, of the reader.

Fourth, the shorter the paragraphs, the more likely they are to be read, and the more likely we are to absorb the material. We simply don't have the patience to read something long. The eye skips ahead and jumps around, whether its owner wills it to or not. Sure, we still read more or less from left to right . . . but the shorter the paragraphs, the more likely they are to be read, and the more likely we are to absorb the material. Your sentences have to be short and sweet, not meandering, labyrinthine, baroque, or adjective-clotted (such as this one). Again, many short sentences are preferable to a few long ones.


A final note: In these real-life scenarios, as in most situations in life, the immediate reaction is the only reaction that matters. When we meet someone new, whether at work or in a social situation, we begin making judgments instantaneously, based on dress, mannerisms, body language, demeanor, and literally dozens of other small details. This process of reasoning and judgment is subtle, often subconscious—but it never stops—and it is the basis of words that work. Sure, this book is full of "rules," but as every good innovator will tell you, even the most basic rules are made to be broken. The meaning of words and actions resides in a kind of flux, their appropriateness never fixed, forever contingent upon individual, unique circumstance. And those circumstances are set by what may be the most important aspect of communication: context.

This chapter has left the world of politics and business to examine how words that work can be fashioned and deployed in everyday life. In the book's next chapter, we return to the public sphere. Applying all that we have learned about the context of American audiences, we examine the lexicon that businesses and politicians will develop to convince and inspire you in the years to come.

## XII

# Twenty-one Words and Phrases for the Twenty-first Century

*"I hope our leaders don't feel like they have to talk to us in monosyllables or break it down to easy-to-understand things. You know, we get smarter by people treating us smarter. . . . You want to be lifted up and told to lead."*
—AARON SORKIN

This book has examined the development and application of words that work. Now it's time to look ahead to the twenty-one words and phrases that you will be hearing often as we move through these early years of the twenty-first century. Some apply to business, others to politics, but they all define the new American lexicon. I choose these words because I believe they will withstand the test of time.

Based on hundreds of thousands of telephone interviews, hundreds of dial sessions and focus groups, and literally a million research hours, I contend that the words and concepts in this chapter will be as essential and powerful tomorrow as they are today. The words that follow are not superficial, timely, or contingent on the ephemeral circumstances of the moment. These words cut to the heart of Americans' most fundamental beliefs and right to the core values that do not change no matter how we vote or shop, or what delivery devices we use to play music, in the year 2020.

The words in this chapter have eminently practical applications. Consider the following example:

---

## VERIZON BUSINESS: THE PERFECT AD COPY FOR THE TWENTY-FIRST CENTURY

### (key words in bold)

"What if you attached an **innovative** wing structure to some bicycle machinery and launched it from a sand dune? *(Black-and-white visuals of early airplane flights)*

That works.

What if you created a thin piece of plastic that could easily be used just like money—anywhere in the world? *(Artistically colorized visuals of money morphing into credit cards)*

That works.

Suppose we created an IP network so far-reaching and expansive, it can make doing business more **efficient** around the globe. *(Visuals of postmodern buildings interspersed with people working at computers)*

Suppose we put your global business network in the hands of world-class professionals. People who know it end-to-end. *(Visuals of multi-ethnic business professionals with confident appearances)*

Verizon has joined with MCI to form Verizon Business, where global capability meets personal **accountability**—to make your business more successful—and your life a little easier. *(A father showing his young daughter pictures of herself on his computer)*

That works!

Introducing Verizon Business.

---

In a single sixty-second spot, Verizon Business managed to incorporate three of the words in this chapter: innovative, efficient, and accountability. These are the words that will sell products and win votes. They will redefine perceptions that need changing and confirm existing ideas that need reinforcing. I have used these words to help more than two dozen *Fortune* 500 companies grow and thrive, and to aid more than two hundred elected officials in winning or keeping their jobs. These are words that work and that will continue to work. They are the language of America.

## WORDS AND PHRASES FOR THE TWENTY-FIRST CENTURY

### 1. *"Imagine"*

*"Imagine"* is one of the most powerful words in the English language. It evokes something different to each person that hears it. Every person has a unique definition of the American Dream that they imagine and someday hope to achieve. The point is that *"imagine"* leads to 300 million different, *personal* definitions—and that's just in the United States alone.

No matter what your company's product or service, the word *"imagine"* has the potential to create and personalize an appeal that is individualized based on the dreams and desires of the person who hears or reads it. The word *"imagine"* is an open, nonrestrictive command—almost an invitation. Its power is derived from the simple fact that it can conjure up anything in the mind of the one doing the imagining. What can be imagined is therefore endlessly personal and targeted in a way that no canned marketing campaign could ever hope to be. When a potential consumer imagines, she's the one doing the most important work, investing her own mental energies to create something new where before there was nothing. You don't have to tell people what to imagine, just encourage them to do so.

The clearest illustration of this process is reading. When you read, you translate the black-and-white symbols on the page into vivid, Technicolor pictures in your mind—but everybody's mental pictures are different. This makes each reader a collaborator with the author in the creation of his or her own entertainment.

Film, for all its wonders, is an infinitely more passive medium for just this reason—and it undermines rather than enhances imagination. Tom Wolfe's *Bonfire of the Vanities* is one of the most read and applauded novels about business and greed ever written because of its visionary and descriptive prose, but the movie was a bust. Even good films suffer in comparison to what we imagine from the pages of a book. *The Natural* is considered by many to be one of the best baseball films of all time—but those same people will assert that the book was better. Same with *Lord of the Rings*.

When an advertisement asks the audience to *"imagine,"* it's inviting them to take ownership of the product or service being sold—to make it their own. But if the ad says too much or shows too much, it undermines the process of imagination that the advertiser is trying to stoke. Conversely, if you show too little, as Infiniti automobiles did when they launched the new brand in 1989, you don't give people the tools they need to create their own images. By not showing the car, they didn't create anticipation or imagination. They created annoyance.

Similarly, AT&T Wireless wanted Americans to imagine (and get) an mLife, digital-speak for mobile life, when it launched a multimillion-dollar branding campaign just before the 2002 Super Bowl. They thought teaser ads asking *"What is mLife"* would *"intrigue"* consumers and pique interest. Like Infiniti, the mLife promotion did become a hot topic of discussion—and debate—and it generated considerable Web traffic, but in this case the product reveal did not live up to the hype, and AT&T Wireless dropped the campaign. If you ask people to imagine the best, you had better deliver the best.

The boundless world of imagination has found an equally boundless partner in the Internet. Samsung, a company that makes everything from microwave ovens to MP3 players, has launched an *"imagine"* inspired campaign, asking its customers to *"become captivated by functions and conveniences you never dreamed possible."* This challenge to consumers to push the boundaries of their own minds is accompanied by an image- and sound-laden Web site that creates an environment in which the versatility and variety of Samsung's products are highlighted.

The concept of imagination also has great salience *within* companies. It's no accident that the designers and builders of the Disney theme parks took for themselves the name *"Imagineers,"* a combination of *"imagine"* and *"engineer."*[1] Every worker wants to feel that he or she is more than just a generic and replaceable cog in a machine. When a company asks its employees to *"imagine,"* it's asking them to forget, at least for a moment, about bureaucratic organizational charts, stodgy bosses, departmental budgets, the established way of doing things, and all the other everyday restrictions that infringe on their work. Asking your employees to *"imagine"* is asking them to contribute a piece of themselves to the enterprise. It can do wonders for morale, of course—but it can also lead to some incredibly innovative ideas.

As in the corporate sphere, *"imagine"* is one of the most powerful words in politics. A political idea is just an idea—but when someone captures your imagination, he or she goes from being a *"politician"* (negative, disreputable, boring) to being a *"leader"* (visionary, statesmanlike, inspiring). The most successful political leaders are those who find a way to inspire. They manifest their own imaginative powers, but, even more importantly, they stimulate the imaginations of their fellow citizens.

Edmund Burke, decrying the onset of the French Revolution, described its cold rationalism this way: "The age of chivalry is gone. That of sophisters, economists and calculators has succeeded."[2] Great political leaders don't come across as human calculators. They exhibit passion, sympathy, and an unbridled belief in a better future. President Kennedy didn't inspire thousands of young Americans to join the Peace Corps by presenting a really persuasive cost-benefit analysis. He appealed to something far greater in our hearts. Imagination, passion, even a touch of poetry—these are the qualities that speed the pulse.

The use of imagination to induce imagery is particularly helpful when talking about a complex subject to a large and diverse audience. In early 2005, when President George W. Bush was attempting the seemingly impossible task of reforming Social Security, he challenged the Congress and the American people to imagine the future for the next generation if the looming threat of Social Security bankruptcy was not properly addressed. In a speech at the University of Notre Dame, Bush explicitly asked the audience to *"imagine if this government of ours does nothing at this point in Social Security, and you've got a five-year-old child."* By doing this the President was not simply asking the audience to think about the future. He was placing every member of the audience in the role of a parent struggling to raise kids and put away enough money for retirement. Bush understood that the combination of the *"imagine"* framework and the intergenerational impact of Social Security would pack a powerful punch. Yet he still failed because the imagination of seniors losing their Social Security in a stock market crash was even more powerful than the dream of their grandchildren getting control of their Social Security savings. Big dreams—or horrific nightmares—are not born from facts and figures. The real emotional impact requires a real imagination—and an appeal to use it.

## 2. "Hassle-free"

The idea that we, as consumers, should not have to think about how we buy a product (quickly), use a product (immediately), or fix a product (easily) has become deeply ingrained in us. And when it comes to how we interact with products, services, and people, *"hassle-free"* is a top priority. In fact, Americans prefer a *"hassle-free"* product to a *"less expensive"* one by an impressive 62 percent to 38 percent. We prize ease of use and convenience to such an extent that we are genuinely willing to pay for it—and it's worth at least another 10 percent and as much as 20 percent on top of the sticker price if the promise is delivered on.

Like *"imagine," "hassle-free"* is in the eyes of the consumer, but there are specific examples that transcend all populations.

In terms of purchasing, haggling with the car dealer is the single best example of a hassle Americans want eliminated (*"Imagine a hassle-free car buying experience"* would be my tagline for any car dealer who asked). CarMax, which famously does not permit haggling over prices on its used cars, is succeeding exactly because they have listened to the consumer, and their tagline says it all: *"The way car buying should be."*

Standing in line waiting at the grocery store after already spending time walking up and down the aisles searching for specific items is a guaranteed hassle producer (*"Easy in, easy out"* best communicates a hassle-free supermarket experience, along with "the five minute guarantee" if you're willing to open up more checkout stands).

Actual product use now needs to be hassle-free as well. Start with the packaging. Too many products are encased so tightly in hard plastic that it seems we have to beat it against the wall and then drop it off a thirty-story building to pop it open or use a chain saw to cut it free from the packaging. We are tired of scraping with our fingernails trying to get the plastic off our CDs and DVDs. We are annoyed when *"batteries [are] not included."* And the solid plastic packaging that encases a new pair of scissors when you buy them? You need scissors to get the scissors open. Pity the people who are buying their very first pair. Companies should stop wrapping and start prepping their products so we can actually get at them when we want to. The value to consumers is immeasurable.

When we take our new laptop out of the box, we want to turn it on and have it work immediately. (My message recommendation to the first manufacturer who produces a truly hassle-free computer: *"Plug it in. Turn it on. Go."*) We are livid when the instructions for setting up our audio system read like the disarmament codes for a North Korean nuclear bomb and are seemingly translated by someone who counted English as their third language. We don't appreciate being switched to a call center in India when our appliance breaks down and someone named "Bob" can't explain how to fix it.

It's often enlightening to look at the etymologies of words and see where they came from. *"Hassle"* originally meant "to hack or saw at." I'd say that sums it up nicely. We don't want to have to hack and saw away at things—we want them to be like butter under a hot knife.

We don't want to think about it. We want it to work—not now, but five minutes ago, dammit! We want the products we use to work as reliably and as instantly as the light does when we flip the switch. Have you tried opening a bottle of medicine lately? The caps are more secure than King Tut's tomb. If it's a prescription for arthritis, you're out of luck—you'll do more damage to your joints trying to get the damned thing open than the medicine will ever be able to alleviate.

### 3. *"Lifestyle"*

*"Lifestyle"* is an example of terminology that was adopted by consumers even before the marketing community. *"Lifestyle,"* like *"imagine"* and the *"American Dream,"* is incredibly powerful because it is at the same time self-defined and aspirational—everyone defines and aspires to his or her own unique lifestyle.

But unlike the "American Dream," the concept of *"lifestyle"* is a relatively new term. The compound word was created in 1929 by Alfred Adler, an Austrian scientist, but today's definition of the word wasn't applied until the 1960s.[3] The word *"lifestyle"* both creates and exemplifies a *Weltanschauung* or *worldview* (speaking of German-derived compound words)[4]—one that is individualistic rather than community-oriented, personalized rather than generic, and forward-looking rather than nostalgic or tethered to tradition. The very notion of *styling* one's life—and that there are many different styles of the good life from which to choose—would have seemed a foreign and bizarre concept to our great-grandparents. Yet *"lifestyle"* is a concept that is essential to understanding our more secular, individualist age.

*"Lifestyle"* implies that there is more than one model of "the good life," and all we have to do is choose. This may be relativistic or self-centered, but we live in an era of individuality, and *choosing a lifestyle* is a crucial component of defining who we are.

Today, *"lifestyle"* has special currency among young people, who use it to describe what they like, what they believe, and what they want to do. It's a catch-all term. Instead of talking about how they eat, what they do for exercise, or how much they work, they talk about their *"lifestyle"* as a whole. All the various facets, instead of being examined individually, are subsumed into the larger *"lifestyle"* context. It's no longer a question of what I want for a career or where I want to live or what I do for fun— that's just a subset of the larger question: *What lifestyle do I want to make for myself?*

### 4. *"Accountability"*

*"Accountability"* is one of the qualities that Americans most want from their political leaders and governing institutions. Yet Americans also think of *"accountability"* as one of the qualities their elected officials and the appointed bureaucrats most lack. Just as Americans don't trust big business and other large institutions, they also don't trust government agencies and systems because they perceive that such large entities are out of control and answerable to no one. The federal bureaucracy has become the world's first genuine perpetual motion machine. It's like a runaway stagecoach in an old Western, its riderless horses racing pell-mell toward a cliff . . . with all of us, the average citizens, as passengers sitting trembling inside. We expect our political leaders to be the heroes on horseback, cutting off the coach before it reaches the precipice and bringing the horses under control before the whole lot of us go tumbling over the edge.

Americans will no longer consent to ride along placidly; we want to know that there's somebody in the saddle. We want *"accountability."* Consider, for instance, the Contract with America; its specific provisions were popular, but the real kicker was the pledge of *"accountability"* that I personally added at the very end of the document. It contained a political first, an accountability and enforcement clause: *"If we break this contract, throw us out. We mean it."* Never before had a group of elected officials been so bold as to suggest to the voters that they ought to even *consider* not returning them to office. And there it was, in writing. That pledge of *"accountability,"* more than any policy detail or ideological argument, is what made possible the Republican takeover of 1994. It's a lesson that Democrats and Republicans alike would do well to remember.

One Democrat who learned that lesson and rode it to the governor's mansion in New Jersey is Jon Corzine. He sought to fill the void of a previous governor who had been forced to resign in disgrace because of scandal and mismanagement, and a temporary placeholder who had been roundly criticized for doing nothing to clean up the political mess. Corzine understood early in the campaign that for voters to trust another Democrat, he needed to prove that he would bring a level of integrity back to the office—and he used an explicit pledge of *"accountability"* to achieve it. Corzine would reiterate his commitment to *"strengthen accountability"* at every speech and public appearance, stressing that increased *"accountability"* and *"transparency"* were essential in restoring the people's trust in state government. It worked. As angry as voters were, Corzine successfully inoculated himself against Republican attacks that he was just as corrupt and unethical as those who came before him.

On Election Day, people invest their trust in democratic institutions and the people who run them, and they expect and demand a return that is worthy of that investment. *"Accountability"* is that return.

Even though you'll hear *"accountability"* talked about in a political context, it's not primarily a political term. The American people universally want corporations held *"accountable"* for their actions as well as their products and how they treat their customers, their employees, and their shareholders. Accountability moved into the corporate lexicon right around the time Enron collapsed.

When it comes to how corporations sell their products, you might think that the word *"accountability"* represents an unambiguously good thing. Not always. A company that tells its customers that it will *"hold ourselves accountable"* for the products and/or services it produces is actually likely to get a horrified response from the people who hear that message. It begs the question: "Accountable for what?" It actually implies that something is going to go wrong to justify that accountability. The most subtle suggestion of a *need* for accountability scares us off. People may demand that companies take responsibility, but they don't want the companies themselves talking about it. By doing so, a company has already conceded too much . . . and has begun to confirm the public's worst fears.

Instead, if you want to profess your *"accountability"* as a company, try a simple, declarative, strong alternative such as *"We deliver."* It says you provide what you promise, and it does not allude to the times when you don't.

## 5. *"Results"* and the *"Can-Do Spirit"*

We Americans are a practical people. We want to understand the bottom line. Theory, abstractions, good intentions—all these are well and good, but in the final analysis, we want to know how many dollar bills we're going to have to peel out of our wallets, whether the on/off button is going to work when we push it, and whether we got a fair shake overall. When we buy something, we want to know that it's going to provide a tangible benefit—something that we can see, hear, feel, or otherwise quantify. We have little patience for "ifs," "ands," "buts," or excuses. Forget about nuances, niceties, or shades of gray. We don't care about the process. We care about *"results."**

In the realms of our personal, family and spiritual lives, we may believe nice ideas such as that "the journey is more important than the destination," but don't dream of trying to tell that to one of your customers. When we're shelling out our hard-earned money, we become single-minded, ruthless, and uncompromising.

A perfect example of where "results" and "can-do" spirit matter is in the fitness industry. In today's world of fad diets and high obesity rates, Americans are looking for realistic options to get in shape and see results. "Results, The Gym," a Washington, D.C.–based fitness center, has embraced the idea of a results-oriented business so much that it named the company after the concept that guides it. It was started in 1994 as a personal training service called "Training for Results," and its current motto, *"Reach your goals, get results,"* serves as both a motivator and a potential solution for consumers looking to get fit. This exemplifies the bottom line of what potential customers are looking for, and what they expect out of a gym.

As in corporate communications, political messages should emphasize bottom-line *"results,"* not process. Americans care where a politician ends up much more than where he or she began, and what he or she does more than what he or she says. They will support policies that pro-

---

*There is a subculture in America that does in fact care about process. They are the people who pay extra for organic groceries from Whole Foods and pay more for their Prius because they care about the environment. But they are still a very small minority.

duce tangible, concrete, quantifiable benefits. Like Vince Lombardi, we don't believe winning is the most important thing—it's the *only* thing. When it comes to evaluating the performance of Washington politicians, there's no more room for excuses. We don't want to hear about the difficulties of the markup process or the intricacies of the Rules Committee. The procedural details are irrelevant. Just *"get it done"* (the best articulation of *"results"*) or we'll find someone who will. The *"Do-Nothing Congress"* of 1948 had its reasons for resisting Harry Truman's program, but they've been forgotten by history; we remember only Truman's denunciation of it. On the eve of the Civil War, President Buchanan faced staggering difficulties and mind-numbing complications—but historians remember only the *"results"* of his presidency and deem him a failure, pure and simple. We Americans are interested in serving no theory, advancing no agenda—we just want our leaders to do what works, we want them to get it done—and we know they can succeed if they put in the effort.

If results are the goal, the *"can-do spirit"* is the effort. Early in 2006 we asked 1,000 adults what phrase best described what Americans were all about. Finishing first: the *"can-do spirit"* (32 percent), followed by *"strong and tough"* (22 percent) and *"self-reliant"* (14 percent). It's one reason why we root for the underdog and appreciate the human interest stories of people who have triumphed over great adversity and eventually succeed after years of failure. A *"can-do"* attitude is uncomplaining, stoic, no-nonsense—all powerful but sadly old-fashioned virtues most often associated with the Greatest Generation. Even though you don't hear the words spoken too often, the term is due for a revival.

For the last seventy-five years, the cinema has been the most common source of can-do pop culture. For much of their careers, Jimmy Stewart and Henry Fonda played characters that were down and out but struggled and eventually succeeded against tremendous odds and tough opponents. Some of the most successful films of the past decade were specifically fashioned around the can-do culture, from the animated blockbuster *Finding Nemo* about a clownfish in search of his father, to Tom Hanks in the Academy Award–winning *Castaway,* which tells a powerful story about the will to survive.

### 6. *"Innovation"*

*"Innovation"* immediately calls to mind pictures of the future. It's the corporate technology version of *"imagine,"* evoking 300 million different,

individual definitions. *"Innovation"* leads to products that are smaller or lighter or faster or cheaper . . . or bigger, more resilient, stronger, longer lasting. It's the road that leads to a laptop battery that will last for twenty-four hours—without causing your keyboard to melt or the fan to whirr so loudly that it distracts you from your work. *"Innovation"* means tourist flights that escape the Earth's orbit and nanotechnology marvels so small that they strain the ability of our comprehension.

Describing your company and products as *"innovative"* is far better than saying they're *"new and improved." "Innovative,"* on the other hand, is bold and forward-looking, progressive (in a nonpolitical sense), confident, and energetic. It's a natural continuation and elaboration of the pioneer spirit that built this country. *"Innovation"* is also entrepreneurial and self-reliant; it suggests initiative, ingenuity, and even passion.

*"Innovation"* can also be used as a call to action. General Electric, citing a study that stated only 9 percent of college students felt the United States was doing enough to foster innovation among young people, launched an *"Innovation Tour"* in 2003. This tour visited campuses across the country, addressing "college students' concerns, feelings, and aspirations relating to innovation and imagination." By actively seeking youth input—often the engine of innovation—GE has been in a better position to hire the next generation of scientists, engineers, technicians, and the other occupations that will drive the twenty-first-century economy.

In our language work for the manufacturing industry, the only other word that is as valued by the American people as *"innovation"* is *"technology."* And with everything becoming more technological, the awareness of technology itself will eventually disappear even as our acceptance and appreciation for what it does in our lives increases—including, among many other outcomes, fostering innovation itself.

## 7. *"Renew, Revitalize, Rejuvenate, Restore, Rekindle, Reinvent"*

These are the so-called *"re"* words, and they are incredibly powerful because they take the best elements or ideas from the past and apply them to the present and the future. *"Nostalgia"* alone has a limited appeal. *"Retro"* may fascinate, but it doesn't necessarily move stuff off the shelves. Younger customers want to buy from companies that are new and fresh and hip. Chances are, a company launching a retro ad campaign is a company whose well of new ideas has run dry.

Instead, take the old and make it new again by putting a fresh spin on it with one or multiple *"re"* words. To *"renew"* is to take an important product or corporate commitment and reassert it. To *"revitalize"* is to take something that is deteriorating and inject new life into it. To *"rejuvenate"* is to take something old and bring it up-to-date with a more youthful feel. To *"restore"* is to take something old and return it to its original luster. To *"rekindle"* is to inject emotion or passion into something tired and staid.

Olay Products, a cosmetics company, is in the business of breathing new life and a sense of restoration into the self-image of its customers. As part of their "Age Defying Series," Olay offers *"renewal creams and lotions"* and *"revitalizing eye gels."* While not directly guaranteeing it, Olay understands that its consumers are looking for the fountain of youth. Words such as *"restore"* and *"rejuvenate"* offer customers a chance to reach back in time to when they had smoother skin and younger-looking eyes.

So mix and match the words and definitions. Apply them liberally. The *"re"* words imply action, movement, progress, and improvement—all essential attributes in the twenty-first-century economy. *"You can't stay who you are,"* says Steve Wynn, who revitalized Vegas with his Mirage Resort in 1989, rejuvenated Vegas with his youth-themed Treasure Island in 1993, reinvented Vegas with his world-renowned luxurious Bellagio resort in 1998, and renewed his position as the great creator of lavish resorts with Wynn Las Vegas in 2005. *"If you don't reinvent, you die."*

As in corporate communications, the *"re-"* words should be applied to politics as well. Better to have programs and policies grounded in tradition, or experience, than launch something that's brand-new. The new Medicare prescription drug program is a case in point. Seniors have been reluctant to enroll in it, unsure about the new rules, resistant to change—this *despite* the fact that they're unsatisfied with the status quo. The most effective way of saying *"new and improved"* from a political standpoint is to employ one of the *"re-"* words.

---

# THE "RE" WORDS THAT
# DEFINE RESPONSIBILITY

**RENEW** our commitment to hardworking American taxpayers;

**REDESIGN** and **REFORM** government programs and services;

**REVITALIZE** the economy;

**REBUILD** confidence in local solutions;

**RESTORE** American faith in the values and principles of accountability, responsibility, and common sense.

---

### 8. *"Efficient"* and *"Efficiency"*

To Americans, the word *"efficiency"* simply means getting more for less— and in the bargain-hungry environment we live in, efficiency is a significant product advantage. *"Efficient"* and *"efficiency"* also have a positive intellectual tone, suggesting the wise use of energy, resources, and so on.

By comparison, *"conserve"* and *"conservation,"* the terminology used until now to describe automobile emissions, gas usage, and the interaction between products and the environment, sound austere. To Americans, *"conservation"* implies paying more to get less, and hints that it may require some sort of onerous effort as well. It also has a backward connotation. But *"efficiency"* is more about innovation and technology—a twenty-first-century approach to twenty-first-century challenges.

One major challenge facing Americans in the twenty-first century is that of rising oil prices. For car companies, being able to tout your product as *"fuel-efficient"* means consumers save money in the long run, a point that is easy to communicate and useful in motivating customers. By the time you read this book, Toyota will be selling more cars than any other manufacturer in the world, and they are surging in popularity because of their Prius hybrid model and its efficient use of gas. Honda has taken advantage of the current oil climate and offers a number of hybrid vehicles that make it the *"overall fuel efficiency leader in America."* While the fact that Honda's hybrid vehicles conserve fuel is important, the use of the word efficiency indicates the innovative way in which this new technology is conserving fuel. This language also appeals to an audience looking to be at the forefront of a technological revolution, seeking to be a part of a movement, as well as part of a solution to a serious political (and ecological) problem.

## 9. *"The Right to . . ."*

Going all the way back to the nation's founding, Americans have always been committed to the concept of *"rights."* Limiting the powers of the federal government wasn't enough; the Founding Fathers demanded that our rights be enumerated formally in the Bill of Rights. And the proliferation of supposed new rights has only accelerated in recent decades. People now argue that there is a right to a job, to a "livable" minimum wage, to health care, to privacy, to abortion, to choice in education, and on and on. Most of those "rights" are promulgated by the political left, though those on the right have their "rights" as well. Presenting a political position within the context of *"rights"* is therefore a difficult but winning approach. *"Rights,"* as opposed to mere policy preferences, are thought to be inalienable. They don't come from us, and no one is allowed to take them away—for any reason. They cannot be abridged, no matter what. And that's what makes the language so powerful.

When an elected official tells you that you have the *"right"* to health care, rather than just that you should have it, he or she is adding intensity to the message. When something is a *"right,"* it's not just nice or reasonable or beneficial—it becomes *essential.*

There's another nuance to the concept of *"rights"* that is equally important. The principle gives people a choice whether or not they'll actually exercise the "right." A parent may not choose to pull his or her child out of the local public school in favor of a better one across town, but having the *"right"*—and therefore the control and the power—to choose the school is important in and of itself. Wanting the *"right"* to choose your doctor, hospital, and health care plan and actually taking the time and making the effort to do so are two different propositions. It's why Americans love the language and the concept of the "Patient's Bill of Rights" health care legislation, even though they don't like the cost and the bureaucracy. But with the *"right to"* lexicon, that decision is in the hands of the voters, not the government.

## 10. *"Patient-Centered"*

Let me begin this discussion with the single dumbest linguistic creation of the last half century: the phrase *"managed care."* Think about it. When you're sick or in pain, do you really want your care *"managed"*? When an operation, procedure, or medication is required to save your life, do you really want some accountant applying a financial equation to your personal situation? The originator of the term *"managed care"* should be thrown in jail for linguistic malpractice—and that word needs to be dropped from the health care lexicon forever.

Here's the replacement. The term *"patient-centered"* obviously has a limited application, but it is included here because that application is so essential to an industry that is expanding on a daily basis. *"Patient-centered"* describes what most people want out of their health care. *"Quality," "affordability,"* and *"choice"* are all important aspects of *"patient-centered"*-ness, but it is the most effective umbrella term for anything related to medicine involving human beings.

The reason why the phrase *"patient-centered"* resonates so strongly is that it draws an unspoken contrast with *"dollar"*-centered and *"insurance"*-centered medicine. When we're sick, or when a family member is hurting, the last thing we want the health care provider to be concerned with is dollars and cents. All we want is to alleviate the pain and suffering and make us or our loved ones better. We want the focus to be squarely on us and on the substance of our care, not on procedural matters such as insurance copayments and plan parameters.

However, when talking about one of the biggest names in health care, Kaiser Permanente, some might not think of a company with a truly personal touch that cares about each customer. Yet one glance at their Web site would lead you to think differently. Under the banner welcoming the visitor to the site, simple text asking consumers to *"please tell us who you are"* is displayed. Upon digging deeper into the site, one is asked questions about the kind of coverage one is looking for, resulting in a listing of plans that best suit the customer. The language is always personal, human, and reassuring, including their recent tagline, *"Live Long and Thrive."*

In a field often considered impersonal and distant as health care, Kaiser Permanente's Web site approach evokes memories of the personal touch of stethoscope-wielding doctors making house calls and the familiarity of the neighborhood pharmacy.

## 11. *"Investment"*

President Clinton came up with one of the most important linguistic innovations of the 1990s when he began to use the term *"investment"* instead of *"spending."* *"Spending"* suggests waste. *"Investment"* suggests the responsible handling of resources. A dollar *"spent"* is a dollar you'll never see again. A dollar *"invested"* is a dollar that comes back to you many times over. *"Spending"* is morally neutral—it could be good or bad, responsible or wasteful. *"Investment"* is by definition reasonable and responsible. *"Investment"* is also by definition forward-looking, whereas *"spending"* implies instant gratification.

Americans understand how important saving and investing are to their own personal finances—even if they don't always (or ever) act on that understanding—and they react favorably toward the application of these principles to politics. You can get an extra 10 percent bump in support for a project or program if you talk about *"investing"* rather than *"spending."*

Just as President Clinton used the word *"investment"* over *"spending"* to defuse the perception of being a "big-spending liberal," President Bush attempted to use different labels to defuse another hot-button issue—Social Security—by changing the definition of his reform from *"privatized accounts"* to *"personal investment."*

A CBS/*New York Times* poll taken in June of 2005 illustrated the power of simple word choice. One question, *"Do you approve or disapprove of the way George W. Bush is handling Social Security?"* yielded only a 25 percent approval rating. But when the same sample in the same questionnaire was asked, *"Do you think allowing individuals to invest a portion of their Social Security taxes on their own is a good idea or a bad idea?"* almost double (45 percent) thought it was a good idea. The president's public approval efforts still fell far short, but he set a more favorable context for the next reform attempt.

*"Investment"* is more than just a political word, however. Companies that invest in technology, invest in their community, invest in job training, or invest in the future will earn a higher level of appreciation. Whether in brand-name pharmaceutical medications or consumer electronics, emerging technologies or online retailers, products and services that promote the significant investments of time or money in their creation can command a price premium. Even on a personal level, *"investing in your future"* is one of the strongest motivations for making long-term purchases. Buying is for now. Investing is forever.

## 12. *"Casual Elegance"*

Like *"patient-centered," "casual elegance"* is another term with an industry-specific application. It's the expression that best defines what Americans want when they travel, more than any other attribute. The United States in the twenty-first century is a casual country—in how we address one another by our first names, in our attitudes, our clothing, and in our *"lifestyle."* There was a time when no man would dream of getting on an airplane without wearing a coat and tie. That country no longer exists. Today you're lucky if the guy next to you in seat 21B showered this week. And it's *"elegance"* we want, rather than *"sophistication."* We like our pleasures simple. *"Casual elegance"* is aspirational; it appeals to our imaginations, our idealized best selves.

This applies to all components of the hospitality industry. *"Clean and comfortable,"* which is what some hotel chains sell, is good, but *"casual elegance"* is even better. A relaxed dining environment is what some restaurants promote, but what people want even more is a sense of *"casual elegance."*

One brand often associated with casual elegance is Ralph Lauren. Using descriptive words like *"timeless"* and *"classic,"* every Ralph Lauren ad for all of its brands say *"relaxation."* This pleasant imagery is meant to transport the consumer to a simpler place in time, where he or she can escape the drudgeries of the daily grind and relax undisturbed; all because the consumer chose the right fabric.

## 13. *"Independent"*

Being *"independent"* is more of a corporate communication effort than a product pitch. It means having no constricting ties, no conflicts of interest, nothing to hide. A company that presents itself as *"independent"* is seen as honest, candid, and responsive to the people it serves. That's one reason why *"independent insurance agents"* tests better than any individual insurance company—the lack of even a hint of bias.

Americans want unique experiences. They want their lives to be tailored to them (once again we see the relevance of *"imagination"* and *"lifestyle"*). Because we identify so closely with the products we use, because they are often such a crucial element of our own self-images, we don't want them to be the same as everybody else's. Everybody's iPod has its own, individual playlist. Everybody's TiVo has a personalized schedule of TV shows. Everyone's cell phone now has its own ring—a must for those under twenty-five.

This *"independence"* and individuality greatly affects how we think about brands and corporations of all kinds. Demonstrate a level of *"independence"* in what you say, what you sell, and what you do, and consumers will *"independently"* reward you. An example of *"independence"* is the successful ad campaign for Tommy Hilfiger's fragrance, Tommy Girl. The slogan, *"A Declaration of Independence,"* suggests that when a woman wears this perfume, she makes it her own. Although anyone can wear the perfume, once she puts it on, it is hers and hers alone.

Politically, our country wasn't born with a Declaration of Rights. We didn't start out with a Declaration of Virtue. It wasn't a Declaration of Justice that fired up the imagination of the "new world" in Philadelphia. Nor was it a Declaration of Equality. America's founding fathers certainly believed in all of these principles and hoped to see them embodied in the nascent nation. But they began this great experiment of ours by declaring *"independence"*—and that anti-authoritarian assertion remains the cardinal American impulse.

*"Independence"* expresses an attitude as much as it does an idea—"Don't tread on me" (also the motto of the United States Marine Corps) . . . "Live and let live" . . . "Smile when you say that, pilgrim" . . . *"Independence"* includes individuality and self-sufficiency. It means we don't want to be tied down like Gulliver by the Lilliputians. It tells the world (often to the world's chagrin) that we Americans will stand on our own two feet and make our own way whether they like it or not.

In contemporary political terms, *"independence"* suggests no ties, no obligations, no conflicts of interest. *"Independent"* politicians are no *politicians* at all—they are transformed into leaders, statesmen. They are candid, fearless, bound only by honor, principle, and the strictures of their own conscience. The independent man or woman is free of all institutional or political encumbrances.

The opposite of *"independence"* is *"partisanship"*—and today it is truly one of the dirtiest words in American politics. We may have divided ourselves into red states and blue states, but partisan identification is down across the country, and the old days of pulling a single lever and voting the party line are long past. Given the option, almost as many Americans self-identify as independents than as either as Democrats or Republicans. More voters are registering their party as "Decline to State" than ever before in American history. Bickering politicians give everyone a splitting headache—and the solution is right there before us: the *"independent,"* maverick politician.

We respect independent politicians because they say what they mean and mean what they say. They buck the party's establishment and its conventional wisdom (to the applause of the media who follows) and go their own way, preferring the road less traveled. We all know the most prominent examples of the *"independent"* leader: Senator John McCain . . . Mayor Rudy Giuliani . . . Senator Joseph Lieberman . . . Mayor Mike Bloomberg . . . the late Senator Daniel Patrick Moynihan . . . Governor Arnold Schwarzenegger . . . and Ross Perot, just to name a few. It's probably no coincidence that most of these mavericks are political centrists rather than inhabitants of the ideological wings of their parties; nevertheless, their independent reputations have as much to do with style and attributes as they do with philosophy. Anyone who appears to put principles, common sense, and results over party loyalty and a rigid agenda can develop a reputation of *"independence."* If you want to truly connect with the American public, it's time to make your own, personal declaration of *"independence."*

### 14. *"Peace of Mind"*

*"Peace of mind"* will eventually supplant *"security"* as a primary political value. It's a kinder, gentler, softer expression of *"security"* that is less politicized, more embracing and all-encompassing.

*"Security"* has a somewhat limited, very specific meaning that is often scary and militant. It is what employees want most in their jobs, but peace of mind wins every other comparison. *"Peace of mind,"* described by Franklin Roosevelt as "freedom from fear," implies the same result, but the tone is far different—and more appealing, especially to women, because it is the positive side of a very negative concern. *"Security"* suggests fences, barbed wire, electronic surveillance, burglar alarms, neighborhood watch programs, and long lines at airport screening. *"Security"* demands from us vigilance in order to prevent something bad. *"Peace of mind,"* by contrast, accentuates the positive. It dwells on a favorable result rather than the disturbing struggle to get there. *"Peace of mind"* is a destination, like the Baseball Hall of Fame in Cooperstown; *"security"* is the six-hour car ride you have to endure to get there.

Americans have enough drama in their daily lives—we don't need our politicians to exacerbate it. Most of us just want to be left alone and live a quiet life. *"Peace of mind"* perfectly encapsulates that disposition.

## 15. *"Certified"*

The reason *"certified"* has begun to enter the lexicon is because trust and confidence in people and promises has evaded. It's not just used-car salesmen that we don't believe anymore. We want and need ironclad agreements that what we buy won't fail us months or even days after our purchase. A warranty only addresses the future of the product. *"Certification"* is an official (usually written) guarantee that what you see is in fact what you get, and that it upholds a higher level of quality and/or reliability. *"Certification"* also implies a specific process of review was followed by a trained professional. Any Tom, Dick, or Harry can offer a guarantee. *"Certification"* suggests something more thorough and serious.

The most common use of *"certified"* or *"certification"* is in the used-car industry, or, as some brands like to call themselves, *"certified pre-owned vehicles."* If you still don't think word choice matters, ask yourself which would you rather own, a used car or a certified pre-owned vehicle? The language of certification is also being used in grocery stores to emphasize the quality of meat, milk, and other perishable items. Within the next half decade, expect dozens of products and industries to apply the *"certified"* label.

Corporations are also finding a value to certification. If you examine the annual reports of the *Fortune* 500 companies, you'll find a number of them emphasize the *"certification"* of their year-end financial report in an effort to convince shareholders that they can trust what they read. We also know from recent market research that corporate officers themselves expect *"certification"* from their accounting firms because of legal ramifications.

## 16. *"All-American"*

The term *"all-American"* and the overt appeal to American pride (rather than patriotism) is not universally appreciated, but those who share the sentiment are absolutely affected by it. It certainly works with older consumers who still see America through red-white-and-blue-colored glasses, particularly when the appeal is forward-looking and values-oriented, such as a reference to the "American Dream."

Yet America is more than a flag flying over a courthouse, or an apple pie cooling near an open window. America is all about progress and innovation, two ways in which All American, the third largest distributor of semiconductors and a top-ten supplier of electronic components, has used its patriotic image to outgrow the competition and become an industry leader. While most consumers won't equate capacitors and inducing cables with the *"American Dream,"* the company's name transcends the complexity of the products and instead sells an image that is easy to convey and understand.

However, younger consumers are less affected by an overt American appeal, both because they are more skeptical about their country and because they are more likely to be ethnically diverse. My research for a number of *Fortune* 500 companies has revealed a greater disapproval toward America among African-Americans and some Latinos, and that mind-set will certainly influence their buying habits.

## 17. *"Prosperity"*

It's long past time to return the word *"prosperity"* to our political lexicon. It was once a prominent part of public debate, in the 1920s and 1930s, but it slipped into obscurity when prosperity fell out of existence for millions of Americans after the Great Depression began in 1929. It does still mean something to people today, and it's overdue for a revival (yet another *"re"* word).

In just ten letters, *"prosperity"* encompasses the idea of more jobs, better careers, employment security, more take-home pay, a stronger economy, and expanded opportunity. In fact, *"prosperity"* is most often described by Americans as the economic component of *"opportunity."* But *"prosperity"* doesn't connote only wealth; it suggests a sense of overall financial well-being and success (with a hint of *"peace of mind"*). You probably wouldn't describe a total loser who wins the lottery as *"prosperous."* You'd reserve it for the neighbor who built up his own small business from scratch, the accountant down the block who just made partner, or your lawyer brother-in-law who just won a large financial settlement for his client. *"Prosperity,"* in other words, has a real-life aspect to it. It's earned. An elected official who says he's seeking to promote prosperity is also, by implication, promoting the good life earned the old-fashioned way—through hard work.

## 18. *"Spirituality"*

The United States remains one of the most religious nations on Earth. Unlike post-Christian Europe, unlike the mostly secular remainder of the Western world, religious faith still has relevance to an overwhelming majority of Americans. If you're an American politician, being religious is not something to run away from or apologize for.

Nevertheless, when appealing to a broad audience (as opposed to a particular niche), evocations of *"spirituality"* are more inclusive and therefore more politically effective than are generic references to *"religion,"* specific denominations, or even *"faith."* Americans reward politicians who talk respectfully but candidly about their core beliefs and who seem grounded and morally centered; we are perfectly comfortable with leaders whose ethics and worldview come from a religious tradition. But the best way to explain our moral compass is by using the broadest, most generally applicable terms possible. Talking about your *"spirituality"* implies an inherent morality and seriousness. Going into detail about your particular denomination, on the other hand, will turn off at least some segment of the population.

## 19. *"Financial Security"*

*"Financial freedom"* used to be one of Americans' top values and the number one definition of the American Dream. But that was before the dot-com bubble burst, the stock market plummeted, and the September 11 attacks occurred.

Alas, in our new century, *"financial freedom"* has dropped to the middle of the priority list. In the terrifying, unstable world we live in today, *"financial security"* is now the higher priority. Eventually there will come a time when Americans' confidence returns, when we not only want *"financial security"* but also aspire to *"financial freedom."* Until then, however, people will continue to be cautious about radical changes—such as Social Security reform, for example—and jealously protective of what they already have. Better, then, to sell tax reform or other policy changes as *"enhancements of financial security"* than as pathways to financial freedom. Sadly, financial freedom is more than most of us are hoping for at the moment. Financial security is still attainable, we hope.

## 20. A *"Balanced Approach"*

Just as professing your independence from partisanship and ideology will win you credibility points with the public (as long as you also appear to practice this philosophy), so too will arguing for a *"balanced approach"* to our nation's problems. People understand that America is faced with multiple, competing priorities. They know it's a juggling act to address numerous issues at the same time. All they ask is that you balance these conflicting needs in a responsible and thoughtful manner.

A *"balanced approach"* refers not only to where you come down on the ideological spectrum for a given political question, but also to the overall pace of political change you endorse. For us, one revolution and one civil war was enough. Temperamentally at least, most of us are quite conservative. Unlike the French Revolution, the Russian Revolution, and the Chinese Revolution, the American Revolution was fundamentally conservative in character. We went to war reluctantly, and only in the interests of preserving the ancient British liberties and rights we felt had been wrongly taken from us.

Americans still take this incremental, cautious approach to political change, and most of us still have an inherent, instinctive dislike of radicalism of all stripes. When Republicans took over the Congress in 1995, they made an immediate and colossal mistake by calling it a *"revolution."* Newt Gingrich spoke in near-messianic terms about saving American civilization—and regardless of any valid substantive points he made, his demeanor and grandiosity made a lot of people jittery. He seemed to want to move too quickly, to do too much. He and others like him would have had more success had they emphasized a *"balanced approach,"* about their desire to enact necessary reforms while still respecting the other side's point of view, about doing things in a new way without throwing overboard all the vestiges of a system that had been developed over 200 years.

### 21. *"A Culture of . . ."*

I hate ending the twenty-one words of the future with this term but it is rapidly increasing in use and has the unfortunate potential to be the most divisive and do the most damage to the civility of politics in these early years of the twenty-first century. Whenever you hear a politician begin a phrase with *"a culture of . . ."* rest assured it is meant as a slam.

The word *culture* used to apply to entire societies, even empires. More and more, however, it has come to be used in a micro sense, to describe every imaginable subculture (and lend to it the dignity of culture as a whole). So today we have the *"culture of"* hate alongside the *"culture of"* fear, a *"culture of"* paintball, the *"culture of"* corruption, the *"culture of"* destruction, the *"culture of"* East Los Angeles, and the *"culture of"* the

Upper East Side. When the U.S. envoy to the United Nations, Ambassador John Bolton, told the Senate Foreign Relations Committee on May 25, 2006, that the U.N. was hopelessly tied to a *"culture of inaction,"* it was only the most recent addition to this growing litany. There are ethnic cultures and religious cultures, political cultures and athletic cultures. The fundamental insight to take from this proliferation of identity groups is that there is no longer any single American culture that unites us all, rich and poor, young and old, white and black (and Latino and Asian), Republicans and Democrats. Regardless of whether you think this balkanization of America is a good thing or whether you deplore it, it is the new reality.

By defining an issue or a cluster of issues as part of a metaphorical *"culture,"* you can lend it new weight and seriousness. If you are a Democrat, it's not a question of a few ethical lapses on the part of a few individual GOP congressmen—they personify a *"culture of corruption."* The problem is bigger than any one individual or any single incident. If you're a conservative Republican, you're not just pro-life on abortion or opposed to euthanasia—you support a *"culture of life."* *"Social"* issues have been supplanted by *"cultural"* issues, which sound less threatening and judgmental.


In the end, how these words are used and delivered is almost as important as the words themselves. This may pain academics, journalists, and some readers, but the fact is, style is almost as important as substance. John McCain is a classic case of language personifying the man and the man personifying the language. In his presidential campaigns, McCain called his bus and his campaign the *"Straight Talk Express"*—and he would use the phrase early in his speeches as a way to set himself and his rhetoric apart from those of his opponents. He was onto something big. *"Straight talk"* is a powerful concept. It's exactly what Americans want from their political leaders—and what they believe is sorely lacking in most of them. By christening his bus the *"Straight Talk Express"* and then, incredibly, getting the media to refer to it by that name repeatedly and uncritically, McCain scored a major communications coup.

But John McCain was not the first person to use the phrase *"Straight Talk."* When I was a student at the University of Pennsylvania back in 1983, I wrote a newspaper column for the *Daily Pennsylvanian* called *"Straight Talk."* As an undergraduate, I was already fascinated by words, and I thought *"straight talk"* was the most explicit way to communicate the notion of matter-of-fact language. A decade later, in several presentations to Senate Republicans just before and just after the 1996 presidential elections, I explicitly advocated that senators pick up on the concept of *"straight talk."* I was somewhat amused to see Senator McCain start using the phrase a year later. I can't be sure whether he got the idea from me—maybe we're just wired the same way. But whatever its origins, *"straight talk"* is a political winner.

To be successful with the words of the twenty-first century, you will have to become comfortable with it. You have to live the words; they have to become you. In the immortal words of Chevy Chase's character in the movie *Caddyshack:* "Be the ball, Danny." It's just that sort of a Zen approach that's required. As Roger Ailes, the greatest media guru of the twentieth century, so accurately put it: *"You are the message."*

# XIII

## *Conclusion*

For most people, language is *functional* rather than being an end in itself. For me, it's the *people* that are the end; language is just a *tool* to reach them, a means to an end. But it's not enough to simply stand there and marvel at the tool's beauty . . . you must realize that it's like fire, and the outcome depends on how it is used . . . to light the way . . . or to destroy.

The real problem with our language today is that it's been so coarsened. Words and expressions once considered horribly vulgar have become a part of the common parlance, their original meanings all but forgotten. Six-year-olds say *"That sucks"* (a crude reference to oral sex), and we giggle at how cute and precocious they are. Adults throw around terms like *"scumbag"* (literally, "a used condom") without a second thought. And that's the problem as I see it—our language has become so unimportant and disposable that we feel we can say anything we want whenever we want to, and after it is spoken, it disappears into the ether.

Beyond the vulgarity of such talk, there's a harshness to it—a disturbing discourtesy, even viciousness, that's relatively new in American life. We seek out words to divide, to demean, to preempt a setup with a putdown. Negativity feels more pervasive than ever before. I hate it, and so

I've dedicated myself to finding the positive in politics and products rather than identifying the faults of others. Surrounded by such meanness and abrasiveness, there is much to be gained by being upbeat and optimistic. When you trash the opposition, you simultaneously demean yourself. The best warrior is a happy warrior. Accentuate the positive . . . eliminate the negative. Negative definitely works, but a solid positive message will triumph over negativity.

Acceptable language varies and changes. The n-word on a sitcom thirty years ago was very edgy but acceptable, but not so in this day and age. Conversely, the slang for certain body parts that would have never made it past network censors a generation ago are heard on television constantly nowadays. Know your audience. Challenge them but don't offend them.


When I was a child, my mother had a Portuguese maid named Maria who would come to the house once a week for half a day. I would wake up every Tuesday morning to hear my mother trying—and inevitably failing—to explain to Maria what she wanted cleaned that day. And with each attempt, my mother would grow more frustrated and her voice would get louder and louder. It fell to me to drag myself out of bed, tramp down the hall in my pajamas, and explain to my mother that Maria wasn't deaf. She just didn't understand English.

If you take away only one lesson from this book, let it be the subtitle, these eleven words: *"It's not what you say, it's what people hear."*

My mom was one of the best writers I ever knew, but sometimes her communication skills failed the test. The American people aren't deaf any more than Maria was. Repeating a faulty message more loudly or vociferously, even if crafted with love and care, won't help people understand you. As you have seen throughout this book, the American elite often creates unnecessary communication barriers that divide them from their audience. It isn't enough to have the correct stance on an issue or the correct positioning for a product or a service; you must also offer it up in such a way that the listener or the consumer can relate to, understand, and appreciate it.

The anecdote about Maria was my original opening for this book. Yet much as in the case of the book's original title, *Killer Words,* neither the people at my publishing house nor my friends and colleagues who helped proofread these pages liked it at all. Everyone, including me, has to practice what we preach and be willing to let go of what we think we are saying and consider what other people are hearing. To me, the Maria story illustrated this very point; ironically, I didn't see that what it meant to me just wasn't coming across to the reader.

Reading about Maria, people got the wrong impression about my childhood and background. Maybe part of that had to do with my use of the word *maid*. These days, many solidly middle class people have "cleaning ladies," but a *maid* or *housekeeper* sounds like someone you'd find on a sprawling estate, along with the butler and the groundskeeper and the personal valet. Even the solidly middle-class Brady Bunch had a housekeeper, not a maid.*

The point is, people read that as an opening anecdote and got the idea that I grew up rich. It wrongly suggested an affluence that I didn't experience as a child, and this distracted from the point I *thought* I was making with the story. Though I did grow up solidly upper middle class (my dad was a dentist), the lifestyle I lived was much closer to that of a working class kid. No allowance. No albums. Almost no toys. My mom would clip dozens of coupons, only buy things on sale, and wear the same clothing day in and day out so that the rest of the family could have what they needed.

I was blind to the fact that none of that came across in the tale of my mom yelling at "the maid." I thought it illustrated perfectly the core message I wanted to convey. Others thought it conveyed that I grew up in a life of privilege. Hardly.

Moral of the story? All together now:

*It's not what you say, it's what people hear.*

---

*While the Alice character liked to refer to herself as a housekeeper, if you Google "Brady Bunch Alice maid," you get more than 76,000 hits. But Google "Brady Bunch Alice housekeeper" and only 40,000 references appear.

# THE MEMOS

The best way to demonstrate how the *Words That Work* actually work is to open up the vault and allow you to read a sampling of actual language memos I have produced for various political and corporate clients. Most of my work is proprietary and cannot be revealed. I have even refused the pressure of journalists and polling associations who have insisted that I disclose these documents because of their impact on the public debate. But several of my more controversial memos did not involve specific clients or require me or my firm to sign confidentiality agreements. Those are the documents I include here publicly for the first time.

Friends who have read this text have found the following three examples to be particularly enlightening because they can see for the first time *Words That Work* in action. All three memos involve either issues, attributes, or politicians that virtually every reader will be familiar with. None of the quotes or recommendations have been edited—you can judge for yourself whether my counsel proved effective and the prognosis accurate. More importantly, these memos will show you how I teach clients to use the *Words That Work*.

What you are about to read isn't always pretty—politics rarely is. But these memos represent my best efforts to reflect the attitudes, concerns, and aspirations of the American people.

# Appendix A

## The 2003 California Gubernatorial Recall: A Case Study in Political Language

In the summer of 2003, my firm did a market research project for an organization called Rescue California that wanted to "recall" Governor Gray Davis and replace him with someone else. Now understand, not many states have recall provisions in their laws or state constitutions, all but one recall effort had failed over the past hundred years, and California had become a pretty safe Democrat bastion over the past decade or so—and Gray Davis was a Democrat. My job was not to turn the state Republican, nor was it to pick a candidate to replace Davis. My only responsibility was to prove that voters were so angry that they would, in fact, vote the governor out of office. I was then to come up with the language that would take that concept and turn it into a reality.

So we went to California and conducted a statewide poll and several dial sessions in key geographic and demographic constituencies. That research, which began even before there were enough signatures to force a recall, revealed four strong reasons to suspect that Davis would probably lose the recall and be removed from office that fall. Here's just a bit of what I reported to Rescue California and how specific words, symbols, and language eventually led to his downfall:

**1.** The mood of the electorate was surly. These weren't anxious voters (like much of America) nor fearful voters (as many were in the days following 9/11 and during the run-up to the Iraq war). They were downright angry, and the focus of their anger sat squarely on the shoulders of Gray Davis:

- An incredible 78 percent of the electorate believed that the state was *"pretty seriously off on the wrong track."* Not just off on the wrong track but *seriously* off on the wrong track.
- The "intensity" factor against Governor Davis was stronger than I had ever measured in a survey, and "the spitting principle" was in full view. Let me explain. While this book is an exposé of language, the emotions that lead to the various articulations are almost as important. When voters either use, respond to, or endorse the most extreme verbiage, you know the desire for change is deep and not going to dissipate until that change occurs. But if their comments are peppered with words like *"kind of," "somewhat,"* and *"moderately,"* you know that intensity doesn't exist.

   And the most extreme expression of intensity is what I call "the spitting principle." When I polled for Ross Perot (the actual term the campaign used was "researched" because Perot repeatedly told reporters he didn't believe in pollsters or polling; hence, my title, "Director of Research"), focus group participants would actually spit on me as they articulated how fed up they were with government. Anything with a "b" or "t" sound would be accompanied by moisture because they couldn't control their emotions . . . or their saliva. To this day, when someone says they're spitting mad during a focus group, I know exactly how they feel (and I prepare to shield myself accordingly).

- The statewide anger in California was directly focused on Governor Gray Davis. As the final question in our statewide survey, we asked whether Californians agreed or disagreed with the following statement: *"When it comes to Gray Davis, I'm mad as hell and I'm not going to take it anymore."* We used this specific question wording because the language, taken straight from Peter Finch's outburst in the movie *Network,* captured in words a mood that is hard to explain and is a measure of intensity that remains unparalleled in the polling profession. More than half the state's electorate agreed, including 35 percent who *"strongly agreed."* Even more remarkably, 31 percent of those who voted for Davis just the year before were *"mad as hell"* by the time we took the survey. This guy was done.

**2.** The issues attached to the direction of the state worked *against* the governor. The state budget deficit was by far the top issue in the minds of California voters. Economic issues dominated public concerns, but no other economic issue came close to the deficit—and it was not difficult for recall proponents to tie the deficit to Davis in the minds of the public. More significantly, the deficit was tied to what many perceived as a deteriorating *"standard of living"* (measured by voters in economic terms) and *"quality of life"* (frustration with day-to-day life). When those two measurements plunge, so do the electoral hopes of incumbents.

There were two related perceptions not addressed in the telephone survey but which came up repeatedly in the dial sessions and cast a pall over everything political: the flight of feet and the fear for their children.

Every Californian we talked to knew of someone personally who had left the state in the past five years because taxes had gotten so high, regulation so stifling, opportunity so limited, and quality of life so poor. The best indicator of this, they told me, was the explosion of real estate "for sale" signs throughout their neighborhoods. Those "for sale" signs, those two words, came to represent and symbolize the political and economic disaster caused by the failed leadership of a failed governor. In this case, the combination of words and symbols was politically lethal. Now take that even one step further by adding the emotional component, the impact on their children. From fear for their safety to anger with the overcrowding of classrooms, from anxiety due to lack of job opportunities to a sense that things were just getting worse and worse, much of the anger expressed toward the governor stemmed from anger about conditions for their kids.

**3.** No one had anything nice to say about the governor or his record. There are a number of polling questions that are used as "leading political indicators" to determine likely strength in an upcoming election. For incumbents, one of the most powerful is the open-ended *"What do you like most about [candidate]?"* They could have said anything, yet four out of ten actually volunteered *"nothing."* (Not *"I don't know"* or *"I'm not sure."* They actually said the word *"nothing."*) Another 15 percent couldn't name even one positive attribute, recent success, or favorable thing about the governor. For a governor who had been in office for four and a half years, this was a total disaster.

**4.** The energy and intensity was in the anti-Davis camp. We asked several questions to measure interest in the recall election and help identify likely voters. In every measurement, those who wanted to recall the governor were more emphatic about their opinions and said they were more likely to vote. An incredible 87 percent of those who said they would definitely or probably vote in favor of the recall said they would *"definitely, positively, absolutely vote,"* while just 53 percent of those who probably or definitely opposed the recall were equally emphatic about their participation.

In addition to doing the research on behalf of recall proponents, I also wrote the actual recall statement that appeared on the ballot. Below, for the first time publicly, is the original draft of that statement that would eventually lead to the governor's ouster. I actually wrote it while sitting at the back of a banquet hall at the Borgata Hotel in Atlantic City while listening to a concert by Hootie and the Blowfish. Literally every word was carefully selected to achieve maximum impact. At just five hundred words, it captures how Californians genuinely felt, and it lays out in living detail almost all of the communication principles we've been discussing. This is the best way to illustrate how language is used to change the political landscape. The bold text is the statement itself. The text in italics is my effort to explain to the reader why each passage was important.

## This recall is about facts.

*(California is a Democrat state with a Democrat ideology. If the recall became a campaign about governing philosophy, we would have lost. "Facts" are the most powerful evidence in a political effort because they are, well, facts. The very first sentence set the context for everything that followed, and that context had to be about something even bigger than the governor himself.)*

**Fact: In the five years that Gray Davis has been governor, he turned all-time record surpluses into all-time record deficits. He increased state spending by 38 percent, even as economists warned him not to.**

*(The length of service mattered to people. We are a nation of forgivers. We will allow people to make mistakes as long as they had good intensions and learned from them. But five years? Voters told us that five years was way too long to keep making mistakes. Two other points here: The "all-time" language communicated to the electorate that the mistakes he made were monumental, and when they learned that he ignored the experts, that made them really angry.)*

**Fact: Thanks to his wasteful government spending, THE BUD-GET DEFICIT INCREASES BY $29 MILLION EVERY SINGLE DAY.**

*("Wasteful government spending" is exactly what the hardworking, over-burdened taxpayers of California most resented about their government. Without it, there would not have been a budget deficit and the need to raise taxes ever higher. But the kicker was the $29 million increase in that deficit—a number low enough for people to relate to but high enough to make them angry.)*

**Fact: California once had one of the best credit ratings in the country. Now it has the worst.**

**California is in deep trouble, yet Gray Davis still has no plan to bring our state out of bankruptcy. And even now, after five years as governor, he still refuses to stand up and take responsibility. Recalling a governor is a serious matter. But so is accountability.**

*(Again, that emphasis on five years. But the operative two words in this portion are the "responsibility" that he refuses to take and the lack of "ac-countability" that everyone wants. Then add to that the lack of any plan, or as voters told us, "a light at the end of the tunnel," and you have the begin-nings of the case for recall. The phrase suggesting that he was unwilling to "stand up" for his actions was a subtle appeal to male voters suggesting that the governor was weak.)*

**Gray Davis made a lot of political promises in his campaigns, but he has not delivered for anyone except the special interest groups, the trial lawyers, and the labor union bosses who already have too much power.**

*(Broken promises are the single most common reason why incumbents are voted out of office, but we took that one step further, linking him with two organizations—unions and trial lawyers—that were unpopular in the state, and the one element of politics that people hate the most, the "spe-cial interest groups." If we had only written that he had broken his prom-ises, that would have been justification enough. But the linkage to his doing so for the benefit of special interests added an emotional intensity, as national Republicans are learning the hard way in 2006.)*

**Fact: He TRIPLED THE CAR TAX—which will cost some fami-lies more than $1,000 every year.**

**Fact: His mismanagement of the energy crisis caused our electricity bills to double.**

**Fact: Instead of bringing new power plants online to solve supply problems, he failed to act, and that caused brownouts all across the state. As a result, CALIFORNIANS PAY SOME OF THE HIGHEST ELECTRICITY RATES IN THE NATION.**

*(The recall had to be more than about fiscal mismanagement. It had to address the day-to-day concerns of Californians and it had to hit them where they'd feel it—in their wallets. All Californians drive, and so the car tax matters, but $350 per person is not that big a deal. But if you focus the impact on families, you can multiply the tax by the three cars in some households, and that's how you get to the magic $1,000 "pain-point" level.*

*Similarly, electric bills are something people pay attention to every day, the doubling in cost was a major drain on personal finances, and the reference to brownouts just reminded people that they had to pay more for unreliable service—raising the level of their own personal anxiety. And just as nobody wants to pay full retail price, nobody wants the distinction of paying the most in the country for their electricity.)*

**California's constitution gives us the right to recall politicians who fail to do their job. Gray Davis has had FIVE YEARS. By any common sense standard, he has failed.**

*(The words here were very carefully chosen. The word "politicians" was used instead of "officeholder," "incumbent," or even "governor" specifically to lower the bar. Asking voters to recall a governor is a big deal. But recalling a politician is not as heavy a lift. Five years is, well, five years. And the reference to common-sense standard came right from the dial sessions. Voters complained bitterly that there was neither any common sense exhibited by the governor nor clear "standards of performance" that he had to meet. We linked the two concepts into a single simple phrase that was devastating.)*

**Fact: Over 150,000 good-paying jobs have left the state, and more are leaving every day. Over one million Californians can't find work, while the rest of the country is adding jobs and recovering from the recession.**

*(To achieve maximum effectiveness, the cost of the Davis administration on a personal level had to be made before voters were asked to consider the statewide economic argument. Similarly, talking about the jobs that had already left the state was powerful, but still not worthy of a recall. To get*

*voters over that hurdle, it was necessary to paint California's future more bleakly than even the present, and remind voters that whereas the rest of the nation was looking up, California was still down-and-out.)*

**Fact: Our schools, once among the best in America, are now among the worst. Gray Davis looked us straight in the eye and promised California a "world-class" education system. Instead, our schools are in crisis, and our teachers are suffering thanks to the slashing of our investment in education. Our kids and our teachers deserve better.**

*(How do you turn the governor into a liar? By reminding them again and again of his "world-class education" pledge that he had offered on many occasions and had so clearly failed to deliver. But the kicker here is how he "looked us straight in the eye and promised." That phrase turned Davis from a liar to a damn liar. This section is also made more powerful by invoking the teachers as well as the students—appealing to a constituency that up to then had been strong public supporters of the governor. It was sending a message to every parent: if even the teachers have suffered, so will your kids.*

**Fact: Our roads are crumbling and traffic is getting worse every day. We have the worst gridlock in the country, and it's only getting worse.**

*(Notice throughout this entire statement that we list three facts in each segment, then a summary paragraph, three more facts, another summary paragraph, and so on. The reason? Voters want proof of any assertion, and three facts is exactly the amount of proof that they want. Anything less is superficial. Anything more is redundant.*

*And in almost every paragraph we gave them something they already knew, from high taxes to the high cost of energy to transportation gridlock, just to verify their perceptions. It is much easier to remind voters of what they already believe and use that verification to lead them to a specific conclusion than to try to convince them of new beliefs.)*

**Something has to change. This recall is about facts. It is about holding our leaders ACCOUNTABLE. And it's about California's future.**

*(Four words expressed in four short simple sentences, all important to voters and all leading them to the conclusion that a recall was necessary: "change," "facts," "accountable," "future.")*

In these tough times, Gray Davis has failed to plan. In our state's time of need, he has failed to acknowledge or take responsibility for his lack of leadership.

Certainly, Gray Davis didn't cause all our problems. But he failed to plan for them. And HE STILL REFUSES TO TAKE RESPONSIBILITY.

*(We have established the context. We have laid out the facts. Now it's time to connect Davis not only to the problem but to the solution. Notice the all-caps in that final sentence. At seven words, it said more than most of the other 493. Amazingly, the California secretary of state's office allowed that all-caps sentence to remain in the official ballot statement. The fact that Davis refused to take responsibility until the final days of the recall said to voters that he could not and would not change.)*

We cannot continue down the path of higher taxes, job losses, wasteful government spending, no accountability, and special interests calling the shots.

*(Five conditions Californians don't want—all collapsed into a single powerful sentence.)*

We cannot wait three more years. WE MUST CHANGE DIRECTION NOW.

FIVE YEARS of failure is too long.

Vote YES. RECALL Gray Davis. We can't afford not to.

*(The "ask" only comes at the very end, within the last ten words. Why? Because a recall is the most extreme political maneuver other than impeachment. Don't ask voters to take an extreme measure until you have told them why. And don't expect them to agree with you unless and until you tell them the consequences of inaction. That's why we added that final sentence.)*

By the time he was voted out of office in October 2003, Gray Davis had lost all credibility with California voters. Sadly for him, credibility is one character attribute that it is almost impossible to regain once it's been lost.

# Appendix B

## The 21 Political Words and Phrases You Should Never Say Again . . . Plus a Few More

Sometimes it is not what you say that matters but what you *don't* say. Other times, a single word or phrase can undermine or destroy the credibility of an otherwise successful pitch or presentation. Effective communication requires that you *stop* saying words and phrases that undermine your ability to educate the American people.

This memo is adopted from a document I originally prepared and presented to Republican congressional spouses in January 2005. From today forward, here are twenty words that should not be said again, and should be replaced permanently with more effective alternatives.

| NEVER SAY | INSTEAD SAY |
|---|---|
| Government | Washington |

Most Americans appreciate their local government. It picks up their trash, cleans their streets, and provides police and transportation services. Local government is okay to them because they often know their locally elected representatives personally and can visit, call, or otherwise yell at them if something goes wrong.

*"Washington"* is the governmental problem. *"Washington"* spending, *"Washington"* waste, *"Washington"* taxation, *"Washington"* bureaucracy, *"Washington"* rules, and *"Washington"* regulations. And now in 2006, *"Washington"* promises and *"Washington"* failures.

When I first sat down to write this book, the war in Iraq was proceeding well, the intelligence that led up to the war had not been fully rebuked, and the words FEMA, Katrina, Abramoff, and "Heckuva job, Brownie" had no relevance whatsoever. Over the past fifty years, it has been Republicans who have railed against Washington government. But thanks to a president they don't like and a dreadfully unsuccessful 2005, Democrats now have equal anti-D.C. fervor.

An anti-Washington ideology is nothing new. From the Articles of Confederation in the 1780s to Jacksonian Democrats in the 1830s to Teddy Roosevelt Republicans at the turn of the twentieth century to the Reagan revolution twenty-five years ago, America goes through cycles of great disdain for centralized power. Today, it's not the size of government or the way it exercises power that is of greatest concern. It's the specific failure of Washington to operate efficiently, effectively, intelligently, and consistently. So if you are an advocate of *"less"* government, better to use the language of *"making Washington accountable"* or *"making Washington more effective"* than arguing over the proper size of government.

As Maryland Lieutenant Governor Michael Steele said at the Republican National Convention, "If we expect to succeed, we must look to ourselves and not to Washington to raise our kids, start our businesses and improve our day-to-day lives." And if you must use the word *"government,"* put it in the context defined by President Bush in his convention acceptance speech: *"Government should help people improve their lives, not try to run their lives."*

| NEVER SAY | INSTEAD SAY |
|---|---|
| Privatization | Personalization |
| Private accounts | Personal accounts |
| Private health care | Free market health care |

Many more Americans would *"personalize"* Social Security than would *"privatize"* it. In fact, even after the failed public effort to reform and modernize Social Security, a majority of individuals younger than fifty would still support *"personalizing"* Social Security, while less than 40 percent would *"privatize"* it. Why? *"Personalizing"* Social Security suggests ownership and control over your own personal retirement savings. *"Privatizing"* Social Security suggests a profit motive, as well as winners and losers.

The word *"private"* and all its derivatives have a negative connotation in today's political environment. Private schools, private clubs, and private health care all suggest a level of exclusivity that's not akin to equal opportunity. While Americans don't believe in the need for equal outcomes, they do believe everyone should start at the same place—and private anything implies an unfair advantage. That's why it is important for advocates of maintaining a *"private health care system"* to instead refer to it as *"free market health care."*

| NEVER SAY | INSTEAD SAY |
|---|---|
| Tax reform | Tax simplification |
| Tax cuts | Tax relief |

While a majority of Americans generally favor *"tax reform,"* one-third of the population fears that they would end up paying more in taxes if the tax code were in fact reformed. However, almost *all* Americans believe they would personally benefit from a tax code that was *"simplified"*—benefit in terms of money they owe, the time they spend on their taxes, and their anxiety about the IRS. When a third of Americans fear the IRS more than root canal surgery, something should be done to simplify the tax code.

Tax cuts are a perennial promise from politicians facing reelection. Even liberal Democrats have found some tax cuts they can support. But the American people have come to distrust politicians who promise *"tax cuts,"* because they often don't happen, and when they do, they're almost always too small and don't materialize when they're expected. A better approach is to talk about *"tax relief"*—giving taxpayers a deserved break—and focus your sympathy toward the *"hardworking, overburdened, underappreciated taxpayer."* The more passion you can get into your defense of taxpayers, the more credible you will become.

| NEVER SAY | INSTEAD SAY |
| --- | --- |
| Inheritance tax<br>Estate tax | Death tax |

The title or label you give a particular tax or government program often determines its popularity. The best example of this is the estate tax that families have to pay if they are beneficiaries of a significant inheritance. While two-thirds of Americans (68 percent) think the *"inheritance tax"* or *"estate tax"* is unfair, fully 78 percent view the *"death tax"* as unfair. And while a narrow majority would repeal the *"inheritance"* or *"estate tax,"* an overwhelming majority would repeal the *"death tax."* If you want to kill it, always refer to it as the *"death tax."*

| NEVER SAY | INSTEAD SAY |
| --- | --- |
| Global economy<br>Globalization<br>Capitalism | Free market economy |

More Americans are afraid of *"globalization"* than even *"privatization."* The reason? *"Globalization"* represents something big, something distant, and something foreign. We distrust *"globalization"* for the same reason we like our local government but dislike Washington—the closer you are, the more control you have. So instead of talking about the principles of *"globalization,"* instead emphasize *"the value and benefits of a free market economy."* True, blue collar and manufacturing audiences probably won't like any terminology you use—to them, anything global is a direct threat to their personal employment.

Similarly, *"capitalism"* reminds people of harsh economic competition that yields losers as well as winners, while *"the free market economy"* provides opportunity to all and allows everyone to succeed. And here's one more economic label: *"Small business owner"* is looked at more favorably than *"entrepreneur,"* even though people think the latter occupation is more financially successful. The difference? A *"small business owner"* is perceived to use her own money, her own skills, and her own sweat to build a business (the gender reference is correct—more women than men are small business owners), while *"entrepreneurs"* are more like speculators who benefit from other people's money and effort.

| NEVER SAY | INSTEAD SAY |
|---|---|
| Outsourcing | The root causes:<br><br>taxation, regulation, litigation, innovation, education, legislation |

When you use the words of your opponents, you are accepting their definitions and by extension their conclusions. If you are a proponent of the free market global economy, you should *never* use the word *"outsourcing,"* because you will then be asked to defend the practice of allowing companies to *"ship American jobs overseas."* Rather, you should talk about *"the root causes"* of why any American company would not want to hire *"the best workers in the world."* The answer:

*"Over-taxation that requires companies to hire high-priced accountants to navigate the tax code . . ."*

*"Over-regulation that requires companies to fill out paperwork that no one reads and no one cares about . . ."*

*"Too much litigation, forcing companies, health care providers, and small businesses to hire an army of lawyers to protect themselves from frivolous lawsuits filed by predatory personal injury lawyers . . ."*

*"Not enough innovation, because companies are spending too much time dealing with taxation, regulation, and litigation . . ."*

*"Insufficient quality education, that trains the next generation of Americans to hold the next generation of jobs . . ."* and

*"Too much legislation, requiring companies to hire lobbyists and Washington insiders to keep up with the changing rules and regulations."*

Taxation, regulation, litigation, innovation, education, legislation . . . because it all rhymes, it will be remembered.

| NEVER SAY | INSTEAD SAY |
|-----------|-------------|
| Foreign trade | International trade |

For many reasons unrelated to this specific issue, the word *"foreign"* conjures up negative images in the minds of many of Americans. We simply don't like *"foreign oil"* or *"foreign products"* or *"foreign nationals."* Even though we are truly a nation of foreigners, we have grave concerns about the motives of foreigners—and that concern has only increased since 9/11. *"International"* is a more positive concept than either *"foreign"* or *"global"* not because of anything positive but because it doesn't come wrapped with all the negative connotations.

In the early days of CNN, network founder Ted Turner forbade anyone to say "foreign" on the air. After all, CNN was an international network and what was "foreign" to one person was likely home to another. The punishment for saying "foreign" rather than "international" was a $50 fine.

| NEVER SAY | INSTEAD SAY |
|-----------|-------------|
| Undocumented workers/aliens | Illegal immigrants |
|  | Border security |

This linguistic distinction may prove to be the political battle of the decade. The label used to describe those who enter America illegally determines the attitudes people have toward them. Those supportive of a guest worker program that would allow illegal immigrants to remain in the country tend to label these people *"undocumented workers"* because it suggests legitimate employees who simply don't have the right paperwork, while those who want to deport these same individuals use the term *"illegal aliens"* because alien has the most negative connotations.

And instead of addressing *"immigration reform,"* which polarizes Americans, you should be talking about *"border security"* issues. Securing our borders and our people has universal support.

| NEVER SAY | INSTEAD SAY |
| --- | --- |
| Drilling for oil | Exploring for energy |

I have been involved in an entire language creation effort involving environmental issues, some of which is included in this book. But the one phrase that stands out more than any other is in some ways an energy issue rather than an environmental concern. *"Drilling for oil"* causes people to paint a picture in their minds of an old-fashioned oil rig that gushes up black goop. *"Exploring for energy"* conjures a picture of twenty-first-century technology and innovation that *"responsibly harvests energy"* and provides us the ability to heat our homes and drive our cars. When you talk about energy, use words such as *"efficient"* and *"balanced,"* and always express concern for the environment.

| NEVER SAY | INSTEAD SAY |
| --- | --- |
| Domestic oil/production | American oil/production |

This may seem like a technicality, but reference to *"domestic oil"* or *"domestic production"* has economic connotations to the listener, while reference to *"American oil"* or *"American production"* generates a reaction of American pride and success. Of course, both phrases are better than dependence on *"foreign oil."*

| NEVER SAY | INSTEAD SAY |
| --- | --- |
| Tort reform | Lawsuit abuse reform |
| Trial lawyer | Personal injury lawyer |

The term *"tort"* means little or nothing to the average American. Most people think it refers to a French pastry. But *"lawsuit abuse"* is something most Americans understand—and resent. There is a universal perception that there are too many lawyers and too many lawsuits—and focusing on abuse rather than torts puts the attention on what the public wants fixed. For an additional touch of intensity, just add the word *"frivolous."*

It is difficult to distrust a *"trial lawyer,"* in part because we see them portrayed so favorably on television and in the movies. But *"personal injury lawyers,"* also known as *"ambulance chasers,"* remind people of those annoying, harassing, middle-of-the-night TV commercials cajoling us to sue someone. If you want to get an additional level of intensity, talk about *"predatory personal injury lawyers."*

| NEVER SAY | INSTEAD SAY |
| --- | --- |
| Corporate transparency | Corporate accountability |
|  | Corporate responsibility |

I constantly hear from people on Wall Street and on Capitol Hill about the need for greater *"corporate transparency."* But in the minds of the American people, *"corporate accountability"* is a much higher priority. The majority of Americans can't explain what *"transparency"* means or recognize it when they see it. But everyone understands and demands *"accountability,"* from all sectors of the economy—and from corporate America most of all. But there is actually one term that is even better received: *"corporate responsibility."* From responsibility for employees and shareholders, for customers and the community, a company that practices *"corporate responsibility"* is seen as a good corporate citizen.

| NEVER SAY | INSTEAD SAY |
|-----------|-------------|
| School choice | Parental choice |
|  | Equal opportunity in education |
| Vouchers | Opportunity scholarships |

Thanks to an effective advertising campaign by national and state teacher unions, Americans remain at best evenly split over whether they support *"school choice."* But they are heavily in favor of *"giving parents the right to choose the schools that are right for their children,"* and there is almost universal support for *"equal opportunity in education."*

*"Vouchers,"* seen as depriving public schools of necessary dollars, have even less support than the principle of school choice. However, *"opportunity scholarships"* do have widespread backing, as they are perceived to be a reward for good students to get a good education. Here again, the words you use determine the support you will receive.

| NEVER SAY | INSTEAD SAY |
|-----------|-------------|
| Health care choice | The right to choose |

This is an important nuance often lost on politicians. Almost all Americans want *"the **right** to choose the health care plan, hospital, doctor, and prescription drug plan that is best for them,"* but far fewer Americans actually want to make that choice. In fact, the older you get, the less eager you are to have a wide range of choices. One reason the Medicare prescription drug card earned only qualified public support when it initially passed, and strong opposition during its actual implementation, is that it offered too many choices and therefore created too much confusion for too many senior citizens.

| NEVER SAY | INSTEAD SAY |
|-----------|-------------|
| Wiretapping<br>Eavesdropping | Electronic intercepts |

An electronic intercept is seen as a high-tech, highly sophisticated, precisely targeted national security effort to root out threats to domestic safety. Wiretapping is a less serious and more informal activity, something that the FBI did to Marilyn Monroe, Martin Luther King, Jr., John Lennon, and John Gotti. And eavesdropping is what prying neighbors do to each other.

| NEVER SAY | INSTEAD SAY |
|-----------|-------------|
| Deny | Not give |

Yes, the two phrases mean exactly the same thing and yield exactly the same result. But *"to deny"* implies that you are preventing someone from receiving something they are entitled to, while *"not to give"* suggests it was only a choice.

# Appendix C

## *The Clinton Impeachment Language*

In the waning days of 1998, the House of Representatives voted to impeach President Bill Clinton in a party line vote. All eyes turned to the Senate and to Senate Majority Leader Trent Lott. Unsure of the style and substance of the upcoming Senate hearings, Lott created an ad-hoc advisory group to help plan the message and the strategy. These meetings took place in the Senator's Capitol office hideaway every weekday morning, and occasionally on weekends, at 8:00 A.M. to discuss the previous day's events and press coverage. I was a member of that message task force, and I attended about three times a week.

The purpose of this book is to give the reader a peek inside the word laboratory. Therefore, what follows is one of the weekly strategic language memos I produced for that task force, written after the House impeachment vote but before Senate action. It appears here unedited, in print for the first time. Nothing in my career prepared me for the challenge of messaging the trial of a president of the United States. I hope I never have to produce a document like the one below again.

MEMORANDUM
To: Senator Lott
Re: Thoughts About the Immediate Future

INTRODUCTION

I will be blunt.

Republicans are in worse shape today than at any time since 1974. The public opinion results of the past ten days are staggering. In three separate polls conducted following the House impeachment vote, Republicans received a favorable response from about 30 percent of the electorate, while Democrats are receiving positive evaluations in the upper 50s and low 60s. Not since Watergate has the public reacted so positively toward the Democrats and so badly toward us.

Why? As public protectors and defenders of Bill Clinton, the Democrats are now receiving the reflected glow of the positive evaluations given the president, while Republicans have come to represent everything that Americans hate about politics.

**1.** They hate what Bill Clinton has so adroitly named *"the politics of personal destruction"* by Washington-style politicians.

**2.** They hate the perceived partisanship.

**3.** And they hate the overall negativity more than anything else.

I emphasize these three points because Republicans have done such a good job of personifying all of them—and there's not that much you can do about it. When Newt Gingrich announced last spring that he would mention the Clinton scandal in every speech, it caused an immediate and sharp decline in how Americans perceived Republicans' role in the scandal. And when Republicans began running ads on the issue, you confirmed exactly what the voters had thought—that you were using Clinton's *"private"* failures for electoral advantage.

At this point you are probably annoyed that I am stating the obvious. Well, no one stood up a year ago, months ago, and even weeks ago to say *enough,* let's get our act together. If someone would have kept Gingrich quiet, or kept the House Judiciary Committee from releasing Clinton's video taped deposition, or even just stopped the national Republican advertising campaign in October, we would not be in this public opinion crisis today. Yes, these were obvious steps, but they were never taken.

Senator, you need to take charge, establish the *"language"* of the upcoming debate, and establish a communication discipline for the GOP conference as well as yourself. That's what this memo seeks to help you do.


## STRATEGY

You are strategically correct to want a quick trial. Conservatives should be reminded that they have long preached the value of *"swift justice,"* and this case should be no different. But how you achieve that objective, and what is said during that process, could be even more important than the process itself.

**1.** Justice Rehnquist should serve as the cover for all otherwise partisan decisions. If you want the Democrats to appear defensive, negative and partisan, you need to pit them against the Chief Justice of the Supreme Court—the symbol of impartial justice in America. That requires Senate Republicans (including yourself) to remove themselves completely from the decision-making process prior to the beginning of the trial. Rehnquist, not you, should rule on the Gorton-Lieberman proposal. Let Rehnquist make all the tough, controversial decisions—and you need to make that clear when you hold your first news conference next week.

**2.** The two-thirds rule for continuing the hearings has conservatives in an uproar. My goal is always to find ideas that represent good politics but in no way undermine good principle. Having personally talked to two members of the House GOP leadership and a half dozen other House members, the reaction to the two-thirds threshold is nothing short of contempt and could lead to a bloody internal war. The objective is correct, but the approach would destroy us.

In the eyes of most Republicans, the goal is the president's removal, but at a very minimum, they need to feel that the president was held *"accountable"* for his actions. Yes, the American people would support a two-thirds requirement to continue, but it would unnaturally short-circuit the trial in a way that conservatives would find totally unacceptable because it would essentially hand control over to the Democratic minority. Allowing a majority vote to suspend the trial is defensible even to most hardliners (you may even want to announce regularly scheduled *"continuation votes"* after a specified number of hours or days). But conservatives will make you pay for the rest of your career if you advocate requiring a two-thirds vote to continue the trial.

**3.** You need to meet with the House managers in advance and they need to be *fully* scripted. It angers me to read Henry Hyde's criticism of you when he was instrumental in releasing Clinton's video deposition against the advice of communication professionals, as well as refusing throughout the hearings to organize a strategic communication effort similar to that waged by the White House. There was never any organized Republican message because Hyde thought it was beneath him (and the impeachment process) to create one.

You must demand that the House managers and your Senate colleagues follow a strategic communication plan. The media will assuredly use unwise or tactless statements by any Republican or conservative against you (just look at how they are treating James Dobson's recent comments). A single misstep by one member will hurt all of you.

Finally, I believe that Clinton's state of the union address will focus on education (targeted at voters under age 50), pension reform (for voters aged 50 to 65) and the combined issues of Medicare and Social Security (for voters over age 60). I urge you to attempt to preempt him—at least on the pension issue. I promise you that *"pension security"* does matter, particularly to those who vote, and could become the sleeper issue of 2000.

## LANGUAGE

I have been testing political rhetoric for six years, and in that time, I have never worked on an issue that tested as consistently badly as this one. It would be easier to sell the legalization of DDT or the dumping of nuclear waste than explaining why the president should be removed from office. That being said, there are a few pearls of wisdom that can be extracted from the pile of dirt we find ourselves in.

Most of what I recommend falls into the soothing category, but that's what the American people want to hear right now. Our numbers are so awful because self-described independents and ticket-splitters have abandoned us in droves, in part because of our harsh rhetoric. The words you and your colleagues need to use should begin building bridges to the center to bring them back.

**1.** *"We need reconciliation, not revenge."* This line should be used at every opportunity. We should mention often the extremist Democrats who attacked us so viciously during the debate in the same way that they used quotes by people like Bob Barr, Bob Dornan, and even Newt Gingrich against us. Americans hate negative politics more than anything else, yet Republicans have given the Democrats a free pass every time they attack.

Use James Carville's quotes wherever you go (threatening us with retribution, that we will be made to pay for voting our conscience) but refer to him as *"White House spin doctor James Carville."* In particular, accuse him of *"instilling ugliness into the political structure."* Note: Attacking *"the White House"* has almost the same impact as attacking Clinton directly but with only a fraction of the backlash.

**2.** *"Character assassination has no place in American democracy."* Talk about the higher degree of discussion and debate in the Senate, and how we need to set a higher tone in all political discourse. Talk about how you hope that this trial *"once and for all will put behind the politics of personal destruction and instill a sense of personal accountability."*

**3.** *"Calm, cool, and collected."* That should be the phrase you use to describe the Senate and what others are encouraged to say to describe you. You may remember a poll I took in 1995 just after the first 100 days when, for the first time since such questions were asked, more people liked and admired the House of Representatives than the Senate. Today, thanks to events of the past year, the House has a lower approval rating than at any time in modern history. We need to evoke the emotions of calming and cooling (e.g., *"cooling the raging tempers in Washington"* ).

**4.** *"We are committed to doing the people's business."* This is something you have said quite effectively. You need to talk about other issues— *"saving and strengthening Social Security for the next generation, cutting wasteful Washington spending, and providing hardworking Americans with much needed tax relief "*—at every opportunity. Even if it is not asked, you need to inject a concentration on issues Americans really care about.

**5.** *"We are listening to the people back home, and we plan to seek common ground to get things done."* Conservatives may get a bit edgy over this, but this sentence is exactly what the independent swing voters most want from their elected officials. *"People want us to do our job. It's time to get to work."* Senator, if we do not bring back those swing voters, 2000 will be a disaster for us. (In numerous tests, we have found that it is better to tell stories about constituents back home rather than family members. For example, when you want to talk about saving Social Security, talk about comments made to you by college students or young adults rather than your mother and daughter.)

Finally, it is important for you personally that you protect the image of the Senate, for in doing so, you are protecting your own image and that of the Republican Party. And the only hope we have of salvaging the congressional GOP's image is for the Senate to conduct a trial without the appearance of either rancor or bitterness. If the public comes to believe that Senate Republicans have behaved in a *"calm, cool, and collected"* manner, you will have successfully restored confidence in Congress and in the Republican Party.

It will also be important for members to prepare op-eds for release at the time of the first vote on whether or not to continue the trial. This is particularly important for Senators up for re-election in 2000. In conversations I've had with individual House members from Democratic districts, those that engaged in a public dialogue with their constituents in November and December were insulated from most of the public outcry, while those that remained silent bore the brunt of the public anger.

## OTHER RECOMMENDATIONS

**1.** The Senate Republican Conference needs to coordinate efforts to convince Americans that we are *"doing the people's business"* despite our other activities. I am extremely afraid of the public reaction against Republicans when Clinton delivers his state of the union address. He will paint himself as a doer fighting the forces of partisanship and negativity (i.e., you). You need the public to know that the Senate is already hard at work on issues they care about. You should ask Connie Mack to prepare sample newsletters and mail that deal with Social Security, cutting wasteful Washington spending, and tax relief—and then ask all senators to get the message out.

**2.** You need to play a greater role in determining who the GOP spokespeople will be. Some of the people who represent us on TV are truly awful, while the Democrats always seem to put their best people forward. This needs to change.

## A FINAL THOUGHT

You have said on more than one occasion that you would rather know in advance what language and strategy works best rather than having that analysis provided after the fact. That will only work if we are talking on a more regular basis. I am quite willing to work through the night on a routine basis to prepare documents such as this one, but the usefulness of the prose is directly proportional to the knowledge I have going in.

If there is anything else you want me to consider before Tuesday, I need you to call me either at home or at work. Otherwise, I want you to see how people reacted to your Iraqi and Social Security comments. They tested well until the word *"impeachment"* was raised.

# NOTES

## Introduction

1. "Politics of the English Language," by George Orwell, 1946
2. Interview with Colin Powell, April 2006
3. Dr. Werner D. Lippert, *Richard Nixon's Détente and Willy Brandt's Ostpolitik: The politics and economic diplomacy of engaging the east.* August 2005, Vanderbilt University, p. 19.
4. Hal Brands, "Progress Unseen: U.S. Arms Control Policy and the Origins of Detente, 1963–1968," *Diplomatic History,* April 2006, Vol. 30, Issue 2, pp. 253–285.
5. http://thinkprogress.org/?s=Frank+Luntz

## Chapter I: The Ten Rules of Effective Language

1. *Simply Speaking,* by Peggy Noonan, Regan Books, 1998, pp. 46–57, as quoted on PBS website: www.pbs.org/wgbh/amex/monkeytrial/sfeature/sf_noonan/html
2. http://kerry.senate.gov/low/record.cfm?id=189831
3. http://www.breitbart.com/news/2005/10/06/D8D2IU703.html
4. "G.K. Chesterton: Prophet of Mirth," by Philip Yancey, in *Orthodoxy* by G.K. Chesterton, page xxi.
5. http://en.wikipedia.org/wiki/A_picture_is_worth_a_thousand_words
6. http://1000words.wordherders.net/archives/000385.html
7. Ken Gross, "First Round to Lexus: Infiniti is outsold four-to-one—but the battle's just begun," *Automotive Industries,* June 1990, Vol. 170, No. 6, p. 21.

8. CNN.com transcript of Harold Ford's speech to Democratic National Convention, August 15, 2000.
9. Fox News Channel, The Beltway Boys, August 17, 2000.
10. Fox News Channel, Hannity & Colmes, August 17, 2000.
11. "The Wonderful Idea of Harold Ford: Hurry Up," by Ryan Lizza, *The New Republic,* Nov. 25, 2002.
12. *Reporting Live,* by Lesley Stahl, as reported by Bob Somerby in the *Daily Howler*

## Chapter II: Preventing Message Mistakes
1. http://isakson.senate.gov/floor/121605taxes.htm
2. Luntz Research survey question
3. http://www.brainyquote.com/quotes/authors/b/bill_gates.html
4. http://www.brainyquote.com/quotes/authors/m/meg_whitman.html
5. http://www.brainyquote.com/quotes/authors/k/kevin_rollins.html
6. *On Directing Film,* by David Mamet
7. Luntz Research, survey of women voters in California
8. Luntz Research survey question
9. www.://www.crf_usa.org/bria/bria14_3.html
10. http://www.lbjlib.utexas.edu/johnson/archives.hom/speeches.hom/640522.asp
11. Luntz Research survey question

## Chapter III: Old Words, New Meaning
1. *The Los Angeles Times,* A-1, two-part story on North Korea, June 2005.
2. George Orwell, *Politics and the English Language*
3. Ibid.
4. Ibid.
5. All these etymologies come from the Online Etymology Dictionary. www.etymonline.com and the *Concise Oxford English Dictionary.*
6. Online Etymology Dictionary (www.etymonline.com) and the *Concise Oxford English Dictionary.*
7. Online Etymology Dictionary (www.etymonline.com).
8. Wikipedia.com, Online Etymology Dictionary (www.etymonline.com).
9. Wikipedia.com, Online Etymology Dictionary (www.etymonline.com).
10. Online Etymology Dictionary (www.etymonline.com) and the *Concise Oxford English Dictionary.*
11. Online Etymology Dictionary (www.etymonline.com), the *Concise Oxford English Dictionary* and Wikipedia.com.
12. Wikipedia.com.
13. Online Etymology Dictionary (www.etymonline.com) and the *Concise Oxford English Dictionary.*
14. Online Etymology Dictionary (www.etymonline.com) and the *Concise Oxford English Dictionary.*
15. Michael Dukakis, Democratic presidential nomination acceptance speech, July 21, 1988.

16. "D.C. Mayor Acted Hastily, Will 'Rehire' Aide," by Yolanda Woodlee, *The Washington Post,* February 4, 1999.
17. "Wisconsin Student Calls for Speech Code Following 'Niggardly' Incident," Cougar News Service, February 1999.
18. Wikipedia.com, "World Wide Web."
19. Wikipedia.com, "World Wide Web."
20. Variety Slanguage Dictionary.
21. Charles Johnson, founder of littlegreenfootballs.com, refuses to reveal where the name came from; see "Frequently Asked Questions" at www.littlegreenfootballs.com.
22. littlegreenfootballs.com, "9/14/2004: The Smoking Memo." Discussed by John Podhoretz on *The O'Reilly Factor,* and widely reported in the press.
23. Powerlineblog.com, archives.
24. "After Blogs Got Hits, CBS Got a Black Eye," by Howard Kurtz, *The Washington Post,* September 20, 2004.
25. Daily Kos archives.
26. "After Blogs Got Hits, CBS Got a Black Eye," by Howard Kurtz, *The Washington Post,* September 20, 2004.
27. The Kerry Spot, National Review Online, archives.
28. *Compact Oxford English Dictionary.*
29. The Online Etymology Dictionary (www.etymonline.com) and the *Concise Oxford English Dictionary.*
30. "Impromptus," by Jay Nordlinger, National Review Online, Feb. 26, 2002. Also see *The American Heritage Book of English Usage, a Practical and Authoritative Guide to Contemporary Usage,* 1996, and the Online Etymology Dictionary (www.etymonline.com) and the *Concise Oxford English Dictionary.*

## Chapter V: Be the Message

1. Interview with Henry Kissinger, March 2006.
2. "He's champing at the bid; Eager to stand out, presidential hopeful Dennis Kucinich takes the 'Seabiscuit' hook by the reins," by Reed Johnson, *The Los Angeles Times,* August 4, 2003.
3. Associated Press, Aug. 1, 2005.
4. Billy Wilder's definition of "the Lubitsch touch" in *Conversations with Wilder,* by Cameron Crowe, p. 113.
5. http://en.wikipedia.org/wiki/2004_Democratic_National_Convention
6. http://www.nationalreview.com/symposium/symposium200407300206.asp
7. http://www.worldnetdaily.com/news/article.asp?ARTICLE_ID=41425
8. "The Vietnam Effect in 2004," (Book Review), *The Hill,* by Deborah Kalb, January 27, 2004.
9. MSNBC Transcript, Scarborough Country, October 22, 2004.
10. Ibid.
11. *True and False: Heresy and Common Sense for the Actor,* by David Mamet
12. "GOP Embraces String of Victories, But It Is Still Seeking Vision for '96," *The New York Times,* Richard Berke, Nov. 7, 1993.

13. http://en.thinkexist.com/quotes/jack_welch
14. http://en.wikiquote.org/wiki/steve_jobs
15. Emergence Slogan Survey, *BusinessWeek,* Kiley, Oct. 2004.
16. *Ad Age,* "Top 10 Advertising Icons of the Century"

## Chapter VI: Words We Remember
1. *Pittsburgh Post-Gazette,* July 19, 2006, pg. C-1.
2. "Top 100 Advertising Campaigns," *Ad Age*
3. Ibid.
4. Ibid.
5. Ibid.
6. http://www.inthe70s.com/generated/commercials.shtml
7. http://www.inthe80s.com/tvcommercials/c.shtml
8. Directed Studies program, Yale University, autumn 1992.
9. Luntz Research "Constitutional Knowledge Survey," August 30, 1998.
10. *Ad Age,* "Top 100 Advertising Campaigns of the Century," by Bob Garfield.
11. Ibid.
12. Ibid.
13. Ibid.
14. Emergence Slogan Survey, *BusinessWeek,* Kiley, Oct. 2004.
15. Emergence Slogan Survey, *BusinessWeek,* Kiley, Oct. 2004.
16. "Ad Track," *USA Today,* May 23, 2005, by Michael McCarthy.
17. *Real Time with Bill Maher,* October 1, 2004.
18. PBS Web site, *The American Experience,* People and Events: Carter's "Crisis of Confidence" Speech.
19. http://en.wikipedia.org/wiki/Daisy_(television_commercial)

## Chapter VII: Corporate Case Studies
1. Interview with Jack Welch, July 2006.
2. Interview with Steve Wynn, June 2006.

## Chapter VIII: Political Case Studies
1. http://www.brainyquote.com/quotes/quotes/e/edwardrmu106342.html
2. Ralph Hallow, "GOP Unveils Down-The-Stretch Ad Blitz," *The Washington Times,* Page A1.
3. Ibid.
4. Ibid.
5. PBS Online, Wisconsin Public Television, Rosser Reeves Collection at the State Historical Society of Wisconsin.
6. "The Presidential Campaign Memorabilia" web site from Duke University Special Collections Library; "Campaigns and Elections" from the PBS website AmericanPresident.org.

## Chapter IX: Myths and Realities About Language and People
1. Interview with Norman Lear, May 2006.
2. Sources for this section include: the 1990 and 2000 census; the 2004 American Community Survey; the 1990 Statistical Abstract; the National League of Cities—"The American Dream in 2004: A Survey of the

American People"; Article: On an "Average" American Day: http://usgov-info.about.com/od/censusandstatistics/a/averageday.htm

3. Luntz Research survey, 1997.
4. 2000 U.S. Census, Table QT-P20 Educational Attainment by sex
5. http://www.news.harvard.edu/glance
6. "Introduction to the Core Curriculum," www.harvard.edu.
7. "The Truth About Harvard: It may be hard to get into Harvard, but it's easy to get out without learning much of enduring value at all. A recent graduate's report," by Ross Douthat, *The Atlantic Monthly,* March 2005.
8. Luntz Research, Constitution Survey, 1998.
9. Luntz Research, Post-Election Survey, 2004.
10. Ronald Reagan, Farewell Address to the Nation, January 11, 1989.
11. Luntz Research survey for America Prepared, November 14, 2003.
12. Write101.com
13. *American Journalism Review,* Paul Farhi, June/July 2005, Volume 27, Issue 3.
14. "Stop the Press!—Newspaper Publishing and Readership," by Peter Francese, *American Demographics,* July 1, 2003.
15. Bureau of Labor Statistics Consumer Expenditure Survey, quoted in "Stop the Press!—Newspaper Publishing and Readership," by Peter Francese, *American Demographics,* July 1, 2003.
16. Newspaper Association of America - *The Source* - http://www.naa.org/thesource/index.asp
17. Nielsen/NetRatings November 2005 press release.
18. Pew Research Center for the People and the Press, quoted in *American Journalism Review,* Paul Farhi, June/July 2005, Volume 27, Issue 3.
19. http://www.washtimes.com/national/20040708-113557-6153r.htm
20. Luntz Research, A&B Americana analysis
21. Ibid.

### Chapter X: What We REALLY Care About

1. Luntz Research, GOP Retreat Final PowerPoint.
2. Luntz Research instant response dial session.
3. Winston Churchill, speech at the Lord Mayor's banquet, Nov. 9, 1954.
4. *Oxford English Dictionary*
5. Ronald Reagan farewell letter, November 1994.
6. Luntz Research, GOP Retreat Final PowerPoint.
7. Ibid.

### Chapter XI: Personal Language for Personal Scenarios

1. http://www.quotationspage.com/quote/403.html

### Chapter XII: Twenty-one Words and Phrases for the Twenty-first Century

1. First used by Richard F. Sailer in the *National Carbon Company Management* magazine, in an article later reprinted by Union Carbide Company.
2. Burke, *Reflections on the Revolution in France*
3. Online Etymology Dictionary
4. Ibid.

# INDEX

# When Words Fail

There was a time when I was willing to take on and face down some of the most powerful politicians in Washington to fight in favor of effective communication and against bad Republican messaging—even when the people I was challenging could and did damage my career.

In 1995, then-Conference Chairman John Boehner told colleagues to talk about "Promises Made, Promises Kept" to their constituents, and I got myself ejected from a conference presentation for telling them that the slogan reminded voters of what a used-car salesman would say.* My alternative? A much more humble and credible "a good first step."

That same year, when Republican leaders began to talk about "devolution," the shifting of national government programs and responsibilities to the states, I insisted that they instead refer to *"local answers and local solutions for local problems."*

Ed Gillespie, then a top staffer to House Majority Leader Dick Armey and later the chairman of the Republican National Committee, berated me so loudly in the halls of the Capitol that Indiana Congressman Steve Buyer had to intervene and tell Ed to back off. What was my offense? Telling members that his too-cute-by-half slogan, *"Clinton Crunch,"* reminded people of a candy bar rather than the economic conditions under Bill Clinton. I didn't back down— and fortunately only a few members repeated the self-defeating phrase.

Good communication doesn't come easily to professional politicians, and the outcome of 2006 was years in the making.

The Republican Party that lost those historic elections was a tired, cranky shell of the articulate, reformist, forward-thinking movement that was swept into office in 1994 on a wave of positive change. I knew those Republicans. I worked for them. They were friends of mine. *These* Republicans were not *those* Republicans.

The leaders of the Republican Party in 1994 were bold, passionate visionaries with the courage to go to the people with a clearly defined new agenda and a freshly minted lexicon around "The Contract with America" that educated

---

*I was hauled into Speaker Gingrich's office in mid-1996 because Boehner and Barry Jackson, his chief of staff, wanted to limit my interaction with members of Congress. There were just five of us in the closed-door meeting: Gingrich; Boehner; Jackson; Arne Christianson, Newt's chief of staff; and me. Gingrich gave me the chance to speak first, and I gave him a laundry list of ineffective messaging that was coming out of the Republican Conference—along with more effective alternatives. He read the list, agreed with the recommendations, and scolded Boehner and Jackson for interfering with my interaction with members. Boehner never forgave me for the supreme embarrassment: One of his first acts as Majority leader was to have me kicked out (once again) of an upcoming members-only retreat.

average Americans, not just political elites. Issues and principles drove them. Words and visions excited them.

But the same youthful activists who were elected on a platform of change and a language of reform became the establishment bulls who destroyed it. The 1994 Republicans held themselves and Congress to a higher ethical standard, attaching the word "accountability" to everything they did—and genuinely meaning it. The 2006 Republicans were an ethical morass, more interested in protecting their jobs than protecting the people they served. The 1994 Republicans came to *"revolutionize"* Washington. Washington won.

The Democrats weren't much better. They launched a hundred criticisms but offered no meaningful solutions. Their leaders rebuffed efforts by some members to introduce a party platform for the midterm election because they felt they could gain more seats by attacking Republicans rather than explaining what they believed. There is no way to dissect the Democrat language playbook, because there was none. They offered only negativity. Just click the postings on YouTube or visit any of the various partisan liberal Web sites and note the ratio of anti-Bush/anti-GOP postings versus anything even remotely pro-anything.

And yet they still won.

Karl Rove, "the architect" of Bush's two presidential campaigns, did a good job in early 2006 of describing the transitory nature of political success:

> "The GOP's progress during the last four decades is a stunning political achievement. But it is also a cautionary tale of what happens to a dominant party—in this case, the Democrat Party—when its thinking becomes ossified; when its energy begins to drain; when an entitlement mentality takes over; and when political power becomes an end in itself rather than a means to achieve the common good.
>
> "We need to learn from our successes—and from the failures of others. As the governing party in America, Republicans cannot grow tired or timid. We have been given the opportunity to govern; we have to continue to show we deserve the trust of our fellow Americans."[1]

How quickly things change. By Election Day 2006, it was Republicans, not Democrats, who had grown *"tired"* and *"timid."* In fact, they went silent. Far too many congressional candidates refused to engage their constituents in a two-way discussion about the challenges facing Social Security. Far too few hosted Medicare prescription drug forums to help seniors sign up and save money. And almost no one stood up to demand an end to the one issue that brought these members to power in the first place: wasteful Washington spending. As Congressman Mike Pence concluded hours after the polls closed, *"the greatest scandal in Washington, D.C. is runaway federal spending."* The accurately labeled *"Bridge to Nowhere"* became the path to a Democrat majority.

These are the exact words of Republican Majority Leader John Boehner in a press conference staged early in 2006. You be the judge of whether this is a party of intellectual conviction, moral clarity, and words that work:

> "I am working with our conference to develop a comprehensive vision, collective vision for our party. It is a long, slow, arduous process. Out of that, I hope that it will dictate a direction that we are going to go this year and long-term. And while I would hope—I would hope that we could agree on one big issue that we would fight for, you know, it is really for the members to decide. What I have got to do is provide the process to see if we can get ourselves there."[2]

At the very moment the American people were demanding real results, the Republican Majority Leader offered them incomprehensible pabulum. Where Republicans once offered vision and direction, they now offered process. Where they were once united behind clearly defined principles, they now stood rudderless with no clearly defined policies. The statement, like the party, was disjointed, out-of-touch, and adrift. As P.J. O'Rourke noted in *The Weekly Standard*, the Republicans had created the best marketing effort since New Coke.[3]


Not everything about what happened to Republicans in 2006 can be explained away by bad language. There was Iraq.

Opponents of the war will protest that there was no way to *"sell"* it to the American public. Perhaps. But for too long, the administration and Republicans in Congress failed even to try. Throughout the entire conflict, Americans raised questions that the administration and congressional Republicans knowingly chose not to answer. They did a poor job of defining the mission, explaining the long-term stakes, and laying out what was going right in Iraq while candidly acknowledging what had gone wrong. In short, Bush and his congressional allies treated the entire matter as if it were self-explanatory, its correctness self-evident, and those who had doubts were treated as unpatriotic.

And whatever explanations they offered were woefully insufficient. President Bush repeated the same identical, tired talking points over and over again. The administration's catchphrase "Stay the Course," originally intended to differentiate "resolute" Republicans from "indecisive" Democrats, came to symbolize the overall message strategy in the White House. In fact, it came to be the only message Americans ever heard about Iraq. No matter what happened, the message was always the same—stay the course, stay the course, stay the course.* Instead of instilling confidence, those three words came to symbolize

---

*In 1982, Ronald Reagan adopted "Stay the Course" as the GOP election mantra. They lost twenty-six seats.

inflexibility and unaccountability. The increasingly difficult "facts on the ground" in Iraq made good communication essential, and yet the worse things got, the less effective the messaging became. The Republicans finally ditched the message days before the election, but it was months too late.

Part of the problem was that Americans had been told that the war would be easy and short. The infamous *"Mission Accomplished"* speech (whomever hung that sign should himself be hanged) on May 1, 2003, aboard the USS *Abraham Lincoln* didn't help. Bush did address the long-term nature of the war against radical Islam, but for too long he refused to acknowledge the violence and bloodshed in Iraq that Americans saw daily.

The American people asked collectively, *"If the war was over and the mission accomplished, why then are our guys still dying?"* The response: silence. That silence was indicative of so many issues—Katrina, Foley, corruption, accountability—whenever voters had questions or doubts, there was only posturing and pithy talking points as answers. The results of 2006 were larger than Iraq; it was, as Strother Martin said to Paul Newman in *Cool Hand Luke, "a failure to communicate."* Weeks of silence became months, even years, and eventually the public's patience gave out. When they didn't get an answer, they communicated their anger at the ballot box, and the so-called *"security moms"* had once again returned to the Democrat fold.

There aren't enough pages in this book to catalogue all the communication failures of 2005–06. From Social Security to illegal immigration, from healthcare costs to gas prices, from Jack Abramoff to Mark Foley, the list of policy blunders and behavioral misconduct goes on and on. But here are five of the communications hurdles that brought about the Republican downfall, in chronological order, with the flawed language that stole defeat from the jaws of victory . . .

## 1. Terri Schiavo
There are times in politics when two competing, irreconcilable core principles come head-to-head with each other. In the case of Terri Schiavo, Republicans chose to ignore the principle of *"limited government"* in favor of the *"defense of life."*

However, most of the public, and even a large majority of Republicans didn't see the Schiavo situation as a matter of supporting life. Rightly or wrongly, most Americans saw federal intervention as a classic case of Washington overreach.*
The Washington Post laid out the facts of the case:

---

*An overwhelming majority of Democrats (89 percent), Republicans (72 percent), liberals (84 percent) and conservatives (76 percent) told pollsters for CBS that the government should not be involved in the Schiavo situation.

"Schiavo's husband and legal guardian, Michael Schiavo, has said that she has no hope of recovery and that, based on their conversations before her heart attack, she would not want to continue living as she is now. Florida courts have repeatedly sided with him, and the U.S. Supreme Court has declined to hear appeals of those rulings.

"Terri Schiavo's parents and siblings have fought to keep her alive, drawing many right-to-life activists and other political groups to their side. In his Senate speech yesterday, [Senate Majority Leader Bill] Frist denounced an unsigned memo circulated to Republican lawmakers over the weekend calling the Schiavo case "a great political issue."[4]

The author of the memo, a Senate staffer, was fired for stupidity, but the damage had been done. To the public, the principle at stake was not life but a disgusting concoction of brazen politics and government intervention—and the memo became the smoking gun. Americans regard family disputes, even those involving life itself, as profoundly private. To them, Washington's very public intervention was nothing more than grandstanding, attempting to draw political benefit at the expense of a family already torn apart.

For a quarter of a century, Republicans argued that Washington was too involved in the daily lives of Americans. And after twenty-five years, the American people agreed. The Terri Schiavo case was no exception . . . and Republicans couldn't very well renounce all they'd been battling since the day Ronald Reagan took the oath of office. It was bizarre to hear some Democrats suddenly speaking out in favor of states' rights and Washington restraint.

And most of the congressional leaders working to keep Terri Schiavo alive did so in good faith. But Republicans would have been better served by taking a less heated, and rhetorically less extreme approach—even if they felt morally obligated to get involved.

## 2. Hurricane Katrina

The profile of President Bush in *Air Force One*, looking down on the flood damage from 12,000 feet, was the most destructive image of him captured on film during his presidency. The physical distance between him and the victims became a metaphor for the gap between the White House and the American people.

Now it is true that the Secret Service and local officials asked him not to appear in New Orleans so that his presence would not divert resources better used to bring people to safety. On the merits, he did the right thing.

But in politics, visuals and images matter—and symbolism often trumps substance. In his understandable aversion to Clinton-esque lip-biting and moral exhibitionism, President Bush has often erred by going to the opposite extreme. After Katrina, he should have repeated his stellar performance at Ground Zero on the Friday after September 11. At that moment, atop the still-smoldering rubble with the bullhorn and the rescue workers, he demonstrated leadership and expressed what 300 million Americans were feeling. Instead, remaining at his ranch in Crawford on a *"working vacation"* as the hurricane bore down and devastated the Gulf was a grave and eventually fatal political mistake.

His language was no better. Upon arriving in Alabama for his first on-site briefing, Bush had this to say:

> "The good news is—and it's hard for some to see it now—that out of this chaos is going to come a fantastic Gulf Coast, like it was before. Out of the rubble of Trent Lott's house—he's lost his entire house—there's going to be a fantastic house. And I'm looking forward to sitting on the porch."[5]

Trent Lott? Sitting on his porch? Talking about the plight of a United States Senator—even one who had indeed lost everything—while people were still struggling and dying on the streets of New Orleans—revealed a political tin ear of the rustiest kind. All of America was witness to the massive suffering normally associated with Third World countries. Bush had three long days to think of what he would say, and the best he could come up with at that first defining moment was *"fantastic?"*

His Jackson Square speech two weeks later merely reinforced the perception that he was distant and emotionally detached. The president's long walk to the podium across the strangely lit square (there was still no electricity in New Orleans, so all the light had to come from trucks) looked eerie on television. The setting, with a Magic Kingdom–like church in the background, gave the impression that he was speaking from a movie set rather than a ravaged community.

Worse yet, his speech was a litany of new federal spending without any apparent limits or accountability, pledging *"we will do what it takes"*[6] to rebuild the Gulf Coast. Rather than laying out a vision and plan for a "new" New Orleans—a New Orleans where children would attend schools that worked, public housing would be fit for human occupancy, and the social structure would be rebuilt and repaired—his message was strictly about money. The president's spending promises tacked onto an already ballooning deficit demoralized the Republican base already embarrassed by an administration seemingly paralyzed by inaction and ineptitude.

But Bush's biggest verbal error in connection with Katrina, the one that really stuck in the public's collective craw, was his infamous *"Brownie, you're doing a heck of a job"*[7] praise of FEMA director Michael Brown (although, curiously, most people remember the phrase flipped, as *"Heck of a job, Brownie"*). Eventually *"Brownie"* would take the fall for the federal government's tepid response to the flooding, but the nickname—its jocularity and good-ol'-boy, frat-boy connotations—stood in stark contrast to the devastation and inept response. Linguistic incompetence, matched by governing incompetence, is a fatal concoction.

### 3. The Bridge to Nowhere

Sometimes a phrase or expression can take on a life of its own, symbolizing something broader and more significant than its original intent. In the fall of 2005, it was revealed that the mammoth federal highway bill contained an earmark to build a bridge from Ketchikan, Alaska to the island of Gravina so that the population would be saved from having to ride a ferry. How many people would be affected? Fifty. Not fifty thousand. Fifty. And the cost? $320 million.[8]

This egregious example of pork-barrel politics represented everything that Americans hated about government spending. Every generation has its symbolic financial management outrage: the $600 Pentagon toilets and *"welfare queens"* in the 1980s, *"midnight basketball"* in the 1990s, and now the *"bridge to nowhere."* It was easy to understand, impossible to defend, an outrage, and a punch line—a comical example of the absurdity of Washington, D.C. As one Republican congressman put it: *"It's on Jay Leno, David Letterman. It's on sitcoms. Everybody knows what the 'Bridge to Nowhere' is, and until we address that, nobody's going to take us seriously."*[9]

It didn't help Republicans in the other forty-nine states when Alaska's sole member of the House, Don Young, defiantly (and shamelessly) defended bringing home the bacon: *"We make no apologies. If I hadn't done fairly well for our state, I'd be ashamed of myself."*[10] And when a reporter from the *Fairbanks Daily News-Miner* suggested diverting some of his state's pork-barrel spending to Hurricane Katrina relief, Congressman Young called it *"the dumbest thing I've ever heard"* followed by, *"they can kiss my ear."*[11]

It was moments like this and words like these that convinced millions of voters that it was time for a change.

### 4. Implementation of the Medicare Prescription Drug Benefit

Republicans began 2003 believing they needed to pass a prescription drug benefit to appeal to the senior vote in 2004. They succeeded, saving the average senior enrollee roughly 40 percent on his or her medications—well above what was promised. But that wasn't the story most seniors read or heard. Democrats were saying, and the media was reporting, that seniors were frustrated with the maze of choices and information, that the process to sign up was too confusing, and that seniors were not really saving money. This message was repeated over and over again until it was largely accepted as fact. Republicans were faced with a strategic communication choice—distance themselves from the drug benefit, or embrace it and help seniors in their districts sign up and save.

Smart Republicans chose to embrace the program—regardless of whether they supported the legislation. The communication approach they took was personal, productive, and positive. I had the opportunity to observe some of the

Medicare Part D Town Hall meetings held in February 2006 by Congressman Jack Kingston of Georgia. The seniors who showed up at each event were often angry and frustrated when they arrived, because they "heard" that the process was arduous and confusing. Some were ready to give up.

Congressman Kingston spent about fifteen minutes explaining and personalizing the program—using his own mother and father as real-life examples. He then took as many questions as the audience could muster. He was sincere, he was patient, and he was informative. At the end of his presentation, seniors were offered the option of signing up on site with the help of a trained staff member. They loved it. I didn't hear a single senior who remained disgruntled. The majority were elated with the amount of money they were going to save. It was political communication and representative government at its best, stripped of all the rancor and rhetorical flourishes—just people in a room, talking out a problem and finding a satisfactory solution.

## 5. The Ports

Historians will most likely write that the Dubai Ports World deal undermined the long-term advantage Republicans held over the Democrats on fighting terrorism. The vehemence with which most of the public—Republicans and Democrats alike—rejected the proposed takeover of several terminals by a United Arab Emirates–owned company clearly took Washington by surprise.

From the White House, the initial response to the public outcry was deafening silence until . . . a vengeful, nasty veto threat from President Bush himself, a man who after more than five years in office had never vetoed a single bill—not for security, not for safety, not for schools or spending. *"There's a mandated process we go through,"* Bush said. *"They ought to listen to what I have to say to this. I'll deal with it with a veto."*[12]

This defiant, stubborn response—Bush's essentially saying, *"Do it because I said so"*—was a personal communications low point for an administration already in trouble because of disintegrating conditions in Iraq. The notion that he would go to the mat for the United Arab Emirates, a country often linked to terrorism, finally wielding a veto pen that he had refused to use on countless bloated spending bills, was a real tipping point.

Reasonable people could disagree on the merits of the ports agreement. But it was a textbook case of an issue that was impossible to explain and defend in a simple and understandable way. The argument against the deal was short, simple . . . and devastating. The argument in favor of it was complicated and required extensive explanations. And right or wrong, it was an electoral loser.

I'm often asked if it had to be this way—if because of Iraq, Katrina, and a host of other "facts on the ground," the GOP had to lose in 2006. The answer is no. A robust economy and a record stock market could have protected them, but the failure of public communication by the political leadership left the country sour and irritable. A wiser, fresher, more in-touch team would have realized it was time to admit mistakes, time to acknowledge voter frustration, and time once again to reaffirm the principles that had kept them in the majority for more than a decade.

Every major event over the past two years had one overarching trait in common: a wholesale collapse in any attempt at preemptive communication. That lack of context-setting led to public outrage, triggering a crisislike response from the White House and the Hill that too often failed the credibility test. Truth is, when you step back and consider all the strategic and communications disasters of 2005–06, it's a wonder that Republicans didn't lose more seats. If the Democrats had smarter leadership and a more compelling message, the outcome could have been much, much worse for the GOP.

All of the issues that came to haunt the Bush White House and congressional Republicans in 2005 and 2006 had that *"out of touch"* component. Every one. In some cases, either out of indifference or laziness, they didn't even try to connect with the people they represent. The reason matters less than the result. That chasm between the elected and their electors was reinforced every time the incumbent used another acronym or referenced some obscure elected official or applied policy-wonk jargon.

I don't want to end this chapter, or this book, without providing a ray of hope. While the rest of the Republican establishment was going down to defeat, something incredibly positive was happening in Florida. A small group of young state legislators led by Marco Rubio, a charismatic thirty-five-year-old Cuban-American and future national leader, decided to change the rules of the political game. Tired of partisan games and personal attacks, his team challenged all of his colleagues to come up with a vision for the future of Florida that was personal, specific, and actionable:

> "In your hands you now hold the first draft of a book that will outline to the people of this state a bold vision of Florida's future. A written public commitment for EVERYONE to read that explains what we think and what we plan to do. If you flip through the pages you will notice that today the pages are blank. But over the next few months, YOU will fill those pages with one hundred innovative ideas. Ideas that will formalize our binding agreement with the people of Florida."

Then came the action. These Florida Republicans crisscrossed the state, holding hundreds of "idea-raisers" (a great phrase) with average people rather than fund-raisers for the special interests. They gathered thousands of ideas from everyday Floridians, and it didn't matter if the idea came from a Republican, a Democrat, or an Independent. The one hundred innovative ideas would know no political boundaries.

The book, "*100 Innovative Ideas for Florida's Future*," was released just after the 2006 election because it was never meant to be a political tool. Instead, it was designed to be a road map for the legislature to rebuild credibility and communication with the people they serve. For the first time, the *people* of Florida, not the special interests, determined the agenda for the future. This innovative exercise in listening will put Florida on the right road for the future, while putting Republicans firmly in the driver's seat.

What happened in Florida shows us what was possible in 2006. A party with ideas that is able to communicate a vision for tomorrow can effectively insulate itself from the negative national political climate. More important, what happened in Florida shows us that congressional Republicans have no one to blame but *themselves*.

They forgot the successful lessons they learned in 1994.

They forgot the power of talking with and listening to their fellow Americans.

Intellectually, they lost their focus.

Linguistically, they got sloppy.

Yet the House and Senate remain very closely divided. The midterm elections of 2006 were just a skirmish before the battle royal of 2008. Whichever party best takes to heart the language lessons of 2006 will emerge victorious next year . . . and beyond.

And remember, it's not what you say that matters. It's what people hear.

—Frank Luntz
November 8, 2006

## Notes

1. Transcript of Karl Rove's speech at the RNC winter meeting, January 20, 2006.
2. Meeting with reporters, March 8, 2006.
3. http://www.weeklystandard.com/Content/Public/Articles/000/000/012/821dfmgg.asp
4. "Congress Passes Schiavo Measure: Bush Signs Bill Giving U.S. Courts Jurisdiction in Case of Fla. Woman," by Charles Babington and Mike Allen, *The Washington Post*, March 21, 2005.
5. Transcript, Sept. 2, 2005, www.whitehouse.gov.
6. "Bush: 'We Will Do What It Takes,'" www.CNN.com, Sept. 15, 2005.
7. Transcript, Sept. 2, 2005, www.whitehouse.gov.
8. "The Bridge to Nowhere: A National Embarrassment," by Ronald D. Utt, Ph.D., Web Memo #889, The Heritage Foundation, Oct. 20, 2005.
9. Rep. Jeff Flake, R-Arizona, quoted by Channel 2 Broadcasting, Inc., "Top 10 of 2005," www.ktuu.com.
10. "Alaska Thanks You," by Nick Jans, *USA Today*, May 17, 2005.
11. "Citizens Against Government Waste Names Reps Tom DeLay and Don Young Co-Porkers of the Month," CAGW press release, Sept. 20, 2005.
12. "Bush Says He Will Veto Any Bill to Stop UAE Port Deal," FOX News, Feb. 22, 2006.